JERRY REMY'S
RED SOX
HEROES

The RemDawg's All-Time Favorite Red Sox,
Great Moments, and Top Teams

Jerry Remy
with Corey Sandler

The Lyons Press
Guilford, Connecticut
An Imprint of The Globe Pequot Press

For my young heroes, my grandchildren
Dominik and Arianna —J.R.

The Lyons Press is an imprint of The Globe Pequot Press.

Photos by the National Baseball Hall of Fame Library, Cooperstown, N.Y. except where otherwise credited.

Project Manager: Jessica Haberman
Text design: Sheryl P. Kober
Layout Artist: Kim Burdick

Library of Congress Cataloging-in-Publication Data is available on file.

ISBN 978-1-59921-406-1

Printed in the United States of America
10 9 8 7 6 5 4 3 2 1

CONTENTS

INTRODUCTION

Every player who gets the privilege of putting on a major league uniform is very good at what he does. Some are great. And some are heroes.

I grew up in New England and I was lucky enough to get to play for the Boston Red Sox for seven seasons. And in 2008 I celebrated my 20th anniversary as a broadcaster of their games.

Baseball has been my life since I was a kid. And except for five years in the minors and three more at the start of my career when I played in California for the Angels, Boston has been the center of my baseball world. Let me tell you: I could have done a lot worse.

The Red Sox are in the blood of New Englanders as well as all of the adopted members of Red Sox Nation across the country and around the world. This team has a rich history and some of the most impassioned fans anywhere.

And so, I realize I am sticking my neck out a bit by coming up with a list of "Red Sox Heroes." Not everyone is going to agree with my choices. Some of you may have a favorite player whom I haven't selected. And others may think I'm just plain wrong in my assessments.

I'm willing to deal with that. It's kind of like what we say when the supporters (or the managers) of two different teams each make a credible argument saying why their squads are better. We say: *That's why we play the game.*

The Fenway Factor

It is worth noting that many of the players we are talking about played almost their entire career in Boston. And Fenway Park is the oldest ballpark in all of major league baseball. That brings up two important things to consider. First of all, the statistics at home for every Red Sox player since 1912 have been earned in a field that has basically retained its shape and character, aside from a few alterations to the upper tier behind home plate that have come and gone. And secondly, the opposite is true for away records for players over the years; stadiums around the league have come and gone while

Fenway remains. All of the players who are on my list of heroes were exceptional, but it is almost impossible to guess what their records would have been if they had played somewhere else.

Many of the early Red Sox teams tried to load up with as many right-handed power hitters as they could. But it is my opinion that Fenway Park has always been a better place for left-handed hitters who understand the mechanics of hitting: Keep your front shoulder on the ball and drive that ball off the Green Monster out there where it is so shallow. Think of Fred Lynn and Wade Boggs.

But then again, it is also very tough for left-handers to hit a home run to right when they pull a ball, because it is so deep out there in the bullpen area. And while we're on the subject, the prevailing theory about pitching to right-handers at Fenway is to pitch them inside and try to tie them up, instead of letting them get their arms extended so they can pull the ball off the wall or over the wall.

What Makes a Hero?

To me, the process of selecting a hero begins with finding guys who go out and play the game the way it should be played, day in and day out. Then I look for the extra talent or the extraordinary moment that highlights someone as not just a very good player, but as a great player.

And finally, let's be honest here: I may be getting on in years, but I cannot claim to have seen Cy Young pitch or Tris Speaker play centerfield like a short-fielder in slow-pitch softball. I know about the legend of Babe Ruth, but the closest I came to him was to work with a coach who was the Bambino's roommate for two years. And I knew next to nothing about Duffy Lewis except that he had something to do with an incline in left field that is now the home of the Green Monster; some old-timers called that piece of landscape "Duffy's Cliff."

But together with my co-author, Corey Sandler, I read the record books and the stories of the history of the Red Sox, from their great early days at the start of the 20th century when they won the very first World Series in 1903 and then four more championships, before their long drought began in 1918. I thought about the players who ran the bases at Fenway 50 and 60 years before I did and weighed their accomplishments against the guys who were on my team and of my era.

Please note that when a player is traded during a season, we list his statistics twice for that year. You will see a *Season* total for the entire year as well as results for Boston and the team he came from or was traded to. The player's career stats include the season numbers; his Boston stats use only the numbers that were achieved in a Red Sox uniform.

I'm not going to claim this list is perfect or even complete, but think of it this way: How would you like to have a 40-man (or 50-man) roster made up of these professionals? What a team!

The Roster

Here are my selections, presented as a depth chart.

Pitchers
Roger Clemens
Dennis Eckersley
Keith Foulke
Lefty Grove
Jim Lonborg
Derek Lowe
Pedro Martinez
Dick Radatz
Babe Ruth
Curt Schilling
Bob Stanley
Luis Tiant
Tim Wakefield
Smoky Joe Wood
Cy Young

Catchers
Rick Ferrell
Carlton Fisk
Jason Varitek

First Base
Jimmie Foxx
George Scott
Mo Vaughn

Second Base
Bobby Doerr
Johnny Pesky

Third Base
Wade Boggs
Jimmy Collins

Shortstop
Rick Burleson
Joe Cronin
Nomar Garciaparra
Rico Petrocelli

Leftfield
Duffy Lewis
Manny Ramirez
Jim Rice
Ted Williams
Carl Yastrzemski

Centerfield
Johnny Damon
Dom DiMaggio
Fred Lynn
Tris Speaker

Rightfield
Tony Conigliaro
Dwight Evans
Harry Hooper
Jackie Jensen
Trot Nixon

Designated Hitter
David Ortiz

We also salute five special moments in Red Sox history. We look at the stories of the 1967 "Impossible Dream" team, the 2004 "Reverse the Curse" team, and the 2007 "Champions of the World, Part II" tour. And then there are two Great Moments that qualify a pair of Daves for special mention: Dave Henderson and Dave Roberts.

And I also have my eye on an up-and-coming crop of young stars who may someday be elevated to an even higher plateau as Red Sox Heroes. Call them the young guns: Jon Lester, Jonathan Papelbon, Dustin Pedroia, and Kevin Youkilis. They're in the chapter called "Heroes in the Making."

THE GOLDEN RED SOX

JIMMY COLLINS
James Joseph Collins
(Boston 1901–1907; career 1895–1908)

Primary position: 3B	
Batted: R	
Threw: R	
Height: 5'9"	
Weight: 178 pounds	
First major league game: April 19, 1895	
Final major league game: August 29, 1908	
Born: January 16, 1870 in Buffalo, New York	
Died: March 6, 1943 in Buffalo, New York	
Baseball Hall of Fame: 1945	
Boston Red Sox Hall of Fame: 1995	

Before Jimmy Collins, corner infielders played the bags; at first and third they guarded the line to try to prevent extra base hits. The second baseman and the shortstop were expected to swoop left or right to grab anything else hit on the ground.

It was because of that sort of alignment that bunting was such an important part of the game in the 1890s and the early part of the twentieth century. All a good bunter had to do was lay down a slow grounder that was far enough away from the catcher or the pitcher and they had a great chance at getting a hit.

In 1895, Collins—an outfielder by trade—was brought in to replace the third baseman for the Louisville Colonels after the original infielder muffed four Baltimore Oriole bunts in a row. Collins made his own plan: instead of standing by the base, he moved a step or two away from the bag and came in to stand at the lip of the grass of the infield. When the next Oriole tried to bunt, Collins ran in toward home plate, picked up the ball with his bare hand, and fired it to first to get the out.

It was such a revolution in defense that it changed the game . . . and established Collins as one of the best fielders of his time. Players still attempted bunts, but some of the ever-changing balance of the game had shifted back in favor of a strong defense.

Horner
Photo

The next year, the National League Bostons (also called the Beaneaters)—who owned his contract—recalled Collins to their team and he began a remarkable career on the field and at the plate.

Collins later moved over to the Boston Americans, the parent team of the Red Sox, and added the role of skipper; as player-manager he had five straight winning seasons including two pennants and a world championship . . . and established the mold for the modern third baseman.

The Boston Americans, led by the still-dominating pitching of 36-year-old Cy Young, won the first-ever World Series in 1903, defeating the Pittsburgh Pirates. On opening day in 1904, Jimmy Collins hoisted the championship flag at the Huntington Avenue Grounds.

Collins was more than just a bunter. He batted .294 for his career and .296 as a member of the Red Sox. His best year came in 1897 as a member of the Boston team from the National League when he batted .346 and drove in 132 runs; he nearly matched those numbers as a player for the Red Sox in 1901 and 1902, batting .332 and .322.

Jimmy Collins

Year	Team	Age	G	AB	R	H	2B	3B	HR	RBI	BA
1895	Season	25	107	411	75	112	20	5	7	57	.273
	LOU (NL)		96	373	65	104	17	5	6	49	.279
	BSN (NL)		11	38	10	8	3	0	1	8	.211
1896	BSN (NL)	26	84	304	48	90	10	9	1	46	.296
1897	BSN (NL)	27	134	529	103	183	28	13	6	132	.346
1898	BSN (NL)	28	152	597	107	196	35	5	15	111	.328
1899	BSN (NL)	29	151	599	98	166	28	11	5	92	.277
1900	BSN (NL)	30	142	586	104	178	25	5	6	95	.304
1901	BOS (AL)	31	138	564	108	187	42	16	6	94	.332
1902	BOS (AL)	32	108	429	71	138	21	10	6	61	.322
1903	BOS (AL)	33	130	540	88	160	33	17	5	72	.296
1904	BOS (AL)	34	156	631	85	171	33	13	3	67	.271
1905	BOS (AL)	35	131	508	66	140	26	5	4	65	.276
1906	BOS (AL)	36	37	142	17	39	8	4	1	16	.275
1907	Season	37	140	522	51	145	29	0	0	45	.278
	BOS (AL)		41	158	13	46	8	0	0	10	.291
	PHA (AL)		99	364	38	99	21	0	0	35	.272
1908	PHA (AL)	38	115	433	34	94	14	3	0	30	.217
Total			1725	6795	1055	1999	352	116	65	983	.294
Boston AL			741	2972	448	881	171	65	25	385	.296

Year	Team	OBP	SLG	OPS	BB	SO	TB	SB	CS	SH	SF	IBB	HBP	GDP
1895	*Season*	*.347*	*.397*	*.744*	*37*	*20*	*163*	*12*	*n/a*	*4*	*n/a*	*n/a*	*10*	*n/a*
	LOU (NL)	.352	.399	.751	33	16	149	12	n/a	3	n/a	n/a	9	n/a
	BSN (NL)	.302	.368	.670	4	4	14	0	n/a	1	n/a	n/a	1	n/a
1896	BSN (NL)	.374	.398	.772	30	12	121	10	n/a	8	n/a	n/a	8	n/a
1897	BSN (NL)	.400	.482	.882	41		255	14	n/a	8	n/a	n/a	7	n/a
1898	BSN (NL)	.377	.479	.856	40		286	12	n/a	13	n/a	n/a	7	n/a
1899	BSN (NL)	.335	.386	.721	40		231	12	n/a	9	n/a	n/a	12	n/a
1900	BSN (NL)	.352	.394	.746	34		231	23	n/a	9	n/a	n/a	10	n/a
1901	BOS (AL)	.375	.495	.870	34		279	19	n/a	12	n/a	n/a	5	n/a
1902	BOS (AL)	.360	.459	.819	24		197	18	n/a	19	n/a	n/a	2	n/a
1903	BOS (AL)	.329	.448	.777	24		242	23	n/a	13	n/a	n/a	2	n/a
1904	BOS (AL)	.306	.379	.685	27		239	19	n/a	13	n/a	n/a	5	n/a
1905	BOS (AL)	.330	.370	.700	37		188	18	n/a	9	n/a	n/a	4	n/a
1906	BOS (AL)	.295	.408	.703	4		58	1	n/a	2	n/a	n/a	0	n/a
1907	*Season*	*.332*	*.333*	*.665*	*34*		*174*	*8*	*n/a*	*15*	*n/a*	*n/a*	*8*	*n/a*
	BOS (AL)	.333	.342	.675	10		54	4	n/a	6	n/a	n/a	0	n/a
	PHA (AL)	.331	.330	.661	24		120	4	n/a	9	n/a	n/a	8	n/a
1908	PHA (AL)	.258	.263	.521	20		114	5	n/a	13	n/a	n/a	4	n/a
Total		**.343**	**.409**	**.752**	**426**	**32**	**2778**	**194**	**n/a**	**147**	**n/a**	**n/a**	**84**	**n/a**
Boston AL		**.336**	**.423**	**.759**	**160**	**0**	**1257**	**102**		**74**			**18**	

Managerial Record

Year	Team	G	W	L	Finish
1901	BOS (AL)	138	79	57	2
1902	BOS (AL)	138	77	60	3
1903	BOS (AL)	141	91	47	AL pennant, won WS
1904	BOS (AL)	157	95	59	AL pennant
1905	BOS (AL)	153	78	74	4
1906	BOS (AL)	115	35	79	8
Totals		**842**	**455**	**376**	

CY YOUNG
Denton True Young
(Boston 1901–1908; career 1890–1911)

Primary position: P	
Batted: R	
Threw: R	
Height: 6'2"	
Weight: 210 pounds	
First major league game: August 6, 1890	
Final major league game: October 6, 1911	
Born: March 29, 1867 in Gilmore, Ohio	
Died: November 4, 1955 in Newcomerstown, Ohio	
Baseball Hall of Fame: 1937	

You've got to figure that the guy whose name is on baseball's top award for pitching had to have put up some pretty good numbers in his career.

Where do we start?

We know he had a great fastball; that's why Denton True Young became known as Cyclone, or Cy.

Young began his career with the Cleveland Spiders of the National League team and then put in two seasons with the St. Louis Browns (later renamed the Cardinals). He had his best years in Boston, from 1901 to 1908 for teams that were called the Boston Americans, Boston Somersets, Boston Pilgrims, and Boston Red Sox. At the end of his career he pitched for the AL Cleveland Naps. He was 44 years old when he returned to Boston, where he pitched his last game, a loss for the Boston Braves of the National League.

And by the time he retired in 1911, he had recorded 511 wins. In nearly a century no other pitcher has ever come within a few thousand fastballs' distance of that remarkable record. And I doubt anyone ever will. Today's superstar pitchers are paid so much money and are so valuable to the team that every pitch is numbered. And we've also got whole squads of relievers, setup men, and closers who specialize in coming in and taking control of the game.

Photo by the National Baseball Hall of Fame Library, Cooperstown, N.Y.

Consider this, too: Cy Young started 815 games and *finished* 749 (or 751, depending who is counting) of them along the way to 511 wins. That's another record not likely to be broken. He also is atop the list of innings pitched, with 7,355.

Cy Young stands all by himself at the top of the list of winningest pitchers. In second place, also pretty much assured of a permanent hold on that rank, is Walter Johnson with 417. Grover Alexander and Christy Mathewson are tied for third place with 373.

The highest-ranking pitcher of the modern era is Warren Spahn, in fifth place, with 363 wins. Spahn began his career in 1942 with the Boston Braves of the National League, and finally hung up his spikes in 1965 when I was just a kid. Greg Maddux moved into eighth place during the 2008 season with 355 wins, just ahead of Roger Clemens who has 354 victories.

As a player for Boston in eight seasons from 1901 and 1908, Young posted a record of 192–112. Interestingly, Roger Clemens ended up in a tie for the team record with a record of 192–111.

Throwing for Boston, Young recorded 33 wins in 1901 and 32 in 1902. He helped lead Boston to a World Series championship in 1903, winning two games in the series. In 1907, he served as player-manager.

Overall, he had 15 seasons with 20 or more wins, and 5 seasons with at least 30 wins.

Included in those totals: a perfect game for Boston against the Philadelphia Athletics on May 5, 1904. Young, at age 37, got the best of the A's star Rube Waddell in what is considered the first perfect game of the modern era of baseball. It's also the only perfect game ever thrown by a Boston pitcher.

He had already pitched a no-hitter against the Cincinnati Reds in 1897 when he played for the Cleveland Spiders of the National League, and he would go on to pitch another no-no (one walk short of a perfect game) on June 30, 1908 at age 41, leading the Boston Red Sox to an 8–0 victory over . . . wait for it . . . New York. The team was called the Highlanders; they officially changed their name to Yankees in 1913.

According to all reports, Young had a strong fastball; he told reporters his nickname of Cy came from "cyclone" although that story is not for certain. Anyhow, like any successful pitcher he had other weapons in his arsenal that he used to set up the batter: a curve, a drop (probably something like what we today call a splitter), a changeup, and a spitball.

Although he fanned 2,803 batters over the course of 22 seasons, he preferred not to throw extra pitches to a batter. One clue to his style: "I aimed to make the batter hit the ball," Young told an interviewer. "That's why I was able to work every other day."

He also had an early understanding of the wear and tear on a pitcher's arm. "When I would go to spring training, I would never touch a ball for three weeks," he said. "Just would do a lot of walking and running. I never did any unnecessary throwing. I figured the old arm had just so many throws in it, and there wasn't any use wasting them."

Major League Baseball first awarded the Cy Young Award in 1956, given to the best pitcher in each league. As a team, the Red Sox have done quite well in bringing home this award. Roger Clemens did it three times for the Red Sox and four more times for other teams. Pedro Martinez owns a pair of the trophies, and Jim Lonborg won the prize for his transcendent 1967 season.

Cy Young

Year	Team	Age	W	L	G	GS	CG	SHO	GF	SV	WHIP	ERA
1890	CLV (NL)	23	9	7	17	16	16	0	1	n/a	1.185	3.47
1891	CLV (NL)	24	27	22	55	46	43	0	8	n/a	1.348	2.85
1892	CLV (NL)	25	36	12	53	49	48	9	4	n/a	1.062	1.93
1893	CLV (NL)	26	34	16	53	46	42	1	7	n/a	1.289	3.36
1894	CLV (NL)	27	26	21	52	47	44	2	5	n/a	1.454	3.94
1895	CLV (NL)	28	35	10	47	40	36	4	7	n/a	1.185	3.26
1896	CLV (NL)	29	28	15	51	46	42	5	4	n/a	1.301	3.24
1897	CLV (NL)	30	21	19	46	38	35	2	7	n/a	1.319	3.80
1898	CLV (NL)	31	25	13	46	41	40	1	5	n/a	1.133	2.53
1899	STL (NL)	32	26	16	44	42	40	4	2	n/a	1.116	2.58
1900	STL (NL)	33	19	19	41	35	32	4	6	n/a	1.161	3.00
1901	BOS (AL)	34	33	10	43	41	38	5	2	n/a	0.972	1.62
1902	BOS (AL)	35	32	11	45	43	41	3	1	n/a	1.048	2.15
1903	BOS (AL)	36	28	9	40	35	34	7	5	n/a	0.969	2.08
1904	BOS (AL)	37	26	16	43	41	40	10	2	n/a	0.937	1.97
1905	BOS (AL)	38	18	19	38	33	31	4	5	n/a	0.867	1.82
1906	BOS (AL)	39	13	21	39	34	28	0	4	n/a	1.088	3.19
1907	BOS (AL)	40	21	15	43	37	33	6	5	n/a	0.982	1.99
1908	BOS (AL)	41	21	11	36	33	30	3	3	n/a	0.893	1.26
1909	CLE (AL)	42	19	15	35	34	30	3	1	n/a	1.105	2.26
1910	CLE (AL)	43	7	10	21	20	14	1	0	n/a	1.078	2.53
1911	*Season*	44	7	9	18	18	12	2	0	n/a	1.306	3.78
	CLE (AL)		3	4	7	7	4	0	0	0	1.446	3.88
	BOS (NL)		4	5	11	11	8	2	0	0	1.225	3.71
Total			**511**	**316**	**906**	**815**	**749**	**76**	**84**	**17**	**1.130**	**2.63**
Boston			**192**	**112**	**327**	**297**	**275**	**38**	**27**	**9**	**1.125**	**2.01**

Year	Team	IP	H	R	ER	HR	BB	SO	HBP	WP	BK
1890	CLV (NL)	147.7	145	87	57	6	30	39	5	7	0
1891	CLV (NL)	423.7	431	244	134	4	140	147	11	12	0
1892	CLV (NL)	453	363	158	97	8	118	168	8	13	0
1893	CLV (NL)	422.7	442	230	158	10	103	102	10	14	0
1894	CLV (NL)	408.7	488	265	179	19	106	108	6	4	0
1895	CLV (NL)	369.7	363	177	134	10	75	121	8	6	0
1896	CLV (NL)	414.3	477	214	149	7	62	140	10	10	0
1897	CLV (NL)	333.7	391	189	141	7	49	88	9	14	0
1898	CLV (NL)	377.7	387	167	106	6	41	101	9	9	0
1899	STL (NL)	369.3	368	173	106	10	44	111	6	6	1
1900	STL (NL)	321.3	337	144	107	7	36	115	4	7	1
1901	BOS (AL)	371.3	324	112	67	6	37	158	8	2	0
1902	BOS (AL)	384.7	350	136	92	6	53	160	13	3	0
1903	BOS (AL)	341.7	294	115	79	6	37	176	9	5	0
1904	BOS (AL)	380	327	104	83	6	29	200	4	4	0
1905	BOS (AL)	320.7	248	99	65	3	30	210	10	6	0
1906	BOS (AL)	287.7	288	137	102	3	25	140	8	5	1
1907	BOS (AL)	343.3	286	101	76	3	51	147	7	6	0
1908	BOS (AL)	299	230	68	42	1	37	150	2	4	0
1909	CLE (AL)	295	267	110	74	4	59	109	8	6	0
1910	CLE (AL)	163.3	149	62	46	0	27	58	4	7	0
1911	*Season*	*126.3*	*137*	*75*	*53*	*6*	*28*	*55*	*4*	*6*	*0*
	CLE (AL)	46.3	54	28	20	2	13	20	1	1	0
	BOS (NL)	80	83	47	33	4	15	35	3	5	0
Total		**7354.7**	**7092**	**3167**	**2147**	**138**	**1217**	**2803**	**163**	**156**	**3**
Boston		**2728.3**	**2347**	**872**	**606**	**34**	**299**	**1341**	**61**	**35**	**1**

TRIS SPEAKER

Tristram E. Speaker ("The Grey Eagle," "Spoke")
(Boston 1907–1915; career 1907–1928)

Primary position: CF	
Batted: L	
Threw: L	
Height: 5′11″	
Weight: 193 pounds	
First major league game: September 14, 1907	
Final major league game: August 30, 1928	
Born: April 4, 1888 in Hubbard, Texas	
Died: December 8, 1958 in Lake Whitney, Texas	
Baseball Hall of Fame: 1937	

Tris Speaker played centerfield as if he were part of the infield; it was his theory that he could help the team more by turning short flies into outs instead of singles. He could use his speed to track down many balls hit over his head. That, combined with a strong arm, helped him set records for assists by an outfielder. He threw runners out at the bases and even made a number of unassisted double plays where he caught the ball and dashed to second base to double off a baserunner.

In 22 years as a player, he recorded 449 assists as an outfielder. No one in the modern era has come even close to that number. The great Carl Yastrzemski posted 195 assists from the outfield across 23 seasons.

Speaker led American League outfielders in putouts seven times, double plays six times, assists three times, and fielding average twice. He was at the center of the great Red Sox outfield of Harry Hooper, Speaker, and Duffy Lewis. Together they were responsible for 396 assists in the five seasons from 1910 to 1914.

He was also one of the best hitters the Red Sox have ever put in the lineup. He still holds a number of records including the highest career and single-season batting averages of any Red Sox centerfielder.

Speaker joined the Boston team in 1907 as a reserve, but it was in 1909 that he caught fire, and he stayed hot for most of the next

Photo by the National Baseball Hall of Fame Library, Cooperstown, N.Y.

20 years. He hit .380 or higher five times in his career, including the 1912 season when he won the Most Valuable Player award batting .383 for the Red Sox, and 1916 when he won the batting title with a .386 average for the Cleveland Indians. Between 1909 when he became a regular in the Boston lineup and his last full season in 1927 as a member of the Washington Senators, he had only one year

with a batting average below .300 and that was only by a hair: .296 in 1919. He scored 100 or more runs in seven seasons.

And his .345 lifetime batting average is sixth on the all-time list of players with 3,000 or more plate appearances, less than three-hundredths of a percent ahead of Ted Williams. (Ty Cobb is in first place with .366, followed by Rogers Hornsby, Joe Jackson, Lefty O'Doul, and Ed Delahanty. Among active players, the only batters who are in the same ballpark are Ichiro Suzuki, Albert Pujols, and Todd Helton, each down in the mid-20th places at about .332 for their careers thus far.)

He leads all major league players with 792 career doubles; in second place and holder of the National League record is Pete Rose with 746 two-base hits. He is fifth all-time in hits, with 3,514, and sixth in triples with 222.

In the Red Sox record book, he set and then equaled the team record for double plays executed by an outfielder with 12 in the 1909 and 1914 seasons. He also holds the mark for the most outfield assists in a season, with 35 in 1909 and again in 1912; he is second in career assists from the outfield with 207 to Harry Hooper's 260. At bat, he holds the team record for most triples in a season, with 22 in 1913. With 222 hits in 1912, he is in second place for the Red Sox season record for hits, behind the mark of 240 set by Wade Boggs in 1985.

Ted Williams owns the two highest single-season batting averages for the Red Sox; Speaker has third place with .383 in 1912. In that same year, Speaker put up a 30-game hitting streak, which is second in Boston only to Dom DiMaggio's 34-game mark in 1949. And to put that great year in perspective, Speaker is the only player in major league history to have three hitting streaks of 20 or more games in one season, again in 1912. All of this happened in the "dead ball" era in baseball.

And finally, the Grey Eagle also had speed. Again in that remarkable year of 1912, he set a team record of eight inside-the-park home runs. As of the start of the 2009 season, Speaker ranked second for stolen bases in a single season by a Red Sox player, with his mark of 52 in 1912. Tommy Harper holds the record with 54, but the speedy young Jacoby Ellsbury swiped 50 in his first full season in 2008 and is a pretty good bet to run past Speaker and Harper.

Speaker ended his career in Boston in 1916 when he was traded to Cleveland after a contract dispute with Red Sox president Joe Lannin.

Lannin wanted Speaker to accept a cut in pay from about $15,000 to $9,000 because his batting average had dropped in 1915 to a mere .322. Speaker refused the offer and was traded away; in his first year with the Indians, he showed Boston he was far from through as he led the American League with a .386 average.

Why is the Gray Eagle relatively less known? Perhaps it is because he played in the supersized shadow of Ty Cobb. If you can look past Cobb, Speaker is clearly one of the greats.

Tris Speaker

Year	Team	Age	G	AB	R	H	2B	3B	HR	RBI	BA	
1907	BOS (AL)	19	7	19	0	3	0	0	0	1	.158	
1908	BOS (AL)	20	31	116	12	26	2	2	0	9	.224	
1909	BOS (AL)	21	143	544	73	168	26	13	7	77	.309	
1910	BOS (AL)	22	141	538	92	183	20	14	7	65	.340	
1911	BOS (AL)	23	141	500	88	167	34	13	8	70	.334	
1912	BOS (AL)	24	153	580	136	222	53	12	10	90	.383	MVP
1913	BOS (AL)	25	141	520	94	189	35	22	3	71	.363	
1914	BOS (AL)	26	158	571	101	193	46	18	4	90	.338	
1915	BOS (AL)	27	150	547	108	176	25	12	0	69	.322	
1916	CLE (AL)	28	151	546	102	211	41	8	2	79	.386	
1917	CLE (AL)	29	142	523	90	184	42	11	2	60	.352	
1918	CLE (AL)	30	127	471	73	150	33	11	0	61	.318	
1919	CLE (AL)	31	134	494	83	146	38	12	2	63	.296	
1920	CLE (AL)	32	150	552	137	214	50	11	8	107	.388	
1921	CLE (AL)	33	132	506	107	183	52	14	3	75	.362	
1922	CLE (AL)	34	131	426	85	161	48	8	11	71	.378	
1923	CLE (AL)	35	150	574	133	218	59	11	17	130	.380	
1924	CLE (AL)	36	135	486	94	167	36	9	9	65	.344	
1925	CLE (AL)	37	117	429	79	167	35	5	12	87	.389	
1926	CLE (AL)	38	150	539	96	164	52	8	7	86	.304	
1927	WASH (AL)	39	141	523	71	171	43	6	2	73	.327	
1928	PHA (AL)	40	64	191	28	51	22	2	3	30	.267	
Total			2789	10195	1882	3514	792	222	117	1529	.345	
Boston			1065	3935	704	1327	241	106	39	542	.337	

Year	Team	OBP	SLG	OPS	BB	SO	TB	SB	CS	SH	SF	IBB	HBP	GDP
1907	BOS (AL)	.200	.158	.358	1	n/a	3	0	n/a	0	n/a	n/a	0	n/a
1908	BOS (AL)	.262	.276	.538	4	n/a	32	3	n/a	3	n/a	n/a	2	n/a
1909	BOS (AL)	.362	.443	.805	38	n/a	241	35	n/a	17	n/a	n/a	7	n/a
1910	BOS (AL)	.404	.468	.872	52	n/a	252	35	n/a	12	n/a	n/a	6	n/a
1911	BOS (AL)	.418	.502	.920	59	n/a	251	25	n/a	17	n/a	n/a	13	n/a
1912	BOS (AL)	.464	.567	1.031	82	n/a	329	52	n/a	7	n/a	n/a	6	n/a
1913	BOS (AL)	.441	.533	.974	65	22	277	46	n/a	16	n/a	n/a	7	n/a
1914	BOS (AL)	.423	.503	.926	77	25	287	42	29	13	n/a	n/a	7	n/a
1915	BOS (AL)	.416	.411	.827	81	14	225	29	25	17	n/a	n/a	7	n/a
1916	CLE (AL)	.470	.502	.972	82	20	274	35	27	15	n/a	n/a	4	n/a
1917	CLE (AL)	.432	.486	.918	67	14	254	30	n/a	15	n/a	n/a	7	n/a
1918	CLE (AL)	.403	.435	.838	64	9	205	27	n/a	11	n/a	n/a	3	n/a
1919	CLE (AL)	.395	.433	.828	73	12	214	15	n/a	20	n/a	n/a	8	n/a
1920	CLE (AL)	.483	.562	1.045	97	13	310	10	13	20	n/a	n/a	5	n/a
1921	CLE (AL)	.439	.538	.977	68	12	272	2	4	12	n/a	n/a	2	n/a
1922	CLE (AL)	.474	.606	1.080	77	11	258	8	3	12	n/a	n/a	1	n/a
1923	CLE (AL)	.469	.610	1.079	93	15	350	8	9	22	n/a	n/a	4	n/a
1924	CLE (AL)	.432	.510	.942	72	13	248	5	7	13	n/a	n/a	4	n/a
1925	CLE (AL)	.479	.578	1.057	70	12	248	5	2	15	n/a	n/a	4	n/a
1926	CLE (AL)	.408	.469	.877	94	15	253	6	1	28	n/a	n/a	0	n/a
1927	WASH (AL)	.395	.444	.839	55	8	232	9	8	15	n/a	n/a	4	n/a
1928	PHA (AL)	.310	.450	.760	10	5	86	5	1	9	n/a	n/a	2	n/a
Total		**.428**	**.500**	**.928**	**1381**	**220**	**5101**	**432**	**129***	**309**			**103**	
Boston		**.414**	**.482**	**.896**	**459**	**61**	**1897**	**267**	**54***	**102**			**55**	

*Incomplete

15

SMOKY JOE WOOD
Howard Ellsworth Wood
(Boston 1908–1915; career 1908–1922)

Primary position: P	
Batted: R	
Threw: R	
Height: 5′11″	
Weight: 180 pounds	
First major league game: August 24, 1908	
Final major league game: September 24, 1922	
Born: October 25, 1889 in Kansas City, Missouri	
Died: July 27, 1985 in West Haven, Connecticut	
Boston Red Sox Hall of Fame: 1995	

For eight years, including two spectacular seasons in 1911 and 1912, Smoky Joe Wood threw smoke past the great hitters of his time. His record in 1912 was 34–5, the highest number of wins ever earned by a Red Sox pitcher in a single season.

Look inside those numbers for 1912: an ERA of 1.91, 10 shutouts, 35 complete games, 258 strikeouts, and only 82 walks in 344 innings pitched. Nearly a century later, no Red Sox pitcher has won as many games in a season or matched his string of 16 consecutive victories. And in that season he set team marks for most wins at Fenway with 18, and most road victories with 16; those records still stand, too.

He grew up as a young phenom, pitching against adults in local teams and even joining the Bloomer Girls, a "female" baseball squad that included several young men. Depending on whose story you believe, the teams either snuck Woods and others onto the team in wigs and drag, or acknowledged that they were fielding a mixed team.

He joined the Red Sox in 1908 at the age of 18 and appeared in six games; in the next two seasons he established himself as a capable pitcher. Then he announced his arrival in 1911 when he appeared in 44 games and posted a record of 23–17 (including 25 complete games and 3 saves), with an ERA of 2.02. That's a lot of innings (275.7) and a tiny number of runs surrendered. His season included a no-hitter against the St. Louis Browns.

Photo by the National Baseball Hall of Fame Library, Cooperstown, N.Y.

Wood's performance in 1911 was a setup for his great 1912 season. During his streak of consecutive wins that year, Wood beat the great Walter Johnson of the Washington Senators in a 1–0 game. In the World Series he went 3–1, winning the eighth and deciding game against Hall of Famer Christy Mathewson of the New York Giants, and was named MVP of the series.

As has happened many times in baseball history, Wood's star shined brightly but not all that long; in July of 1913 he slipped and fell while fielding a bunt in Detroit, breaking the thumb on his right (pitching) hand. According to reports of the time, he lost some of his smoke after the injury, although he continued to pitch successfully for the remainder of the 1913 season and two more after that. In 1915, pitching in pain, he had his last season as a starter for the Red Sox and posted a 15–5 record with an ERA of 1.49.

He sat out the 1916 season and most of 1917 before the Red Sox sold his contract to the Cleveland Indians, and he had a second career there . . . as an outfielder. From 1918 to 1922, he batted .298 with 275 RBIs. In his final year, he had 150 hits, 92 RBIs, and 8 home runs. It was not quite as notable a conversion from the pitcher's mound to the batter's box as Babe Ruth's, but it shows Wood's dedication and athletic ability.

After retirement, Wood became the baseball coach for Yale University for more than 20 seasons. His son, also named Joe Wood, had a cup of coffee with the Red Sox in the 1944 season during World War II. He appeared in three games and posted a 0–1 record. That was his entire major league career.

In 1984, Smoky Joe returned to Fenway Park for an Old Timer's Day event. He died a year later.

We'll never know what kind of numbers Smoky Joe would have put up if he hadn't gotten injured at age 23. His record of 117–57 and a career ERA of 2.03 as a pitcher give us a hint of his greatness.

Smoky Joe Wood

Year	Team	Age	W	L	G	GS	CG	SHO	GF	SV	WHIP	ERA
1908	BOS (AL)	18	1	1	6	2	1	1	3	0	1.324	2.38
1909	BOS (AL)	19	11	7	24	19	13	4	3	0	1.021	2.18
1910	BOS (AL)	20	12	13	35	17	14	3	13	0	1.062	1.68
1911	BOS (AL)	21	23	17	44	33	25	5	11	3	1.096	2.02
1912	BOS (AL)	22	34	5	43	38	35	10	5	1	1.015	1.91
1913	BOS (AL)	23	11	5	23	18	12	1	5	2	1.243	2.29
1914	BOS (AL)	24	10	3	18	14	11	1	4	1	1.129	2.62
1915	BOS (AL)	25	15	5	25	16	10	3	8	2	1.042	1.49
1917	CLE (AL)	27	0	1	5	1	0	0	3	1	1.532	3.45
1919	CLE (AL)	29	0	0	1	0	0	0	1	1	0.000	0.00
1920	CLE (AL)	30	0	0	1	0	0	0	1	0	3.000	22.50
Total			**117**	**57**	**225**	**158**	**121**	**28**	**57**	**11**	**1.085**	**2.03**
Boston			**117**	**56**	**218**	**157**	**121**	**28**	**52**	**9**	**1.078**	**1.99**

Year	Team	IP	H	R	ER	HR	BB	SO	HBP	WP	IBB	BK
1908	BOS (AL)	22.7	14	12	6	0	16	11	1	0	n/a	0
1909	BOS (AL)	160.7	121	51	39	1	43	88	6	5	n/a	0
1910	BOS (AL)	198.7	155	81	37	3	56	145	10	5	n/a	0
1911	BOS (AL)	275.7	226	113	62	2	76	231	11	10	n/a	0
1912	BOS (AL)	344	267	104	73	2	82	258	12	7	n/a	0
1913	BOS (AL)	145.7	120	54	37	0	61	123	8	8	n/a	0
1914	BOS (AL)	113.3	94	38	33	1	34	67	0	5	n/a	0
1915	BOS (AL)	157.3	120	32	26	1	44	63	1	3	n/a	0
1917	CLE (AL)	15.7	17	7	6	0	7	2	0	0	n/a	0
1919	CLE (AL)	0.7	0	0	0	0	0	0	0	0	n/a	0
1920	CLE (AL)	2	4	5	5	0	2	1	0	0	n/a	0
Total		**1436.3**	**1138**	**497**	**324**	**10**	**421**	**989**	**49**	**43**	**n/a**	**0**
Boston		**1418**	**1117**	**485**	**313**	**10**	**412**	**986**	**49**	**43**	**n/a**	**0**

Batting

Year	Team	Age	G	AB	R	H	2B	3B	HR	RBI	BA
1908-15	BOS (AL)		226	496	63	121	26	6	5	50	.244
1917	CLE (AL)	27	10	6	0	0	0	0	0	0	.000
1918	CLE (AL)	28	119	422	41	125	22	4	5	66	.296
1919	CLE (AL)	29	72	192	30	49	10	6	0	27	.255
1920	CLE (AL)	30	61	137	25	37	11	2	1	30	.270
1921	CLE (AL)	31	66	194	32	71	16	5	4	60	.366
1922	CLE (AL)	32	142	505	74	150	33	8	8	92	.297
Total			**696**	**1952**	**266**	**553**	**118**	**31**	**23**	**325**	**.283**
Boston			**226**	**496**	**63**	**121**	**26**	**6**	**5**	**50**	**.244**

Year	Team	OBP	SLG	OPS	BB	SO	TB	SB	CS	SH	SF	IBB	HBP	GDP
1908-15	BOS (AL)	.304	.351	.655	40	n/a	174	4	n/a	23	n/a	n/a	3	n/a
1917	CLE (AL)	.000	.000	.000	0	3	0	0	n/a	0	n/a	n/a	0	n/a
1918	CLE (AL)	.356	.403	.759	36	38	170	8	n/a	20	n/a	n/a	3	n/a
1919	CLE (AL)	.367	.370	.737	32	21	71	3	n/a	9	n/a	n/a	2	n/a
1920	CLE (AL)	.390	.401	.791	25	16	55	1	1	12	n/a	n/a	2	n/a
1921	CLE (AL)	.438	.562	1.000	25	17	109	2	0	10	n/a	n/a	0	n/a
1922	CLE (AL)	.367	.442	.809	50	63	223	5	1	22	n/a	n/a	6	n/a
Total		**.357**	**.411**	**.768**	**208**	**189**	**802**	**23**	**n/a**	**96**	**n/a**	**n/a**	**16**	**n/a**
Boston		**.304**	**.351**	**.655**	**40**	**n/a**	**174**	**4**	**n/a**	**23**	**n/a**	**n/a**	**3**	**n/a**

HARRY HOOPER
Harry Bartholomew Hooper ("Hoop")
(Boston 1909–1920; career 1909–1925)

Primary position: RF	
Batted: L	
Threw: R	
Height: 5'10"	
Weight: 168 pounds	
First major league game: April 16, 1909	
Final major league game: October 4, 1925	
Born: August 24, 1887 in Bell Station, California	
Died: December 18, 1974 in Santa Cruz, California	
Baseball Hall of Fame: 1971	
Boston Red Sox Hall of Fame: 1995	

Winning the World Series in 2004 and again in 2007 was a wonderful experience for players and fans, but we all remember that there was a slight delay of 86 years before the trophy arrived back in Boston.

That's one reason why Harry Hooper is one of our heroes. Consider this: He was the rightfielder in the "million dollar outfield" that had Tris Speaker in center and Duffy Lewis in left, and they all but owned the World Series. The Red Sox were champions in 1912, 1915, 1916, and 1918 and Hooper was there: the only Boston player to ever bring home four World Series trophies.

The "million dollar" label was strictly hyperbole. It might have been more like the $25,000 outfield. Babe Ruth, already a star on the team as a pitcher and looking toward becoming an outfielder, was paid $3,500 in 1916 by the Red Sox. Hooper held out for a salary of $15,000 after the 1920 season, but was traded away to the White Sox.

A line drive hitter in the dead ball era, Hooper apparently knew how to choose his spots. In 1915 he had only two home runs all season, but he hit two more in the deciding game of the World Series against the Philadelphia Phillies that year: one tied the score early and the second produced the go-ahead run in the top of the ninth. It was also the first time a player had ever hit two long balls in a single World Series game.

Photo by the National Baseball Hall of Fame Library, Cooperstown, N.Y.

Hooper was also an excellent fielder, and the very first to patrol the difficult right field of Fenway Park, which opened in 1912. In the eighth and deciding game of the World Series that year (the second game ended in a tie because of darkness), Hooper robbed Larry Doyle of the New York Giants of a home run, falling into the stands after making a leaping, bare-handed catch. The Sox won the game and the Series 3–2 in 10 innings.

He still holds the Red Sox club record for most triples, with 130, way out in front of teammates who have come since. The closest among recent players is Jim Rice, in sixth place with 79. Hooper also has the most career stolen bases, with 300; to give you an idea how much of a lead he has in this statistic, Tris Speaker had 267 and Carl Yastrzemski is in third place with 168.

Hooper has three other footnotes in Boston baseball history. He was the first player (and among the few to ever do this) to pinch hit for Babe Ruth; this happened in 1914 when Ruth was making his debut as a rookie pitcher. In 1915, he was in the lineup when Ruth hit his first home run. And then in 1935, after he had retired and was working as traveling secretary for the Boston Braves, Hooper was in attendance when Ruth hit his 714th and last home run.

Harry Hooper

Year	Team	Age	G	AB	R	H	2B	3B	HR	RBI	BA
1909	BOS (AL)	21	81	255	29	72	3	4	0	12	.282
1910	BOS (AL)	22	155	584	81	156	9	10	2	27	.267
1911	BOS (AL)	23	130	524	93	163	20	6	4	45	.311
1912	BOS (AL)	24	147	590	98	143	20	12	2	53	.242
1913	BOS (AL)	25	148	586	100	169	29	12	4	40	.288
1914	BOS (AL)	26	142	530	85	137	23	15	1	41	.258
1915	BOS (AL)	27	149	566	90	133	20	13	2	51	.235
1916	BOS (AL)	28	151	575	75	156	20	11	1	37	.271
1917	BOS (AL)	29	151	559	89	143	21	11	3	45	.256
1918	BOS (AL)	30	126	474	81	137	26	13	1	44	.289
1919	BOS (AL)	31	128	491	76	131	25	6	3	49	.267
1920	BOS (AL)	32	139	536	91	167	30	17	7	53	.312
1921	CHW (AL)	33	108	419	74	137	26	5	8	58	.327
1922	CHW (AL)	34	152	602	111	183	35	8	11	80	.304
1923	CHW (AL)	35	145	576	87	166	32	4	10	65	.288
1924	CHW (AL)	36	130	476	107	156	27	8	10	62	.328
1925	CHW (AL)	37	127	442	62	117	23	5	6	55	.265
Total			**2309**	**8785**	**1429**	**2466**	**389**	**160**	**75**	**817**	**.281**
Boston			**1647**	**6270**	**988**	**1707**	**246**	**130**	**30**	**289**	**.272**

Year	Team	OBP	SLG	OPS	BB	SO	TB	SB	CS	SH	SF	IBB	HBP	GDP
1909	BOS (AL)	.337	.325	.662	16	n/a	83	15	n/a	6	n/a	n/a	5	n/a
1910	BOS (AL)	.346	.327	.673	62	n/a	191	40	n/a	34	n/a	n/a	8	n/a
1911	BOS (AL)	.399	.395	.794	73	n/a	207	38	n/a	13	n/a	n/a	4	n/a
1912	BOS (AL)	.326	.327	.653	66	n/a	193	29	n/a	21	n/a	n/a	7	n/a
1913	BOS (AL)	.359	.399	.758	60	51	234	26	n/a	13	n/a	n/a	5	n/a
1914	BOS (AL)	.336	.364	.700	58	47	193	19	14	7	n/a	n/a	4	n/a
1915	BOS (AL)	.342	.327	.669	89	36	185	22	20	17	n/a	n/a	3	n/a
1916	BOS (AL)	.361	.350	.711	80	35	201	27	11	14	n/a	n/a	1	n/a
1917	BOS (AL)	.355	.349	.704	80	40	195	21	n/a	22	n/a	n/a	6	n/a
1918	BOS (AL)	.391	.405	.796	75	25	192	24	n/a	16	n/a	n/a	4	n/a
1919	BOS (AL)	.374	.360	.734	79	28	177	23	n/a	12	n/a	n/a	5	n/a
1920	BOS (AL)	.411	.470	.881	88	27	252	16	18	5	n/a	n/a	2	n/a
1921	CHW (AL)	.406	.470	.876	55	21	197	13	7	12	n/a	n/a	1	n/a
1922	CHW (AL)	.379	.444	.823	68	33	267	16	12	10	n/a	n/a	5	n/a
1923	CHW (AL)	.370	.410	.780	68	22	236	18	18	14	n/a	n/a	7	n/a
1924	CHW (AL)	.413	.481	.894	65	26	229	16	13	14	n/a	n/a	4	n/a
1925	CHW (AL)	.351	.380	.731	54	21	168	12	8	17	n/a	n/a	5	n/a
Total		**.368**	**.387**	**.755**	**1136**	**412**	**3400**	**375**	**121**	**247**			**76**	
Boston		**.272**	**.367**	**.639**	**826**	**289**	**2303**	**300**	**300**	**180**			**54**	

GEORGE DUFFY LEWIS
George Edward Lewis ("Duffy")
(Boston 1910–1917; career 1910–1921)

Primary position: LF	
Batted: R	
Threw: R	
Height: 5'10"	
Weight: 165 pounds	
First major league game: April 16, 1910	
Final major league game: June 6, 1921	
Born: April 18, 1888 in Los Angeles, California	
Died: June 17, 1979 in Salem, New Hampshire	
Boston Red Sox Hall of Fame: 2002	

Before there was the Green Monster in Fenway Park's leftfield, there was an incline that rose ten feet to meet the wall from the leftfield foul pole to the flagpole in centerfield. The mound helped hold up the wall, and when overflow crowds showed up at the ballpark, fans would camp out on the incline.

The first Red Sox player to play there—and master it with great skill—was Duffy Lewis, and with a bit of hyperbole the mound was nicknamed "Duffy's Cliff." The incline mound was removed in 1934, putting the base of the wall a few feet below Lansdowne Street on the other side of the Monster. There may have been a slight incline toward the wall for years afterward, but Fenway's field was completely redone after the 2004 season.

For nearly all of his time in Boston, Lewis was part of the superb defensive outfield that also included Tris Speaker in center and Harry Hooper in right. Cartoonists of the time sometimes depicted Lewis as a mountain climber with a fielder's mitt.

In eight years with Boston, Lewis batted .289 with 629 RBIs and played on three World Series championship teams: 1912, 1915, and 1916. He missed the 1918 season because of World War I.

In 1919, he was traded to the New York Yankees, preceding Babe Ruth by a year. He played two years for New York and a partial season

Photo by the National Baseball Hall of Fame Library, Cooperstown, N.Y.

in 1921 with the Washington Senators. He continued his career as a player-manager in the minor leagues.

Throughout the history of the Red Sox, leftfield at Fenway has been a difficult place to play, because of the "cliff" and more importantly because of the Green Monster. Think of the great players who have patrolled there: Ted Williams, Carl Yastrzemski, Jim Rice, Mike Greenwell, and Manny Ramirez. They're all following in the footsteps of the original mountain climber, Duffy Lewis.

Duffy Lewis

Year	Team	Age	G	AB	R	H	2B	3B	HR	RBI	BA
1910	BOS (AL)	22	151	541	64	153	29	7	8	68	.283
1911	BOS (AL)	23	130	469	64	144	32	4	7	86	.307
1912	BOS (AL)	24	154	581	85	165	36	9	6	109	.284
1913	BOS (AL)	25	149	551	54	164	31	12	0	90	.298
1914	BOS (AL)	26	146	510	53	142	37	9	2	79	.278
1915	BOS (AL)	27	152	557	69	162	31	7	2	76	.291
1916	BOS (AL)	28	152	563	56	151	29	5	1	56	.268
1917	BOS (AL)	29	150	553	55	167	29	9	1	65	.302
1919	NYY (AL)	31	141	559	67	152	23	4	7	89	.272
1920	NYY (AL)	32	107	365	34	99	8	1	4	61	.271
1921	WSH (AL)	33	27	102	11	19	4	1	0	14	.186
Total			**1459**	**5351**	**612**	**1518**	**289**	**68**	**38**	**793**	**.284**
Boston			**1184**	**4325**	**500**	**1248**	**254**	**62**	**27**	**629**	**.289**

Year	Team	OBP	SLG	OPS	BB	SO	TB	SB	CS	SH	SF	IBB	HBP	GDP
1910	BOS (AL)	.328	.407	.735	32		220	10	n/a	27	n/a	n/a	4	n/a
1911	BOS (AL)	.355	.437	.792	25		205	11	n/a	23	n/a	n/a	10	n/a
1912	BOS (AL)	.346	.408	.754	52		237	9	n/a	31	n/a	n/a	3	n/a
1913	BOS (AL)	.336	.397	.733	30	55	219	12	n/a	29	n/a	n/a	2	n/a
1914	BOS (AL)	.357	.398	.755	57	41	203	22	31	24	n/a	n/a	5	n/a
1915	BOS (AL)	.348	.382	.730	45	63	213	14	7	28	n/a	n/a	4	n/a
1916	BOS (AL)	.313	.343	.656	33	56	193	16	n/a	24	n/a	n/a	4	n/a
1917	BOS (AL)	.342	.392	.734	29	54	217	8	n/a	33	n/a	n/a	5	n/a
1919	NYY (AL)	.293	.365	.658	17	42	204	8	n/a	26	n/a	n/a	0	n/a
1920	NYY (AL)	.320	.332	.652	24	32	121	2	8	16	n/a	n/a	2	n/a
1921	WSH (AL)	.252	.245	.497	8	10	25	1	1	3	n/a	n/a	1	n/a
Total		**.333**	**.384**	**.717**	**352**	**353**	**2057**	**113**	**n/a**	**264**	**n/a**	**n/a**	**40**	**n/a**
Boston		**.340**	**.394**	**.734**	**303**	**269**	**1707**	**102**	**n/a**	**219**	**n/a**	**n/a**	**37**	**n/a**

*Strikeout and Caught Stealing stats are incomplete

BABE RUTH

George Herman Ruth ("The Babe,"
"The Bambino," "The Sultan of Swat")
(Boston 1914–1919; career 1914–1935)

Primary position: RF, P	
Batted: L	
Threw: L	
Height: 6'2"	
Weight: 215 pounds	
First major league game: July 11, 1914	
Final major league game: May 30, 1935	
Born: February 6, 1895 in Baltimore, Maryland	
Died: August 16, 1948 in New York, New York	
Baseball Hall of Fame: 1936	

The Babe: Perhaps the greatest ballplayer of all time, he was the one that got away from the Red Sox when he was traded before the 1920 season to that American League team in New York. He qualifies as a hero in this book based on his six seasons in Boston . . . despite the pain he caused generations of Red Sox fans in the 1920s and early 1930s, achievements that still echoed until Boston finally won it all in 2004.

Babe was bigger than life, in his actions on the field and even more so off the field. He had a prodigious appetite for almost everything, from food to partying. No matter what people say about today's players appearing in ads, in movies, or on the non-sports pages of the newspapers, it was all done before—in a very big way—by Babe Ruth.

When I was with the Angels, one of my coaches was Jimmy Reese, who was Babe Ruth's roommate on the Yankees in 1930 and 1931. Jimmy told me he never saw him. He said that when they were on the road, the only things in the hotel room they shared were the Babe's suitcases.

Ruth signed a professional contract with the minor league Baltimore Orioles in February of 1914. He played half a season with that team, and then because of the financial needs of the Orioles, he was

sold to the Boston Red Sox and made his major league debut that same year at the age of 19.

He was obviously very talented, but also very green. And according to stories of the time, he did not get along very well with the mere mortals on the team. Twenty years later, the same sort of things were said about another rising Red Sox phenom, Ted Williams.

Ruth pitched well after arriving in 1914 in July, but the team wasn't doing that well and Ruth was sent back down to the minor leagues. He played for the Providence Grays, winning nine games in less than two months and helping them grab the International League pennant; on September 5, 1914, Ruth threw a 9–0 shutout for the Grays playing in Toronto against the Maple Leafs and also hit the first home run of his professional career.

In his six years with the Red Sox, the Babe had a pitching record of 89–46, including 17 shutouts and 105 complete games. He had an impressively low ERA of 2.19. And, in an interesting bit of irony, he yielded only a total of 9 home runs in 1,190 innings or the equivalent of about 1 every 13 games.

The Red Sox used the Babe exclusively as a pitcher from 1914 to 1916, but he began to shine as a hitter on those days he was also throwing and soon was playing in the field as well.

The Babe pitched for the Red Sox in the 1916 World Series against Brooklyn and in 1918 against the Chicago Cubs, winning all three games he started and posting a total ERA of 0.87: just 3 earned runs across 31 innings pitched. The Sox won both Series; the 1918 championship would be the last one captured by Boston for 86 years until the great season of 2004.

And from 1915 to 1917 he put up some spectacular numbers as a pitcher. Across those three years he won 65 games and lost only 33. In 1916 his ERA was a miniscule 1.75. By 1918, though, the Red Sox were beginning to see that he could be even more valuable as an everyday player. In that year, the Babe appeared in 95 games (including 20 as a pitcher, 59 in the outfield, 13 at first base, and 3 times as a pinch-hitter), batting .300 with 11 home runs while posting a 13-7 record as a starter.

As a member of the Red Sox lineup, across the equivalent of two-and-a-half seasons as a batter, Ruth had 49 home runs, 230 RBIs, and a batting average of .308. In 1919, his final year in Boston, he only pitched in 17 games and played the outfield for 111 games and first base for 5 more; that season he showed hints of the greatness he would attain as a hitter: In 1919, in 432 at-bats, he swatted 29 home runs, drove in 114 runs, and batted .322. He also hit 12 triples, the rare hit that generally requires both power and speed. (And in those 17 games started as a pitcher, he went 9–5 with an ERA of 2.97.)

We'll never know the sort of numbers he would have put up as a member of the Red Sox if he had been allowed to stay in Boston. We do know that in 1921, his second year as a member of the Yankees, he had an explosive season: he hit 59 home runs, 16 triples, 44 doubles, and drove in 171 runs, and batted .378 for the season. And apparently just for the fun of it, he pitched in two games that year, winning both.

As of this writing, Ruth still holds the record for the highest OPS for a career, at 1.1638. (As a part-time hitter for the Red Sox, his OPS was still an impressive 0.978.) To some people, OPS is a very valuable measure of a hitter. It is calculated as the total of a player's on-base percentage plus his slugging percentage. On-base percentage tells you how often a player reaches base as the result of a hit or a walk or hit-by-pitch, and it deducts from the calculation productive sacrifice flies. Anything over about .400 is very good, meaning that on average a player is on base about 4 out of 10 times he comes to the plate. Slugging percentage looks at the total bases produced per at-bat. Walks and singles are worth a base, doubles two bases, triples three bases, and home runs . . . you've figured this out, right? . . . are worth four bases. So Babe Ruth's career OPS means he was good for about six bases for every five plate appearances.

Here are the all-time leaders in OPS (through the start of the 2009 season, with active players in **bold**):

Babe Ruth	1.1638
Ted Williams	1.1155
Lou Gehrig	1.0798
Barry Bonds	1.0512
Albert Pujols	**1.0489**
Jimmie Foxx	1.0376
Hank Greenberg	1.0169
Rogers Hornsby	1.0103
Manny Ramirez	**1.0044**
Todd Helton	**1.0020**

And here is the list of all-time single-season OPS records throughout the history of baseball:

Barry Bonds	1.4217	(2004)
Babe Ruth	1.3818	(1920)
Barry Bonds	1.3807	(2002)
Barry Bonds	1.3785	(2001)
Babe Ruth	1.3586	(1921)
Babe Ruth	1.3089	(1923)
Ted Williams	1.2875	(1941)
Barry Bonds	1.2778	(2003)
Babe Ruth	1.2582	(1927)
Ted Williams	1.2566	(1957)

One of Babe Ruth's most famous pitching performances was the opening act of what has to be the strangest no-hitter in baseball history. On June 23, 1917, Ruth was the starting pitcher against Washington. Ruth walked the first batter on four pitches, and he complained bitterly and loudly to umpire Brick Owens. To make a short story even shorter, he eventually directed at least one of the magic words at an umpire that cannot go unanswered and Ruth was tossed from the game. Ruth was so hot he tried to punch the ump on his way to the showers.

Boston pitcher Ernie Shore—who had a short but successful career with the Red Sox that was interrupted and all but ended by a year of military service in World War I—came in to replace Ruth. The runner on first was thrown out trying to steal a base and Shore went on to retire every one of the next 26 batters; it was put down in the record books as a perfect game, later amended to a two-pitcher no-hitter. You can look it up.

The story of the sale of Babe Ruth to the Yankees is one of those tales often told and often told wrongly. It's a complicated story, but it begins with a successful showman and producer named Harry Frazee. He began his career in 1899 promoting barnstorming exhibitions by minor league teams in the Midwest and by 1910 he had moved on to building and owning theaters in New York. He had a string of successful shows, mostly light musical comedies.

About the same time he set his eyes on buying a baseball team, trying for the Boston Braves of the National League and later for the Chicago Cubs and the New York Giants; none of the deals worked out. By 1916, he was a millionaire—back when a million dollars was a whole lot of money—and in 1917 he was able to make a substantial offer for the Red Sox. Together with a partner, Frazee offered about $675,000 for the team (and its increasingly valuable real estate in the Fens).

And if you think that fancy financial deals were only invented recently, think again. Frazee did not even have to come up with the full purchase price; only half the money was in the form of cash with the rest in the form of notes that would be paid off over time from the profits of the club. Frazee also promised to devote his full attention to running the baseball team, although he did continue to dabble a bit in New York.

So how did Babe Ruth, who was obviously a fine pitcher, end up playing in the outfield? The most obvious answer, of course, is that he turned out to be a tremendous hitter and also possessed other essential tools: hitting for power, speed on the bases, and athletic skill as a fielder. The second answer is that in 1918 the ranks of the Red Sox were depleted because a number of players were in uniform, military not baseball. And so Ruth was needed to fill in as a position player, at first base or right field.

He began to hit, and hit balls far. And soon his regular appearances in the lineup produced some spectacular feats such as homering in four consecutive games, including one in which he was also the starting pitcher.

It was also true that at the time he was hitting against second- and third-string pitchers much of the time because some of the game's best hurlers were off to war. In any case, Ruth seemed to enjoy hitting more than pitching, and at one point reported a sore arm and asked to play the field instead of the mound. Management wanted it both ways, but Ruth solved the problem for the moment when he went into a slump in mid-summer in 1918. A left-handed hitter, he was apparently trying to pull every ball into right field, and other teams began successfully getting him out with left-handed pitchers. Ruth went back to being a pitcher for the remainder of the season and helped lead the Red Sox to the American League title and into the World Series against the Chicago Cubs.

The weaker competition that year, and the fact that the season was shortened by a few weeks to 126 games because of the war, are often overlooked. In any case, the Red Sox won the World Series in 1918. World War I ended on November 11, 1918, and as any Red Sox fan knows, it would be a long, long time before they would do it again: World War II, the Korean War, the Vietnam War, and 85 years would come and go before another World Series title would come to Boston.

Even with his slump, Ruth had hit 11 home runs in the 1918 season, an astounding number in the dead ball era; the total for the entire American League that year was 98.

And then came the 1919 season, which was Ruth's last in Boston. The widely held belief is that owner Frazee was having financial difficulties with his Broadway and other theatrical productions and sold Ruth to finance a show. That story is not correct.

The American League had suffered during the final years of World War I as players were in the service and as "non-essential" activities were curtailed. And there was another sort of war among some of the owners of teams in the AL as well as the older National League.

Oddly enough, the Red Sox and the New York Yankees were allies in many of the internal battles. At the end of the 1918 season, Frazee sold some of his former stars—Duffy Lewis, Ernie Shore, and Dutch Leonard—to the Yankees. Lewis and Shore were on the decline and as it turned out, Leonard refused to go to New York and ended up in Cleveland. One of the reasons Frazee could spare these players was Babe Ruth's emergence as a very valuable outfielder while still holding a spot in the pitching rotation.

Before the 1919 season, Ruth demanded a new contract that reflected his double duties; he wanted $15,000 for a one-year deal, a pretty large amount of money for the time. Frazee refused; Ruth threatened to retire or become an actor, neither very likely for a talented 24-year-old ballplayer not yet at his prime.

Frazee threatened to trade Ruth; Ruth did not show up at spring training. At the last minute, Frazee and Ruth agreed to a three-year contract paying a total of $30,000.

In spring training, while still working out as a pitcher, Ruth again took his turn in the outfield and in April of 1919 he clubbed a ball an estimated 587 feet at a stadium at what was to become the University of Tampa in Florida.

As the 1919 season got underway, Ruth had streaks of great hitting interspersed with slumps and regular battles with his manager Ed Barrow. And when he did hit well, his success came mostly against right-handers, and he had problems with the deep recesses of right field at Fenway Park. (Of the 49 homers Ruth hit as a member of the Red Sox, only 11 came at home.)

Ruth was a spot pitcher in 1919, pitching regularly mostly in the second half of the season after the troubled Carl Mays was traded . . . to the Yankees. The Babe set the record for home runs at 29 for the season, but overall Boston had a dismal record, finishing in sixth place and 20.5 games behind the Chicago White Sox. (Some of the members of these same White Sox conspired to fix the 1919 World Series; they became known as the Black Sox.)

Meanwhile, despite having Babe Ruth, Boston's attendance tumbled that year; fans wanted a winning team. And it was also no secret that Ruth was a big handful of trouble in many ways; he got into trouble in all sorts of ways off the field. That's the PG-rated version of a very wild story. If you think Manny being Manny drove Boston management mad, when the Babe was in Boston the ride was wild.

In the off-season, Ruth traveled around the country to play in exhibitions and make special appearances. He even headed to Hollywood to try to gain a bit more exposure in the movie industry. When the 1920 season approached, he told reporters that he once again wanted to renegotiate his contract; this time he wanted $20,000 for a year, which was more than any other player was receiving at the time.

Frazee again said no, and the Boston newspapers were filled with leaks from both sides. Some praised Ruth as indispensable to the coming success of the team, while others took ownership's side, saying that a contract was in place and any changes to the Babe's deal could result in every player on the Red Sox also demanding a raise.

In any case, on December 26, 1919, Harry Frazee apparently decided that Ruth was more trouble than he was worth. He agreed to sell him to the New York Yankees for $125,000, the largest transaction in the history of professional baseball to that time; the deal would take effect if the Yankees and Ruth could come to a contract agreement. And there was a second, side deal that obligated Yankees owner Jacob Ruppert to arrange a loan of $350,000 to Frazee, using Fenway Park as collateral; the agreement was obviously connected to the sale of Ruth but was not dependent upon it.

So, the story is obviously a lot more complicated than the common explanation that Frazee sold the Babe to the Yankees to pay his debts or to finance a Broadway show. You can read all about it: Frazee issued a statement to the press that was published on January 7, 1920, a day after Ruth agreed to terms with the Yankees.

"Ruth had simply become impossible and the Boston Club could no longer put up with his eccentricities," Frazee wrote. "While Ruth, without question is the greatest hitter that the game has ever seen, he is likewise one of the most selfish and inconsiderate men that ever wore a baseball uniform. Had he possessed the right disposition, had he been willing to take orders and work for the good of the club like the other men on the team, I would never have dared let him go."

I guess it's fair to say that would not be the first time the Red Sox—or other teams—would believe they had no choice but to part with a great hitter or pitcher. A player has to want to play to put up big numbers.

Anyhow, the rest you probably know about: He took his 49 home runs in 6 seasons to New York and went on to hit 659 more for the Yankees across 15 seasons. In 1935, the Babe came back to Boston—to the National League Braves—and played in 28 games (hitting 6 dingers) before hanging up his cleats at age 40.

(For the record, he only started four more games and threw in a fifth after he was sold to the Yankees in 1920; they decided that as great as he was as a pitcher, he was even better when he was in the lineup as a hitter.)

Oh, and one more thing for the record. In Ruth's day, balls that hit the foul pole were counted as doubles and balls that left the park fair but hooked out of bounds on the other side of the pole were called foul balls. We'll never know . . . but Ruth probably hit a few hundred more homers than are on his Hall of Fame plaque.

Babe Ruth

Hitting

Year	Team	Age	G	AB	R	H	2B	3B	HR	RBI	BA	
1914	BOS (AL)	19	5	10	1	2	1	0	0	2	.200	
1915	BOS (AL)	20	42	92	16	29	10	1	4	21	.315	
1916	BOS (AL)	21	67	136	18	37	5	3	3	15	.272	
1917	BOS (AL)	22	67	123	14	40	6	3	2	12	.325	
1918	BOS (AL)	23	95	317	50	95	26	11	11	66	.300	
1919	BOS (AL)	24	130	432	103	139	34	12	29	114	.322	
1920	NYY (AL)	25	142	457	158	172	36	9	54	137	.376	
1921	NYY (AL)	26	152	540	177	204	44	16	59	171	.378	
1922	NYY (AL)	27	110	406	94	128	24	8	35	99	.315	
1923	NYY (AL)	28	152	522	151	205	45	13	41	131	.393	MVP
1924	NYY (AL)	29	153	529	143	200	39	7	46	121	.378	
1925	NYY (AL)	30	98	359	61	104	12	2	25	66	.290	
1926	NYY (AL)	31	152	495	139	184	30	5	47	150	.372	
1927	NYY (AL)	32	151	540	158	192	29	8	60	164	.356	
1928	NYY (AL)	33	154	536	163	173	29	8	54	142	.323	
1929	NYY (AL)	34	135	499	121	172	26	6	46	154	.345	
1930	NYY (AL)	35	145	518	150	186	28	9	49	153	.359	

Hitting cont.

Year	Team	Age	G	AB	R	H	2B	3B	HR	RBI	BA	
1931	NYY (AL)	36	145	534	149	199	31	3	46	163	.373	
1932	NYY (AL)	37	133	457	120	156	13	5	41	137	.341	
1933	NYY (AL)	38	137	459	97	138	21	3	34	103	.301	AS
1934	NYY (AL)	39	125	365	78	105	17	4	22	84	.288	AS
1935	BSN (NL)	40	28	72	13	13	0	0	6	12	.181	
Total			**2518**	**8398**	**2174**	**2873**	**506**	**136**	**714**	**2217**	**.342**	
Boston			**406**	**1110**	**202**	**342**	**82**	**30**	**49**	**230**	**.308**	

Year	Team	OBP	SLG	OPS	BB	SO	TB	SB	CS	SH	SF	IBB	HBP	GDP
1914	BOS (AL)	.200	.300	.500	0	4	3	0	n/a	0	n/a	n/a	n/a	n/a
1915	BOS (AL)	.376	.576	.952	9	23	53	0	n/a	2	n/a	n/a	0	n/a
1916	BOS (AL)	.322	.419	.741	10	23	57	0	n/a	4	n/a	n/a	0	n/a
1917	BOS (AL)	.385	.472	.857	12	18	58	0	n/a	7	n/a	n/a	0	n/a
1918	BOS (AL)	.411	.555	.966	58	58	176	6	n/a	3	n/a	n/a	2	n/a
1919	BOS (AL)	.456	.657	1.113	101	58	284	7	n/a	3	n/a	n/a	6	n/a
1920	NYY (AL)	.533	.849	1.382	150	80	388	14	14	5	n/a	n/a	3	n/a
1921	NYY (AL)	.512	.846	1.358	145	81	457	17	13	4	n/a	n/a	4	n/a
1922	NYY (AL)	.434	.672	1.106	84	80	273	2	5	4	n/a	n/a	1	n/a
1923	NYY (AL)	.545	.764	1.309	170	93	399	17	21	3	n/a	n/a	4	n/a
1924	NYY (AL)	.513	.739	1.252	142	81	391	9	13	6	n/a	n/a	4	n/a
1925	NYY (AL)	.393	.543	.936	59	68	195	2	4	6	n/a	n/a	2	n/a
1926	NYY (AL)	.516	.737	1.253	144	76	365	11	9	10	n/a	n/a	3	n/a
1927	NYY (AL)	.486	.772	1.258	137	89	417	7	6	14	n/a	n/a	0	n/a
1928	NYY (AL)	.463	.709	1.172	137	87	380	4	5	8	n/a	n/a	3	n/a
1929	NYY (AL)	.430	.697	1.127	72	60	348	5	3	13	n/a	n/a	3	n/a
1930	NYY (AL)	.493	.732	1.225	136	61	379	10	10	21	n/a	n/a	1	n/a
1931	NYY (AL)	.495	.700	1.195	128	51	374	5	4	0	n/a	n/a	1	n/a
1932	NYY (AL)	.489	.661	1.150	130	62	302	2	2	0	n/a	n/a	2	n/a
1933	NYY (AL)	.442	.582	1.024	114	90	267	4	5	0	n/a	n/a	2	n/a
1934	NYY (AL)	.448	.537	.985	104	63	196	1	3	0	n/a	n/a	2	n/a
1935	BSN (NL)	.359	.431	.790	20	24	31	0		0	n/a	n/a	0	2
Total		**.474**	**.690**	**1.164**	**2062**	**1330**	**5793**	**123**	**117**	**113**	**n/a**	**n/a**	**43**	**2**
Boston		**.409**	**.568**	**.977**	**190**	**184**	**631**	**13**	**n/a**	**19**	**n/a**	**n/a**	**8**	

Note: OBP and OPS do not include HBP

Pitching

Year	Team	W	L	G	GS	CG	Shutouts	GF	S	WHIP	ERA
1914	BOS (AL)	2	1	4	3	1	0	0	0	1.217	3.91
1915	BOS (AL)	18	8	32	28	16	1	3	0	1.153	2.44
1916	BOS (AL)	23	12	44	41	23	9	3	1	1.075	1.75
1917	BOS (AL)	24	13	41	38	35	6	2	2	1.079	2.01
1918	BOS (AL)	13	7	20	19	18	1	0	0	1.046	2.22
1919	BOS (AL)	9	5	17	15	12	0	2	1	1.545	2.97
1920	NYY (AL)	1	0	1	1	0	0	0	0	1.250	4.50
1921	NYY (AL)	2	0	2	1	0	0	1	0	2.556	9.00
1930	NYY (AL)	1	0	1	1	1	0	0	0	1.444	3.00
1933	NYY (AL)	1	0	1	1	1	0	0	0	1.667	5.00
Total		**94**	**46**	**163**	**148**	**107**	**17**	**11**	**4**	**1.159**	**2.28**
Boston		**89**	**46**	**158**	**144**	**105**	**17**	**10**	**4**	**1.142**	**2.19**

Year		IP	H	R	ER	HR	BB	SO	HBP	WP	IBB	BK
1914	BOS (AL)	23	21	12	10	1	7	3	0	0	n/a	0
1915	BOS (AL)	217.7	166	80	59	3	85	112	6	9		1
1916	BOS (AL)	323.7	230	83	63	0	118	170	8	3		1
1917	BOS (AL)	326.3	244	91	73	2	108	128	11	5		0
1918	BOS (AL)	166.3	125	51	41	1	49	40	2	3		1
1919	BOS (AL)	133.3	148	59	44	2	58	30	2	5		1
1920	NYY (AL)	4	3	4	2	0	2	0	0	0		0
1921	NYY (AL)	9	14	10	9	1	9	2	0	0		0
1930	NYY (AL)	9	11	3	3	0	2	3	0	0		0
1933	NYY (AL)	9	12	5	5	0	3	0	0	0		0
Total		**1221.3**	**974**	**398**	**309**	**10**	**441**	**488**	**29**	**25**		**4**
Boston		**1190.3**	**934**	**376**	**290**	**9**	**425**	**483**	**29**	**25**		**4**

RICK FERRELL
Richard Benjamin Ferrell
(Boston 1933–1937; career 1929–1947)

Primary position: C	
Batted: R	
Threw: R	
Height: 5'10"	
Weight: 160 pounds	
First major league game: April 19, 1929	
Final major league game: September 14, 1947	
Born: October 12, 1905 in Durham, North Carolina	
Died: July 27, 1995 in Bloomfield Hills, Michigan	
Baseball Hall of Fame: 1984	
Boston Red Sox Hall of Fame: 1995	

Rick Ferrell is considered one of the best defensive catchers in baseball history. If you have any doubt, consider the fact that in 1945 as a member of the Washington Senators he handled a starting rotation that included four knuckleball pitchers, a fact that is prominent on Ferrell's Hall of Fame plaque.

Four knucklers: That had to be like eating soup with a fork. The Senators had Dutch Leonard, Johnny Niggeling, Mickey "Itsy Bitsy" Haefner, and Roger Wolff. Together they won 60 games that year and Ferrell was charged with only 21 passed balls for the 1945 season.

He was also remarkably durable. When he retired in 1947 at age 41 he held the American League record with 1,806 games caught; that mark stood until another player who starred in Boston, Carlton Fisk, surpassed it with 2,226.

In his career with Boston, which included most of 1933, full seasons in 1934, 1935, and 1936, and 18 games in 1937, Ferrell batted .302. His best season came in 1936 when he hit .312 and had 55 RBIs. In his career, he hit .300 or higher four times.

He was mostly a singles hitter, hitting only 28 home runs in his career; his brother Wes Ferrell had slightly more power, with a lifetime total of 38 homers as a pitcher. Rick also had an exceptional eye at the plate, striking out only 277 times in 6,028 at-bats and drawing 931 walks for his career.

Photo by the National Baseball Hall of Fame Library, Cooperstown, N.Y.

In 1933, the brothers were both selected to represent the American League in the first All-Star Game played; Wes was in his last year with the Cleveland Indians while Rick had joined the Red Sox two months earlier. Rick caught all nine innings.

The brothers both were members of the Red Sox from 1934 through 1937 and were regular battery mates, one Ferrell pitching to another. They were traded to Washington as part of a package for Ben Chapman and Bobo Newsom.

Rick Ferrell was elected to the Baseball Hall of Fame in 1984 by the Veterans Committee and earned automatic entrance to the Red Sox Hall of Fame. In 2008, brother Wes Ferrell was chosen for Boston's Hall in recognition of his four years on the team as a successful pitcher and one of the best-hitting pitchers in baseball: 62–40 as a pitcher and 17 home runs and a .308 batting average at the plate.

Rick Ferrell

Year	Team	Age	G	AB	R	H	2B	3B	HR	RBI	BA	
1929	SLB (AL)	23	64	144	21	33	6	1	0	20	.229	
1930	SLB (AL)	24	101	314	43	84	18	4	1	41	.268	
1931	SLB (AL)	25	117	386	47	118	30	4	3	57	.306	
1932	SLB (AL)	26	126	438	67	138	30	5	2	65	.315	
1933	*Season*	*27*	*140*	*493*	*58*	*143*	*21*	*4*	*4*	*77*	*.290*	AS
	SLB (AL)		22	72	8	18	2	0	1	5	.250	
	BOS (AL)		118	421	50	125	19	4	3	72	.297	
1934	BOS (AL)	28	132	437	50	130	29	4	1	48	.297	AS
1935	BOS (AL)	29	133	458	54	138	34	4	3	61	.301	AS
1936	BOS (AL)	30	121	410	59	128	27	5	8	55	.312	AS
1937	*Season*	*31*	*104*	*344*	*39*	*84*	*8*	*0*	*2*	*36*	*.244*	AS
	BOS (AL)		18	65	8	20	2	0	1	4	.308	
	WSH (AL)		86	279	31	64	6	0	1	32	.229	
1938	WSH (AL)	32	135	411	55	120	24	5	1	58	.292	AS
1939	WSH (AL)	33	87	274	32	77	13	1	0	31	.281	
1940	WSH (AL)	34	103	326	35	89	18	2	0	28	.273	
1941	*Season*	*35*	*121*	*387*	*38*	*99*	*19*	*3*	*2*	*36*	*.256*	
	WSH (AL)		21	66	8	18	5	0	0	13	.273	
	SLB (AL)		100	321	30	81	14	3	2	23	.252	
1942	SLB (AL)	36	99	273	20	61	6	1	0	26	.223	
1943	SLB (AL)	37	74	209	12	50	7	0	0	20	.239	
1944	WSH (AL)	38	99	339	14	94	11	1	0	25	.277	AS
1945	WSH (AL)	39	91	286	33	76	12	1	1	38	.266	AS
1947	WSH (AL)	41	37	99	10	30	11	0	0	12	.303	
Total			**1884**	**6028**	**687**	**1692**	**324**	**45**	**28**	**734**	**.281**	
Boston			**522**	**1791**	**221**	**541**	**111**	**17**	**16**	**240**	**.302**	

Year	Teams	OBP	SLG	OPS	BB	SO	TB	SB	CS	SH	SF	IBB	HBP	GDP
1929	SLB (AL)	.373	.285	.658	32	10	41	1	2	4	n/a	n/a	1	
1930	SLB (AL)	.363	.360	.723	46	10	113	1	4	11	n/a	n/a	1	
1931	SLB (AL)	.394	.427	.821	56	12	165	2	3	3	n/a	n/a	0	
1932	SLB (AL)	.406	.420	.826	66	18	184	5	5	9	n/a	n/a	1	
1933	*Season*	*.381*	*.373*	*.754*	*70*	*23*	*184*	*4*	*2*	*15*	*n/a*	*n/a*	*2*	
	SLB (AL)	.357	.319	.676	12	4	23	2	0	1	n/a	n/a	0	
	BOS (AL)	.385	.382	.767	58	19	161	2	2	14	n/a	n/a	2	
1934	BOS (AL)	.390	.389	.779	66	20	170	0	0	4	n/a	n/a	0	
1935	BOS (AL)	.388	.413	.801	65	15	189	5	8	13	n/a	n/a	0	
1936	BOS (AL)	.406	.461	.867	65	17	189	0	1	5	n/a	n/a	0	
1937	*Season*	*.366*	*.285*	*.651*	*65*	*33*	*98*	*1*	*1*	*2*	*n/a*	*n/a*	*1*	
	BOS (AL)	.438	.385	.823	15	4	25	0	0	0	n/a	n/a	0	
	WSH (AL)	.348	.262	.610	50	18	73	1	1	2	n/a	n/a	1	
1938	WSH (AL)	.401	.382	.783	75	17	157	1	0	9	n/a	n/a	0	
1939	WSH (AL)	.377	.336	.713	41	12	92	1	1	7	n/a	n/a	1	4
1940	WSH (AL)	.365	.340	.705	47	15	111	1	1	2	n/a	n/a	0	7
1941	*Season*	*.366*	*.336*	*.702*	*67*	*26*	*130*	*3*	*1*	*3*	*n/a*	*n/a*	*0*	*12*
	WSH (AL)	.407	.348	.755	15	4	23	1	0	1	n/a	n/a	0	3
	SLB (AL)	.357	.333	.690	52	22	107	2	1	2	n/a	n/a	0	9
1942	SLB (AL)	.307	.253	.560	33	13	69	0	1	6	n/a	n/a	0	5
1943	SLB (AL)	.348	.273	.621	34	14	57	0	0	2	n/a	n/a	1	3
1944	WSH (AL)	.364	.316	.680	46	13	107	2	1	2	n/a	n/a	0	10
1945	WSH (AL)	.366	.325	.691	43	13	93	2	4	4	n/a	n/a	2	10
1947	WSH (AL)	.389	.414	.803	14	7	41	0	0	2	n/a	n/a	0	4
Total		**.378**	**.363**	**.741**	**931**	**277**	**2190**	**29**	**35**	**103**	**n/a**	**n/a**	**10**	**55***
Boston		**.393**	**.410**	**.803**	**269**	**75**	**734**	**7**	**11**	**36**	**n/a**	**n/a**	**2**	**0**

(HBP and SF not included in OBP)

*GDP Incomplete

LEFTY GROVE
Robert Moses Grove ("Lefty")
(Boston 1934–1941; career 1925–1941)

Primary position: P	
Batted: L	
Threw: L	
Height: 6'3"	
Weight: 190 pounds	
First major league game: April 14, 1925	
Final major league game: September 28, 1941	
Born: March 6, 1900 in Lonaconing, Maryland	
Died: May 22, 1975 in Norwalk, Ohio	
Baseball Hall of Fame: 1947	

We all stand in awe of Pedro Martinez, who compiled an amazing record of 117–37 in six years with the Red Sox, and a winning percentage of .760. And there is the almost unstoppable Roger Clemens, who posted a mark of 192–111 (.634) in 13 seasons in Boston.

For his time—an era that included some of the greatest hitters in the history of baseball—Lefty Grove was nearly as dominant. Grove is on almost any baseball historian's list of the greatest left-handed pitchers of all time.

Grove was injured and seemed to be on an irreversible decline when he came to the Red Sox at age 34 in 1934; he posted an 8–8 record and a 6.50 ERA that season. But in 1935, Grove recovered some of his earlier brilliance and in that season he won 20 games against 12 losses with a 2.70 ERA. Over the course of his eight years in Boston, he won 105 games against 62 losses for a .629 winning percentage. He retired at the age of 41.

Let's back up for a moment and consider the entire careers of all three.

Lefty Grove pitched for 17 seasons (beginning with the American League's Philadelphia Athletics and finishing in Boston) and ended with a 300–141 record, a winning percentage of .680 and an ERA of 3.06. He won the pitching Triple Crown in 1930 and 1931 and was the Most Valuable Player for 1931, and led the league in strikeouts for seven consecutive seasons.

Pedro Martinez was with the New York Mets in 2007 (he began his career with the Los Angeles Dodgers, moving to the Montreal Expos, then the Red Sox, and on to the Mets). Plagued with injuries in New York, he posted a still-respectable 32–23 record in the equivalent of about two seasons spread across four years. Through the end of the 2008 season, his career mark stood at 214–99, a winning percentage of .684 and an ERA of 2.91.

And the Rocket, Roger Clemens, came up with the Red Sox and then moved to Toronto, the New York Yankees, the NL Houston Astros, and then back to the Yankees (with a few retirements and semi-retirements along the way). Clemens did not play in 2008, and as we go to press his career mark stood at 354–184, a winning percentage of .658 and an ERA of 3.12. So I'd take a right-left-right rotation of Clemens, Grove, and Martinez any time. Wouldn't you?

Lefty Grove was discovered by Jack Dunn, the owner of the minor league Baltimore Orioles; Dunn was also responsible for spotting and eventually delivering Babe Ruth to the Red Sox. Grove was sold to the Philadelphia Athletics of the AL in 1925 and was almost unbeatable from the start. In the three seasons from 1929 to 1931, Grove won 75 games and lost just 15, crowned by the 1931 season in which he posted a 31–4 record and an ERA of 2.06.

Grove is one of only three pitchers in the history of the game to have struck out the side on nine pitches twice in their careers. (The others are Sandy Koufax in 1962 and 1964, and Nolan Ryan in 1968 and 1972.) Grove's accomplishment came in 1928, about a month apart near the end of that one season.

Grove, by all accounts, was not a particularly pleasant fellow. He did not get along with fans, and was known for publicly telling off his own team if they failed to make a play behind him. And way before his time, he also negotiated special privileges in his contract including his own workout schedule and midseason vacations (not because he needed the rest but because he could pick up some extra cash by pitching exhibition games for barnstorming teams.)

Lefty Grove

Year	Team	Age	W	L	G	GS	CG	SHO	GF	SV	WHIP	ERA	
1925	PHA (AL)	25	10	12	45	18	5	0	12	1	1.716	4.75	
1926	PHA (AL)	26	13	13	45	33	20	1	9	6	1.271	2.51	
1927	PHA (AL)	27	20	13	51	28	14	1	18	9	1.258	3.19	
1928	PHA (AL)	28	24	8	39	31	24	4	6	4	1.116	2.58	
1929	PHA (AL)	29	20	6	42	37	19	2	5	4	1.304	2.81	
1930	PHA (AL)	30	28	5	50	32	22	2	17	9	1.144	2.54	
1931	PHA (AL)	31	31	4	41	30	27	4	10	5	1.077	2.06	MVP
1932	PHA (AL)	32	25	10	44	30	27	4	13	7	1.193	2.84	
1933	PHA (AL)	33	24	8	45	28	21	2	16	6	1.318	3.20	AS
1934	BOS (AL)	34	8	8	22	12	5	0	6	0	1.655	6.50	
1935	BOS (AL)	35	20	12	35	30	23	2	4	1	1.223	2.70	AS
1936	BOS (AL)	36	17	12	35	30	22	6	3	2	1.192	2.81	AS
1937	BOS (AL)	37	17	9	32	32	21	3	0	0	1.344	3.02	AS

Year	Team	Age	W	L	G	GS	CG	SHO	GF	SV	WHIP	ERA	
1938	BOS (AL)	38	14	4	24	21	12	1	3	1	1.350	3.08	AS
1939	BOS (AL)	39	15	4	23	23	17	2	0	0	1.246	2.54	AS
1940	BOS (AL)	40	7	6	22	21	9	1	1	0	1.363	3.99	
1941	BOS (AL)	41	7	7	21	21	10	0	0	0	1.470	4.37	
Total			**300**	**141**	**616**	**457**	**298**	**35**	**123**	**55**	**1.278**	**3.06**	
Boston			**105**	**62**	**214**	**190**	**119**	**15**	**17**	**4**	**1.321**	**3.34**	

Year	Team	IP	H	R	ER	HR	BB	SO	HBP	WP	IBB	BK
1925	PHA (AL)	197	207	120	104	11	131	116	5	9	n/a	0
1926	PHA (AL)	258	227	97	72	6	101	194	6	5	n/a	0
1927	PHA (AL)	262.3	251	116	93	6	79	174	2	5	n/a	1
1928	PHA (AL)	261.7	228	93	75	10	64	183	1	4	n/a	0
1929	PHA (AL)	275.3	278	104	86	8	81	170	3	8	n/a	0
1930	PHA (AL)	291	273	101	82	8	60	209	5	2	n/a	0
1931	PHA (AL)	288.7	249	84	66	10	62	175	1	2	n/a	0
1932	PHA (AL)	291.7	269	101	92	13	79	188	1	0	n/a	0
1933	PHA (AL)	275.3	280	113	98	12	83	114	4	1	n/a	0
1934	BOS (AL)	109.3	149	84	79	5	32	43	1	1	n/a	0
1935	BOS (AL)	273	269	105	82	6	65	121	3	2	n/a	0
1936	BOS (AL)	253.3	237	90	79	14	65	130	4	0	n/a	0
1937	BOS (AL)	262	269	101	88	9	83	153	1	5	n/a	0
1938	BOS (AL)	163.7	169	65	56	8	52	99	1	3	n/a	0
1939	BOS (AL)	191	180	63	54	8	58	81	1	0	n/a	0
1940	BOS (AL)	153.3	159	73	68	20	50	62	1	1	n/a	0
1941	BOS (AL)	134	155	84	65	8	42	54	2	3	n/a	0
Total		**3941**	**3849**	**1594**	**1339**	**162**	**1187**	**2266**	**42**	**51**		**1**
Boston		**1540**	**1587**	**665**	**571**	**78**	**447**	**743**	**14**	**15**		**0**

JOE CRONIN
Joseph Edward Cronin
(Boston player 1935–1945, manager 1935–1947; career 1926–1945)

Primary position: SS, Manager

Batted: R

Threw: R

Height: 5'11"

Weight: 180 pounds

First major league game: April 29, 1926

Final major league game: April 19, 1945

Born: October 12, 1906 in San Francisco, California

Died: September 7, 1984 in Osterville, Massachusetts

Baseball Hall of Fame: 1956

Boston Red Sox Hall of Fame: 1995

Boston Red Sox Retired Uniform Number: 4

Joe Cronin was a hard-hitting shortstop, posting a .301 batting average across 20 seasons in the major leagues. Cronin batted .300 or higher in eight seasons, drove in at least 100 runs in eight seasons, and recorded slugging averages of .500 or better in four full seasons, three of them as a member of the Red Sox.

He began his career as a 19-year-old player with the Pittsburgh Pirates and then developed his stroke (and his strategic skills) in seven seasons with the Washington Senators.

After a so-so start at Pittsburgh, Cronin blossomed in Washington. And by 1930 he was player of the year; in 1933 he was also given the job of manager and he led the Senators to the World Series. At the end of the 1934 season, he was sold to the Red Sox for $225,000; that was actually more than the amount paid by the Yankees for Babe Ruth. (Boston received $125,000 for Ruth in 1919, plus a loan on the side.)

By the time he came over to Boston he was an established player/manager. He held the dual roles for the Red Sox from 1935 to 1945, then moved upstairs to be Boston's general manager from 1948 to 1958. And in 1959 he was elected president of the American League, a post he held until 1973.

Photo by the National Baseball Hall of Fame Library, Cooperstown, N.Y.

As a manager, he apparently knew how to manage himself late in his career: he still holds the AL record for the most pinch-hit home runs in a season, with five in 1943. (The National League record is seven, shared by Dave Hansen and Craig Wilson.) On June 17 of that year he also became the first player to hit pinch-hit homers in both games of a doubleheader.

Cronin's best years as a player were in 1930 for the Washington Senators (.346 average, 13 home runs, and 126 RBIs), and in 1938 as a member of the Red Sox (.325 average, 17 home runs, and 94 RBIs).

As a manager for Washington and then Boston, he had a record of 1,236–1,055. While he was making up the lineup for the Red Sox, the team had four second-place finishes (alas, each time trailing the Yankees), and then won the American League crown in 1946. His 1941 team included Ted Williams (with a .406 average that season), Jimmie Foxx (.300), Bobby Doerr (.282), and Dom DiMaggio (.283).

Although he hit .311 with 16 home runs and 95 RBIs in 1941, he took himself out of the starting lineup in 1942 to make room for a promising rookie: Johnny Pesky.

And Cronin has his own place in the great history of Red Sox–Yankee brawls. On May 30, 1938, at a game that drew the largest crowd in the history of Yankee Stadium, more than 81,000 fans squeezed in to see a doubleheader. In the first game Red Ruffing ended the eight-game winning streak of Boston's Lefty Grove. In the second game, Boston pitcher Archie McKain hit Yankee outfielder Jake Powell with a pitch; Powell charged the mound but ended up in an extended fight with player-manager Cronin. Both players were ejected, but the fight continued under the stands.

Early in the 1945 season, Cronin broke his leg, and that was the end of his time as a player. But in the next season he managed the Red Sox to the World Series, losing to the St. Louis Cardinals; the seventh and deciding game of that series included Enos Slaughter's "mad dash" from first base in the Cardinals' eighth inning. Red Sox shortstop Johnny Pesky's throw was late, and the Cardinals broke a tie and went on to win the game and the Series.

On May 29, 1984 the Red Sox retired their first two uniform numbers: Ted Williams' number 9 and Joe Cronin's 4.

This book is about accomplishments on the field, but it wouldn't be proper to write about Cronin without acknowledging two facts. The Boston Red Sox were the last major league team to integrate their roster, and the first African-American player— Pumpsie Green—joined the squad six months after Cronin left to become president of the American League. Along the way, Boston passed on the chance to sign players like Jackie Robinson in 1945 and Willie Mays in 1949.

Howard Bryant, a Boston native and a former sports columnist, now a senior writer for *ESPN The Magazine*, wrote a book about the

Red Sox and their racial history. We spoke with him about Cronin. He said blame could be spread pretty broadly through the organization at the time, from ownership to the front office to the scouts and minor league operations. At best, Bryant told us, Cronin as general manager did not fight for change.

What we now can say, though, is that the current Red Sox management has both acknowledged the team's past and taken a number of positive steps to foster interest in baseball among minorities. And today's team color is not white or black; it's red.

Joe Cronin

Year	Team	Age	G	AB	R	H	2B	3B	HR	RBI	BA	
1926	PIT (NL)	19	38	83	9	22	2	2	0	11	.265	
1927	PIT (NL)	20	12	22	2	5	1	0	0	3	.227	
1928	WSH (AL)	21	63	227	23	55	10	4	0	25	.242	
1929	WSH (AL)	22	145	494	72	139	29	8	8	61	.281	
1930	WSH (AL)	23	154	587	127	203	41	9	13	126	.346	
1931	WSH (AL)	24	156	611	103	187	44	13	12	126	.306	
1932	WSH (AL)	25	143	557	95	177	43	18	6	116	.318	
1933	WSH (AL)	26	152	602	89	186	45	11	5	118	.309	AS
1934	WSH (AL)	27	127	504	68	143	30	9	7	101	.284	AS
1935	BOS (AL)	28	144	556	70	164	37	14	9	95	.295	AS
1936	BOS (AL)	29	81	295	36	83	22	4	2	43	.281	AS
1937	BOS (AL)	30	148	570	102	175	40	4	18	110	.307	AS
1938	BOS (AL)	31	143	530	98	172	51	5	17	94	.325	AS
1939	BOS (AL)	32	143	520	97	160	33	3	19	107	.308	AS
1940	BOS (AL)	33	149	548	104	156	35	6	24	111	.285	
1941	BOS (AL)	34	143	518	98	161	38	8	16	95	.311	AS
1942	BOS (AL)	35	45	79	7	24	3	0	4	24	.304	
1943	BOS (AL)	36	59	77	8	24	4	0	5	29	.312	
1944	BOS (AL)	37	76	191	24	46	7	0	5	28	.241	
1945	BOS (AL)	38	3	8	1	3	0	0	0	1	.375	
Total			2124	7579	1233	2285	515	118	170	1424	.301	
Boston			1134	3892	645	1168	270	44	119	737	.300	

Year	Team	OBP	SLG	OPS	BB	SO	TB	SB	CS	SH	SF	IBB	HBP	GDP
1926	PIT (NL)	.315	.337	.652	6	15	28	0	x	3	x	x	0	x
1927	PIT (NL)	.292	.273	.565	2	3	6	0	x	0	x	x	0	x
1928	WSH (AL)	.309	.322	.631	22	27	73	4	0	10	x	x	0	x
1929	WSH (AL)	.388	.421	.809	85	37	208	5	9	21	x	x	1	x
1930	WSH (AL)	.422	.513	.935	72	36	301	17	10	22	x	x	5	x
1931	WSH (AL)	.391	.480	.871	81	52	293	10	9	4	x	x	4	x
1932	WSH (AL)	.393	.492	.885	66	45	274	7	5	3	x	x	3	x
1933	WSH (AL)	.398	.445	.843	87	49	268	5	4	5	x	x	2	x
1934	WSH (AL)	.353	.421	.774	53	28	212	8	0	9	x	x	1	x
1935	BOS (AL)	.370	.460	.830	63	40	256	3	3	8	x	x	3	x
1936	BOS (AL)	.354	.403	.757	32	21	119	1	3	6	x	x	1	x
1937	BOS (AL)	.402	.486	.888	84	73	277	5	3	11	x	x	6	x
1938	BOS (AL)	.428	.536	.964	91	60	284	7	5	11	x	x	5	x
1939	BOS (AL)	.407	.492	.899	87	48	256	6	6	20	x	x	0	18
1940	BOS (AL)	.380	.502	.882	83	65	275	7	5	13	x	x	1	6
1941	BOS (AL)	.406	.508	.914	82	55	263	1	4	14	x	x	1	20
1942	BOS (AL)	.415	.494	.909	15	21	39	0	1	1	x	x	0	3
1943	BOS (AL)	.398	.558	.956	11	4	43	0	0	0	x	x	0	3
1944	BOS (AL)	.358	.356	.714	34	19	68	1	4	5	x	x	1	7
1945	BOS (AL)	.545	.375	.920	3	2	3	0	0	0	x	x	0	0
Total		.390	.468	.858	1059	700	3546	87	71*	166	x	x	34	57*
Boston		.394	.484	.878	585	408	1883	31	34	89	x	x	18	57*

x Statistic not recorded

*Incomplete statistic

JIMMIE FOXX
James Emory Foxx ("The Beast," "Double X")
(Boston 1936–1942; career 1925–1945)

Primary position: 1B	
Batted: R	
Threw: R	
Height: 6'0"	
Weight: 195 pounds	
First major league game: May 1, 1925	
Final major league game: September 23, 1945	
Born: October 22, 1907 in Sudlersville, Maryland	
Died: July 21, 1967 in Miami, Florida	
Baseball Hall of Fame: 1951	
Boston Red Sox Hall of Fame: 1995	

Double X was one of the best right-handed hitters ever to play for the Red Sox, and many of the records he set more than 70 years ago still stand. In some ways he was the right-handed Babe Ruth, but instead of leaving the Red Sox in his prime he came to Boston to play.

Foxx made it to the majors in 1925 at age 17 for the Philadelphia Athletics. After three partial seasons, he stuck with the club in 1928. By 1932, he was a phenomenon, batting .364 for the A's and hitting 58 homers; he set an American League record that year—later tied by Hank Greenberg of the Detroit Tigers in 1938—for the most home runs by a right-handed hitter.

Foxx came up to Philadelphia as a catcher, but that spot was already taken by Mickey Cochrane, a future Hall of Famer. He saw only spot duty behind the plate, at first base, and in the outfield. But in 1929, he found a spot at first base.

After his 58-homer season in 1932, he went on to win the Triple Crown in 1933 with a league-leading batting average of .356, 163 RBIs, and 48 home runs. He was chosen as MVP for both of those seasons.

Just as Babe Ruth left the Red Sox mostly for financial reasons, Jimmie Foxx came to Boston because Philadelphia owner Connie Mack had trouble meeting his payroll during the Depression. In 1933, he

Photo by the National Baseball Hall of Fame Library, Cooperstown, N.Y.

traded away the great pitcher Lefty Grove to Boston for a pair of play-ers and $125,000; in 1935 Jimmie Foxx, in a dispute with Mack over his salary, was dealt to Boston in a $150,000 deal.

Jimmie Foxx's 1938 season was among the best by a Red Sox player, leading the league in batting average at .349 and in RBIs with 175. He also hit 50 home runs—still the record for a right-handed Red Sox hitter—and was rewarded for his efforts with the MVP award.

Other Red Sox records still held by Double X:

- Most RBIs in a season: 175 in 1938
- Most extra-base hits in a season: 92 in 1938
- Highest slugging average (right-handed batter): .704 in 1938
- Most multi-homer games: 10 in 1938
- Most walks in a game: 6 in 1938 (tied for major league record)
- Highest career on-base percentage (right-handed batter, at least 1,500 AB): .429

His .360 batting average in 1939 is the 12th highest for a Red Sox player. Foxx was the second major league player in the history of the game to reach the 500 home run mark, doing so in 1940 as a member of the Red Sox. (Babe Ruth had passed that plateau 11 years before.) Foxx was just short of 33 years old at the time, and thus is the second youngest player ever to hit 500 homers, behind only Alex Rodriguez who popped his just after his 32nd birthday.

Lefty Gomez, a Hall of Fame pitcher for the Yankees, always said that Foxx was one of the most difficult batters he had to face in his career, saying "He's got muscles in his hair." Yankees catcher Bill Dickey—also in the Hall of Fame—told a *New York Times* reporter about a time when Gomez shook off every pitch call he gave him against Foxx. Dickey went to the mound for a conference and asked Gomez what he wanted to throw. "I don't wanna throw him nothin'," Gomez told Dickey. "Maybe he'll just get tired of waitin' and leave."

When Double X retired in 1945, he had a 20-year career with 534 home runs, 1,922 RBIs, and a lifetime .325 batting average. He briefly managed the Fort Wayne Daisies of the All-American Girls Professional Baseball League, and the character of Jimmy Dugan—played by Tom Hanks—was loosely based on Foxx. When Double X went into the Hall of Fame in 1951, he wore a Red Sox cap.

Jimmie Foxx

Year	Team	Age	G	AB	R	H	2B	3B	HR	RBI	BA	
1925	PHA (AL)	17	10	9	2	6	1	0	0	0	.667	
1926	PHA (AL)	18	26	32	8	10	2	1	0	5	.313	
1927	PHA (AL)	19	61	130	23	42	6	5	3	20	.323	
1928	PHA (AL)	20	118	400	85	131	29	10	13	79	.328	
1929	PHA (AL)	21	149	517	123	183	23	9	33	118	.354	
1930	PHA (AL)	22	153	562	127	188	33	13	37	156	.335	
1931	PHA (AL)	23	139	515	93	150	32	10	30	120	.291	
1932	PHA (AL)	24	154	585	151	213	33	9	58	169	.364	MVP
1933	PHA (AL)	25	149	573	125	204	37	9	48	163	.356	MVP, AS
1934	PHA (AL)	26	150	539	120	180	28	6	44	130	.334	AS
1935	PHA (AL)	27	147	535	118	185	33	7	36	115	.346	AS
1936	BOS (AL)	28	155	585	130	198	32	8	41	143	.338	AS
1937	BOS (AL)	29	150	569	111	162	24	6	36	127	.285	AS
1938	BOS (AL)	30	149	565	139	197	33	9	50	175	.349	MVP, AS
1939	BOS (AL)	31	124	467	130	168	31	10	35	105	.360	AS
1940	BOS (AL)	32	144	515	106	153	30	4	36	119	.297	AS
1941	BOS (AL)	33	135	487	87	146	27	8	19	105	.300	AS
1942	Season	34	305	43	69	12	0	8	33	1	.226	
	BOS (AL)		30	100	18	27	4	0	5	14	.270	
	CHC (NL)		70	205	25	42	8	0	3	19	.205	
1944	CHC (NL)	36	15	20	0	1	1	0	0	2	.050	
1945	PHI (NL)	37	89	224	30	60	11	1	7	38	.268	
Total			**2317**	**8134**	**1751**	**2646**	**458**	**125**	**534**	**1922**	**.325**	
Boston			**887**	**3288**	**721**	**1051**	**181**	**45**	**222**	**788**	**.320**	

Year	Team	OBP	SLG	OPS	BB	SO	TB	SB	CS	SH	SF	IBB	HBP	GDP
1925	PHA (AL)	.667	.778	1.445	0	1	7	0	0	0	n/a	n/a	0	n/a
1926	PHA (AL)	.333	.438	.771	1	6	14	1	0	2	n/a	n/a	0	n/a
1927	PHA (AL)	.393	.515	.908	14	11	67	2	1	1	n/a	n/a	1	n/a
1928	PHA (AL)	.416	.548	.964	60	43	219	3	8	12	n/a	n/a	1	n/a
1929	PHA (AL)	.463	.625	1.088	103	70	323	9	7	16	n/a	n/a	2	n/a
1930	PHA (AL)	.429	.637	1.066	93	66	358	7	7	18	n/a	n/a	0	n/a
1931	PHA (AL)	.380	.567	.947	73	84	292	4	3	4	n/a	n/a	1	n/a
1932	PHA (AL)	.469	.749	1.218	116	96	438	3	7	0	n/a	n/a	0	n/a
1933	PHA (AL)	.449	.703	1.152	96	93	403	2	2	0	n/a	n/a	1	n/a
1934	PHA (AL)	.449	.653	1.102	111	75	352	11	2	1	n/a	n/a	1	n/a
1935	PHA (AL)	.461	.636	1.097	114	99	340	6	4	0	n/a	n/a	0	n/a

Year	Team	OBP	SLG	OPS	BB	SO	TB	SB	CS	SH	SF	IBB	HBP	GDP
1936	BOS (AL)	.440	.631	1.071	105	119	369	13	4	2	n/a	n/a	1	n/a
1937	BOS (AL)	.392	.538	.930	99	96	306	10	8	4	n/a	n/a	1	n/a
1938	BOS (AL)	.462	.704	1.166	119	76	398	5	4	1	n/a	n/a	0	n/a
1939	BOS (AL)	.464	.694	1.158	89	72	324	4	3	5	n/a	n/a	2	17
1940	BOS (AL)	.412	.581	.993	101	87	299	4	7	2	n/a	n/a	0	18
1941	BOS (AL)	.412	.505	.917	93	103	246	2	5	2	n/a	n/a	0	21
1942	*Season*	*.320*	*.344*	*.664*	*40*	*70*	*105*	*0*		*0*	*n/a*	*n/a*	*0*	*10*
	BOS (AL)	.392	.460	.852	18	15	46	0	0	0	n/a	n/a	2	1
	CHC (NL)	.282	.288	.570	22	55	59	1		0	n/a	n/a	0	9
1944	CHC (NL)	.136	.100	.236	2	5	2	0		0	n/a	n/a	0	0
1945	PHI (NL)	.336	.420	.756	23	39	94	0		1	n/a	n/a	0	3
Total		**.428**	**.609**	**1.037**	**1452**	**1311**	**4956**	**87**	**72**	**71**	**n/a**	**n/a**	**13**	**69**
Boston		**.429**	**.605**	**1.033**	**624**	**568**	**1988**	**38**	**31**	**16**	**n/a**	**n/a**	**6**	**57**

Pitching

Year	Team	Age	W	L	G	GS	CG	SHO	GF	SV	WHIP	ERA
1939	BOS (AL)	31	0	0	1	0	0	0	1	0	0	0
1945	PHI (NL)	37	1	0	9	2	0	0	8	0	1.191	1.59
Total			**1**	**0**	**10**	**2**	**0**	**0**	**9**	**0**	**1.141**	**1.52**
Boston			**0**	**0**	**1**	**0**	**0**	**0**	**1**	**0**	**0**	**0**

Year	IP	H	R	ER	HR	BB	SO	HBP	WP	IBB	BK
1939	1.0	0	0	0	0	0	1	0	0	0	0
1945	22.7	13	4	4	0	14	10	1	0	0	0
Total	**23.7**	**13**	**4**	**4**	**0**	**14**	**11**	**1**	**0**	**0**	**0**
Boston	**1.0**	**0**	**0**	**0**	**0**	**0**	**1**	**0**	**0**	**0**	**0**

BOBBY DOERR
Robert Pershing Doerr
(Boston 1937–1951)

Primary position: 2B	
Batted: R	
Threw: R	
Height: 5'11"	
Weight: 175 pounds	
First major league game: April 20, 1937	
Final major league game: September 7, 1951	
Born: April 7, 1918 in Los Angeles, California	
Baseball Hall of Fame: 1986	
Boston Red Sox Hall of Fame: 1995	
Boston Red Sox Retired Uniform Number: 1	

Bobby Doerr may have been the greatest second baseman in Red Sox history. He played 1,865 games, never at any position other than second. And he spent every day of his 13-year major league career as a member of the Red Sox: 2,042 hits in 8,028 plate appearances and a career batting average of .288.

I'm always honored to be mentioned in the same breath as Doerr, but what we have most in common is that we both played second base and wore the uniform of the Boston Red Sox. I may be a better dancer, but I'm not completely certain of that.

Doerr was a star on both sides of the game. A nine-time All-Star, he batted .300 or better three times and had six seasons with at least 100 RBIs. He had some serious punch in his swing: 223 home runs, 381 doubles, and 89 triples.

On defense, he once held the American League record for a second baseman for handling 414 chances in a row without an error; it still stands as a Boston record. His streak extended 73 games, from June 23 to September 19, 1948; some guy named Jerry Remy is in second place in the Red Sox record book with 67 games spanning from July 24, 1983 through April 4, 1984. In 2008, Dustin Pedroia came into the same neighborhood in his second year in the major leagues, with a streak of 61 games.

Photo by the National Baseball Hall of Fame Library, Cooperstown, N.Y.

Doerr became a member of the Red Sox in 1937 at the age of 19 and became a starter the next year; it was a pretty impressive infield with Jimmie Foxx at first, Doerr at second, Joe Cronin at shortstop, and Pinkie Higgins at third. Oh, and sorry to have to tell you, though Boston finished with a record of 88–61, they were second in the American League . . . to the New York Yankees.

Even with his power, he was also an excellent bunter, leading the league in 1938 with 22 sacrifice bunts. In 1939, the year Boston added Ted Williams, Doerr found his long-ball swing and had the first of 12 consecutive years with ten or more home runs. He batted .325 in 1944, and on May 17 of that year he hit for the cycle (single, double, triple, and home run in a single game) against the St. Louis Browns. And he had another cycle, on May 13, 1947 against the Chicago White Sox. Both of those rare batting feats were accomplished at home at Fenway Park; he is the only Red Sox ever to do it twice.

In 1944, while baseball continued during World War II, he led the league with a slugging percentage of .528, and his .325 batting average was just two points behind Lou Boudreau for the batting title.

In August of 2007, Doerr—the oldest living member of the Baseball Hall of Fame—was honored in a ceremony at Fenway Park. He stopped to pass along some advice to Boston's Dustin Pedroia. "Just keep playing hard and have fun," Doerr said. It must have worked, since Pedroia went on to win the Rookie of the Year Award and had an even better 2008 season.

If there is any question about his place among Red Sox heroes, look up at the placards in the outfield that show the retired uniform numbers. Number 1 is Bobby Doerr.

I got to meet Doerr a few times at Fenway, and he was a true gentleman, a class act. And his numbers speak for themselves.

Bobby Doerr

Year	Team	Age	G	AB	R	H	2B	3B	HR	RBI	BA	
1937	BOS (AL)	19	55	147	22	33	5	1	2	14	.224	
1938	BOS (AL)	20	145	509	70	147	26	7	5	80	.289	
1939	BOS (AL)	21	127	525	75	167	28	2	12	73	.318	
1940	BOS (AL)	22	151	595	87	173	37	10	22	105	.291	
1941	BOS (AL)	23	132	500	74	141	28	4	16	93	.282	AS
1942	BOS (AL)	24	144	545	71	158	35	5	15	102	.290	AS
1943	BOS (AL)	25	155	604	78	163	32	3	16	75	.270	AS
1944	BOS (AL)	26	125	468	95	152	30	10	15	81	.325	AS
1946	BOS (AL)	28	151	583	95	158	34	9	18	116	.271	AS
1947	BOS (AL)	29	146	561	79	145	23	10	17	95	.258	AS
1948	BOS (AL)	30	140	527	94	150	23	6	27	111	.285	AS
1949	BOS (AL)	31	139	541	91	167	30	9	18	109	.309	
1950	BOS (AL)	32	149	586	103	172	29	11	27	120	.294	AS
1951	BOS (AL)	33	106	402	60	116	21	2	13	73	.289	AS
Total			1865	7093	1094	2042	381	89	223	1247	.288	

Year	Team	OBP	SLG	OPS	BB	SO	TB	SB	CS	SH	SF	IBB	HBP	GDP
1937	BOS (AL)	.313	.313	.626	18	25	46	2	4	4	n/a	n/a	1	
1938	BOS (AL)	.363	.397	.760	59	39	202	5	10	22	n/a	n/a	0	
1939	BOS (AL)	.365	.448	.813	38	32	235	1	10	10	n/a	n/a	1	17
1940	BOS (AL)	.353	.497	.850	57	53	296	10	5	6	n/a	n/a	0	16
1941	BOS (AL)	.339	.450	.789	43	43	225	1	3	6	n/a	n/a		6
1942	BOS (AL)	.369	.455	.824	67	55	248	4	4	12	n/a	n/a	1	11
1943	BOS (AL)	.339	.412	.751	62	59	249	8	8	9	n/a	n/a	1	11
1944	BOS (AL)	.399	.528	.927	58	31	247	5	2	10	n/a	n/a	0	3
1946	BOS (AL)	.346	.453	.799	66	67	264	5	6	9	n/a	n/a	1	18
1947	BOS (AL)	.329	.426	.755	59	47	239	3	3	4	n/a	n/a	0	25
1948	BOS (AL)	.386	.505	.891	83	49	266	3	2	4	n/a	n/a	4	13
1949	BOS (AL)	.393	.497	.890	75	33	269	2	2	7	n/a	n/a	0	31
1950	BOS (AL)	.367	.519	.886	67	42	304	3	4	9	n/a	n/a	1	21
1951	BOS (AL)	.378	.448	.826	57	33	180	2	1	3	n/a	n/a	1	10
Total		**.362**	**.461**	**.823**	**809**	**608**	**3270**	**54**	**64**	**115**	**n/a**	**n/a**	**11**	**182**

DOM DIMAGGIO
Dominic Paul DiMaggio
("The Little Professor")
(Boston 1940–1953)

Primary position: CF	
Batted: R	
Threw: R	
Height: 5'9"	
Weight: 168 pounds	
First major league game: April 16, 1940	
Final major league game: May 9, 1953	
Born: February 12, 1917 in San Francisco, California	
Boston Red Sox Hall of Fame: 1995	

The Little Professor would have been a star even if his last name had been Smith; he batted .298 for his career—ten full seasons with the Red Sox—and was one of the team's all-time best leadoff hitters. He still holds Boston's record for a hitting streak of 34 consecutive games.

His older brother, of course, was Joltin' Joe DiMaggio of the New York Yankees, not a bad player himself. And there was another older brother, Vince, who also preceded him to the major leagues, playing in 1937 and 1938 for the Boston Bees of the National League and then putting up decent numbers for eight more seasons.

Brother Joe DiMaggio was already a star with the Yankees when Dom began playing in the minor leagues for the San Francisco Seals of the Pacific Coast League. After a season in which he batted .361, the Red Sox purchased Dom's contract from the Seals in 1939 and he was on Boston's major league roster in 1940. The numbers he put up in his rookie year were pretty close to the consistent production he would have for all 11 seasons with the Red Sox; in his first year he batted .301 with 8 home runs and 81 runs scored. By 1941 he was the starting centerfielder with Ted Williams in left and Lou Finney in right.

In 1941 and 1942 he scored 117 and then 110 runs, near the top in that category in the American League. When he came back in 1946

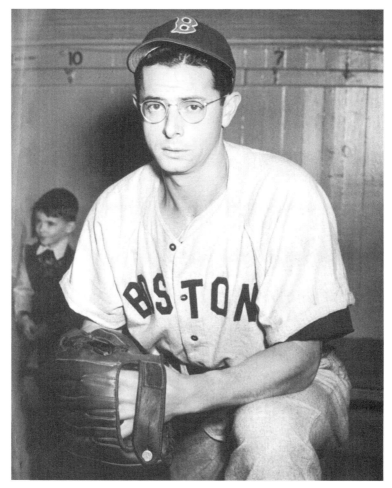

Photo by the National Baseball Hall of Fame Library, Cooperstown, N.Y.

from three years served in the Coast Guard during World War II he had his best season, batting .316 and driving in 73 runs.

DiMaggio (along with Williams) lost 1943 to 1945 to service in World War II, but like the Splendid Splinter when he returned he picked up right where he had left off, batting .316 in 1946 as the Red Sox won their first pennant since 1918.

(Boston lost the 1946 World Series to St. Louis despite DiMaggio's clutch hitting in Game 7; he doubled home two runs to tie the score in the bottom of the eighth inning but was injured running and had to be removed from the game. In the bottom of the eighth, Harry Walker doubled into left-center field and Enos Slaughter scored from first on his famous "Mad Dash." This was the play where some fans—unfairly, I think—blamed Johnny Pesky for a moment's hesitation as the cutoff man on the throw; the other way to look at is that DiMaggio might have caught the ball or at least made a stronger throw from the outfield.)

A seven-time All-Star, DiMaggio batted at least .300 in four seasons and led the American League in runs twice, and one season each in triples and stolen bases. In 1949 he got a hit in 34 consecutive games, a Boston record that still stands; team records show the second-longest hitting streak as 30, a mark jointly held by Nomar Garciaparra (in 1997) and Tris Speaker in 1912. (Big Brother Joe DiMaggio, of course, is way out in front in MLB history with his 56-game streak for New York. And in one of those strange ironies that are part of baseball, brother Joe made a great catch in the eighth inning at Yankee Stadium on August 9, 1949 to end Dom's 34-game streak.)

DiMaggio enjoyed a close friendship with teammates Ted Williams, Bobby Doerr, and Johnny Pesky, and one of their last times together was chronicled in David Halberstam's book *The Teammates*.

Dom stood 5'9" and wore glasses; put them together and that was the source of his nickname of "The Little Professor." He was a dandy of a fielder and a consistent and productive leadoff hitter.

Dom DiMaggio

Year	Team	Age	G	AB	R	H	2B	3B	HR	RBI	BA	
1940	BOS (AL)	23	108	418	81	126	32	6	8	46	.301	
1941	BOS (AL)	24	144	584	117	165	37	6	8	58	.283	AS
1942	BOS (AL)	25	151	622	110	178	36	8	14	48	.286	AS
1946	BOS (AL)	29	142	534	85	169	24	7	7	73	.316	AS
1947	BOS (AL)	30	136	513	75	145	21	5	8	71	.283	
1948	BOS (AL)	31	155	648	127	185	40	4	9	87	.285	
1949	BOS (AL)	32	145	605	126	186	34	5	8	60	.307	AS
1950	BOS (AL)	33	141	588	131	193	30	11	7	70	.328	AS
1951	BOS (AL)	34	146	639	113	189	34	4	12	72	.296	AS
1952	BOS (AL)	35	128	486	81	143	20	1	6	33	.294	AS
1953	BOS (AL)	36	3	3	0	1	0	0	0	0	.333	
Totals			**1399**	**5640**	**1046**	**1680**	**308**	**57**	**87**	**618**	**.298**	

Year	Team	OBP	SLG	OPS	BB	SO	TB	SB	CS	SH	SF	IBB	HBP	GDP
1940	BOS (AL)	.367	.464	.831	41	46	194	7	6	5	n/a	n/a	2	5
1941	BOS (AL)	.385	.408	.793	90	57	238	13	6	7	n/a	n/a	7	7
1942	BOS (AL)	.364	.437	.801	70	52	272	16	10	4	n/a	n/a	6	9
1946	BOS (AL)	.393	.427	.820	66	58	228	10	6	9	n/a	n/a	1	16
1947	BOS (AL)	.376	.390	.766	74	62	200	10	6	9	n/a	n/a	3	12
1948	BOS (AL)	.383	.401	.784	101	58	260	10	2	5	n/a	n/a	2	11
1949	BOS (AL)	.404	.420	.824	96	55	254	9	7	3	n/a	n/a	2	10
1950	BOS (AL)	.414	.452	.866	82	68	266	15	4	7	n/a	n/a	4	14
1951	BOS (AL)	.370	.418	.788	73	53	267	4	7	4	n/a	n/a	2	13
1952	BOS (AL)	.371	.377	.748	57	61	183	6	8	4	n/a	n/a	2	10
1953	BOS (AL)	.333	.333	.666	0	1	1	0	0	0	n/a	n/a	0	0
Totals		**.383**	**.419**	**.802**	**750**	**571**	**2363**	**100**	**62**	**57**	**n/a**	**n/a**	**31**	**107**

JOHNNY PESKY

John Michael Paveskovich ("The Needle")
(Boston player 1942–1952; manager 1963–1964, 1980; career 1942–1954)

Primary position: SS, 3B	
Batted: L	
Threw: R	
Height: 5'9"	
Weight: 168 pounds	
First major league game: April 14, 1942	
Final major league game: September 24, 1954	
Born: September 27, 1919 in Portland, Oregon	
Boston Red Sox Hall of Fame: 1995	
Boston Red Sox Retired Uniform Number: 6	

Johnny Pesky first put on a Red Sox uniform at the start of the 1942 season. Aside from a few years off during World War II and a short stint out of town at the end of his career, he's worn one ever since.

In his career with the Red Sox, he was shortstop, coach, manager, radio and television broadcaster, and mentor to generations of players. And if there is a fan in Red Sox Nation who hasn't seen Johnny, met him, or received his autograph . . . well, they've just not tried very hard.

Johnny Pesky is a link from Ted Williams, Bobby Doerr, and Dom DiMaggio to David Ortiz, Dustin Pedroia, and Jacoby Ellsbury. He is a baseball lifer, so connected to the Red Sox that he has a part of Fenway Park named after him.

Pesky played for the Red Sox from 1942 to 1952, minus three years lost to World War II. In 1942, after Pearl Harbor but before many ballplayers left the majors to join the military, Johnny Pesky won the job as starting shortstop for the Red Sox. He replaced the great player-manager Joe Cronin, who had put himself into the field for most of the past eight seasons. His 1942 rookie season batting average of .331 is tied with Fred Lynn for the third highest in Red Sox history.

Photo by the National Baseball Hall of Fame Library, Cooperstown, N.Y.

Between the last game of 1942 and the start of the 1943 season, the Red Sox lost nearly its entire starting team. Of the stars, only Bobby Doerr remained.

Pesky was a dependable singles hitter, batting as high as .335 with 208 hits in 1946 and compiling a career batting average with Boston of .313. He played the last two-and-a-half seasons of his career with Detroit and Washington.

A right-hander who batted from the left side, he was an excellent bunter, leading the league in sacrifice hits in 1943 and making at least 200 hits in each of his first three seasons. One thing he was not, though, was a home run hitter; he had only 17 in his career.

Now about that yellow marker on the rightfield line at Fenway. According to the sign on the wall, the pole is 302 feet away from home plate; some say it may be a few feet closer. In any case, if you can manage to hit the pole or wrap a fair ball to the left of the pole you can pick up the shortest possible rightfield home run in major league baseball; if you don't manage to land the ball in the stands along the line, the distance to the back wall in rightfield is a more respectable 380 feet.

(And though it is called the foul pole, just as in other parks it actually stands in fair territory. If a ball hits the pole, it's a home run; if it lands in the stands to the right of the pole, it is foul. At Fenway, it is called the "Pesky Pole.")

So, you might imagine that the left-handed hitter Pesky must have pulled a whole bunch of balls down the line . . . except that the records don't show that. He only hit 13 homers as a member of the Red Sox, and only 6 came at Fenway.

It seems that the pole was first given a name by Red Sox pitcher Mel Parnell in the 1940s, after one of Pesky's rare "long" shots landed near it. According to the records, Pesky hit one home run in a game pitched by Parnell, but it did not win the game; in fact the Red Sox lost in extra innings.

In any case, Parnell went on to be part of the Red Sox radio and television broadcast team from 1965 to 1968, and his name for the pole became a local landmark. In 2006 the Red Sox made it official with a plaque.

Pesky is also associated—fairly or unfairly—with a notable moment in the unhappy history of World Series mishaps for the Red Sox. It came during the seventh and final game of the 1946 Series, which pitted the Red Sox against the St. Louis Cardinals; Boston was a win away from taking home their first championship since 1918.

The Sox had tied the game 3–3 in the top of the eighth inning. Enos Slaughter was on first base with two outs; Slaughter was not held on, and he broke for second base as Harry Walker hit a dying quail into short leftfield. Slaughter reached second and kept on running as Boston outfielder Leon Culberson retrieved the ball and threw it back to the infield—not all that well—to Pesky who had his back to the plate to receive the ball. Slaughter never stopped, rounding third and heading for home.

Now, I wasn't there, and I don't want to get involved in trying to analyze a play from 1946. I'll just report here what is on the record.

Although it was claimed at the time—and repeated over the years—that for some reason Pesky "held" the ball, old news films of the play show that he caught the relay, spun around, and was surprised to see Slaughter heading for home plate. He released the ball quickly but the throw was up the third base line and the runner was safe.

Culberson had come in the game to replace Dom DiMaggio, who had been injured on the basepaths in the top of the eighth inning after he had doubled home the tying runs. The speedy DiMaggio might have caught the ball, or might have made a better throw to Pesky. Mel Allen's broadcast of the play said that Culberson fumbled the ball momentarily.

It took until 1986 and a famous error by a fine but injured player—Bill Buckner—before some Red Sox fans could come up with another supposed goat in the World Series. (Interestingly, Buckner returned to Fenway Park in 2008 to throw out the first pitch at the home opener, to the forgiving cheers of the fans.)

After ending his playing career, Pesky got his first coaching job in the Yankees organization, working in 1955 for manager Ralph Houk and the minor-league Denver Bears. From 1956 to 1960, he was a manager for Detroit minor league teams. And then in 1961 he rejoined the Red Sox as manager of their AAA team, the Seattle Rainiers.

At the end of the 1962 season, Pinky Higgins was promoted from manager of the Red Sox to general manager and Pesky was brought back to Boston to run the club on the field. He had the bad luck of having a pretty mediocre team for the time he was in charge. In his first year the Red Sox improved from eighth to seventh place; in 1964 they dropped back to eighth and Pesky was replaced with two games to go in the season.

From 1965 to 1967, Pesky worked for the Pittsburgh Pirates organization. For the first two years, he was first base coach for manager Harry Walker—the same guy who hit the double that scored Enos Slaughter in the 1946 World Series. In 1968 Pesky managed the AAA Columbus Jets for Pittsburgh.

And then in 1969, Pesky came back to Boston. His first assignment—from 1969 to 1974—was as color analyst on radio and television broadcasts, which is nice work if you can get it. He partnered with Ken Coleman and Ned Martin on television and did some games with Joe Castiglione on radio.

And then in 1975 he put on a Red Sox uniform once again, as first base coach for manager Darrell Johnson; that team made it all the way to the seventh game of the World Series against Cincinnati. By 1980, he was a bench coach for Don Zimmer, and when Zim was fired near the end of that season he took over for the final five games of a fifth-place season.

In the years that followed, with his friend Ralph Houk as manager in Boston, Pesky was a bench and batting coach; he worked very closely with Jim Rice. His final year as a full-time coach was in 1984, but in the years since he has filled a number of roles as a special instructor and representative of the team. He sat on the bench with the players at Fenway regularly until the start of the 2007 season, when Major League Baseball limited the number of coaches who could be in uniform during a game.

The rightfield pole was officially named the "Pesky Pole" in September 2006. And then in 2008 Pesky's number 6 was retired by the Red Sox, joining the pantheon of greats on the outfield wall of Fenway. At age 89, he still had a locker in the clubhouse at Fenway Park.

Retiring Pesky's number was an exception to the Red Sox practice of limiting that honor to teammates who had played at least 10 years with the Red Sox, finished their careers here, and were inducted into the Baseball Hall of Fame. In Pesky's case, he had eight years in Boston, and if not for the three full seasons he lost to service in World War II he might have had ten . . . and been chosen for the Hall of Fame.

At least here in Boston, though, Pesky will forever be a part of the Red Sox.

Johnny Pesky

Year	Team	Age	G	AB	R	H	2B	3B	HR	RBI	BA	
1942	BOS (AL)	22	147	620	105	205	29	9	2	51	.331	
1946	BOS (AL)	26	153	621	115	208	43	4	2	55	.335	AS
1947	BOS (AL)	27	155	638	106	207	27	8	0	39	.324	
1948	BOS (AL)	28	143	565	124	159	26	6	3	55	.281	
1949	BOS (AL)	29	148	604	111	185	27	7	2	69	.306	
1950	BOS (AL)	30	127	490	112	153	22	6	1	49	.312	
1951	BOS (AL)	31	131	480	93	150	20	6	3	41	.313	
1952	*Season*	*32*	*94*	*244*	*36*	*55*	*6*	*0*	*1*	*11*	*.225*	
	BOS (AL)		25	67	10	10	2	0	0	2	.149	
	DET (AL)		69	177	26	45	4	0	1	9	.254	
1953	DET (AL)	33	103	308	43	90	22	1	2	24	.292	
1954	*Season*	*34*	*69*	*175*	*22*	*43*	*4*	*3*	*1*	*10*	*.246*	
	DET (AL)		20	17	5	3	0	0	1	1	.176	
	WASH (AL)		49	158	17	40	4	3	0	9	.253	
Total			**1270**	**4745**	**867**	**1455**	**226**	**50**	**17**	**404**	**.307**	
Boston			**1029**	**4085**	**776**	**1277**	**196**	**46**	**13**	**361**	**.313**	

Year	Team	OBP	SLG	OBP	BB	SO	TB	SB	CS	SH	SF	IBB	HBP	GDP
1942	BOS (AL)	.375	.416	.791	42	36	258	12	7	22	n/a	n/a	2	8
1946	BOS (AL)	.401	.427	.828	65	29	265	9	8	14	n/a	n/a	3	8
1947	BOS (AL)	.393	.392	.785	72	22	250	12	9	9	n/a	n/a	0	10
1948	BOS (AL)	.394	.365	.759	99	32	206	3	5	7	n/a	n/a	6	10
1949	BOS (AL)	.408	.384	.792	100	19	232	8	4	5	n/a	n/a	4	12
1950	BOS (AL)	.437	.388	.825	104	31	190	2	1	6	n/a	n/a	5	13
1951	BOS (AL)	.417	.398	.815	84	15	191	2	2	7	n/a	n/a	2	10
1952	*Season*	*.372*	*.262*	*.634*	*56*	*16*	*64*	*1*	*5*	*6*	*1*	n/a	*3*	
	BOS (AL)	.313	.179	.492	15	5	12	0	3	1		n/a	1	1
	DET (AL)	.394	.294	.688	41	11	52	1	2	5		n/a	0	2
1953	DET (AL)	.353	.390	.743	27	10	120	3	7	5		n/a	2	4
1954	*Season*	*.296*	*.320*	*.616*	*13*	*8*	*56*	*1*	*1*	*2*	*1*	n/a	*0*	*4*
	DET (AL)	.300	.353	.653	3	1	6	0	0	0	0	n/a	0	2
	WASH (AL)	.296	.316	.612	10	7	50	1	1	2	1	n/a	0	2
Total		**.394**	**.386**	**.780**	**662**	**218**	**1832**	**53**	**49**	**83**	**1***	**n/a**	**25**	**82**
Boston		**.401**	**.393**	**.794**	**581**	**189**	**1604**	**48**	**39**	**71**	**0***	**n/a**	**23**	**72**

*Incomplete statistic

JACKIE JENSEN
Jack Eugene Jensen
(Boston 1954–1961; career 1950–1961)

Primary position: RF	
Batted: R	
Threw: R	
Height: 5'11"	
Weight: 190 pounds	
First major league game: April 18, 1950	
Final major league game: October 1, 1961	
Born: March 9, 1927 in San Francisco, California	
Died: July 14, 1982 in Charlottesville, Virginia	
Boston Red Sox Hall of Fame: 2000	

It's a story that sounds like it came from the mind of a Hollywood scriptwriter.

How many players can claim this combination of accomplishments? He was a player in both the Rose Bowl and the World Series; won the Most Valuable Player award (as a Red Sox player); was featured (along with Ted Williams) in a painting by Norman Rockwell that appeared on the cover of the *Saturday Evening Post*; and was the subject of a television movie called *The Jackie Jensen Story* that aired before the peak of his career. And to add to the Hollywood drama, he retired (twice) while still playing close to his peak because expansion baseball was taking teams off the trains and onto airplanes, and he was deathly afraid of flying.

A young athlete from a broken home, brought up by his mother, Jensen joined the Navy near the end of World War II. He enrolled at the University of California and became an All-American in two sports. As a pitcher and outfielder, he helped Cal win the first College World Series in 1947, defeating a team from Yale that included future President George H. W. Bush.

Playing halfback in 1948, he became the first Cal player to rush for more than 1,000 yards. The Golden Bears completed the season undefeated with 10 wins. He scored a touchdown in the 1949 Rose Bowl (Cal was upset 20–14 by Northwestern) and placed fourth in the voting for the Heisman Trophy.

Photo by the National Baseball Hall of Fame Library, Cooperstown, N.Y.

He signed a minor league baseball deal in 1949, and in 1950 his contract was sold (along with Billy Martin's) to the New York Yankees, where he was groomed as the backup for Joe DiMaggio. He appeared in the 1950 World Series only briefly, as a pinch runner. In 1952, he was displaced by a phenomenal rookie, Mickey Mantle. After playing part of 1952 and all of the 1953 season with the Washington Senators, he was traded again, this time to the Boston Red Sox.

At age 26 he became the rightfielder for Boston, playing with Jimmie Piersall in center and Ted Williams in left. (Williams said

Jensen was one of the best outfielders he had ever seen.) By 1957 he was considered one of the game's best and most underrated players but he was poised for fame . . . and a fall.

Jensen hit more than 20 home runs in each year from 1954 to 1959 and batted about .280 for the period. And in 1958—the year after his television movie, his *Saturday Evening Post* cover, and a *Sports Illustrated* cover story (without a jinx)—he had his breakout year.

In 1958 he led the league with 122 RBIs, batted .286, and hit 35 home runs. He won the MVP award, topping Bob Turley, Rocky Colavito, and Bob Cerv. The next year he again led the league in RBIs, with 112, and added a Gold Glove; he had a great arm and led the league in double plays from right field.

Jensen drove in 100 or more runs in five of his seven years with the Red Sox, and he led the American League in RBIs in 1955, 1958, and 1959. On August 2, 1956 he drove in nine runs in an 18–3 blowout over Detroit; he had a three-run homer, a bases-loaded triple, a two-run single, and a sacrifice fly. He used his speed to lead the league in stolen bases with 22 in 1954 and in triples with 11 in 1956.

In 1958, the Dodgers had moved to Los Angeles and the Giants to San Francisco. Luckily for Jensen, the furthest-west team in the American League was Kansas City, and most teams traveled by train with occasional airplane flights for long hauls. The occasional flights were still too much for Jensen, and the AL was due to move into California with the Angels. Red Sox owner Tom Yawkey arranged for psychotherapy to try to help Jensen get over his terrific fear of flying. But Jensen announced his retirement in 1960 and returned home to California—presumably by ground transportation.

(In 1959, Chuck Essegian became the only other athlete to play in both the Rose Bowl and World Series; he appeared for Stanford in the 1952 football game and played for the Los Angeles Dodgers in the 1959 Series, delivering two pinch-hit home runs against the Chicago White Sox.)

Jensen unretired in 1961—the year the Los Angeles Angels joined the American League—and tried hypnotherapy to get him through airplane flights. But he had a decent though sub-par year, hitting .263 with 13 home runs and 66 RBIs, and he retired again at the end of the season.

Since 1990, the Boston Chapter of the Baseball Writers Association of America has bestowed an annual Jackie Jensen Award to the player who shows exemplary "spirit and determination." Recent winners have included Mike Lowell and Kevin Youkilis.

Jackie Jensen

Year	Team	Age	G	AB	R	H	2B	3B	HR	RBI	BA	
1950	NYY (AL)	23	45	70	13	12	2	2	1	5	.171	
1951	NYY (AL)	24	56	168	30	50	8	1	8	25	.298	
1952	*Season*	25	*151*	*589*	*83*	*165*	*30*	*6*	*10*	*82*	*.280*	AS
	NYY (AL)		7	19	3	2	1	1	0	2	.105	
	WSH (AL)		144	570	80	163	29	5	10	80	.286	
1953	WSH (AL)	26	147	552	87	147	32	8	10	84	.266	
1954	BOS (AL)	27	152	580	92	160	25	7	25	117	.276	
1955	BOS (AL)	28	152	574	95	158	27	6	26	116	.275	AS
1956	BOS (AL)	29	151	578	80	182	23	11	20	97	.315	
1957	BOS (AL)	30	145	544	82	153	29	2	23	103	.281	
1958	BOS (AL)	31	154	548	83	157	31	0	35	122	.286	MVP, AS
1959	BOS (AL)	32	148	535	101	148	31	0	28	112	.277	GG
1961	BOS (AL)	34	137	498	64	131	21	2	13	66	.263	
Total			**1438**	**5236**	**810**	**1463**	**259**	**45**	**199**	**929**	**.279**	
Boston			**1039**	**3857**	**597**	**1089**	**187**	**28**	**170**	**733**	**.282**	

Year	Team	OBP	SLG	OPS	BB	SO	TB	SB	CS	SH	SF	IBB	HBP	GDP
1950	NYY (AL)	.247	.300	.547	7	8	21	4	0	1	n/a	n/a	0	3
1951	NYY (AL)	.369	.500	.869	18	18	84	8	2	1	n/a	n/a	1	1
1952	*Season*	*.357*	*.402*	*.759*	*67*	*44*	*237*	*18*	*6*	*5*	*n/a*	*n/a*	*3*	*16*
	NYY (AL)	.261	.263	.524	4	4	5	1	0	0	n/a	n/a	0	1
	WSH (AL)	.360	.407	.767	63	40	232	17	6	5	n/a	n/a	3	15
1953	WSH (AL)	.357	.408	.765	73	51	225	18	8	1	n/a	n/a	5	19
1954	BOS (AL)	.359	.472	.831	79	52	274	22	7	1	11	n/a	2	32
1955	BOS (AL)	.369	.479	.848	89	63	275	16	7	3	12	8	3	20
1956	BOS (AL)	.405	.497	.902	89	43	287	11	3	1	4	5	1	23
1957	BOS (AL)	.367	.469	.836	75	66	255	8	5	1	5	3	2	22
1958	BOS (AL)	.396	.535	.931	99	65	293	9	4	1	4	7	3	13
1959	BOS (AL)	.372	.492	.864	88	67	263	20	5	1	12	3	0	20
1961	BOS (AL)	.350	.392	.742	66	69	195	9	8	2	4	2	3	16
Total		**.375**	**.460**	**.835**	**812**	**546**	**2409**	**143**	**55**	**18**	**52**	**28**	**23**	**185**
Boston		**.374**	**.478**	**.852**	**585**	**425**	**1842**	**95**	**39**	**10**	**52**	**28**	**14**	**146**

HEROES OF MY YOUTH

TED WILLIAMS
Theodore Samuel Williams
("The Kid," "The Splendid Splinter,"
"Teddy Ballgame")
(Boston 1939–1960)

Primary position: LF	
Batted: L	
Threw: R	
Height: 6'3"	
Weight: 205 pounds	
First major league game: April 20, 1939	
Final major league game: September 28, 1960	
Born: August 30, 1918 in San Diego, California	
Died: July 5, 2002 in Inverness, Florida	
Baseball Hall of Fame: 1966	
Boston Red Sox Hall of Fame: 1995	
Boston Red Sox Retired Uniform Number: 9	

There are some guys—I think of Muhammad Ali or Michael Jordan—who walk into a room and you know they are there. That's what Ted Williams was like.

Brash right from the start, by all reports he all but ignored most of the time-honored traditions of baseball. He was a showoff, applauding his abilities by himself. He disregarded the rookie rules and pushed his way into the batting cage and into the limelight any time he wanted.

He also could play.

Ted Williams came to spring training in 1938, but it was obvious that even with all of his talent at the plate he was way too green to stay with the big club for the season. And so he was optioned to the minors. He came up to Boston for the start of the 1939 season and stuck; he played his entire career for the Red Sox.

Let's look at the 1941 season, one of the greatest years ever recorded by a ballplayer in the modern era. Teddy Ballgame stroked 185 hits including 37 homers, drove in 120 runs, and drew 147 walks. He had an on-base percentage of .553 and a slugging average of .735, for an OPS (On-Base Plus Slugging) of 1.288.

Photo by the National Baseball Hall of Fame Library, Cooperstown, N.Y.

In the past century of baseball, a player has posted an OPS of 1.257 or higher only ten times. And there have been only three players involved: four times by Barry Bonds (1.422 in 2004, 1.381 in 2002, 1.379 in 2001, 1.278 in 2003), four times by Babe Ruth (1.379 in 1920, 1.359 in 1921, 1.309 in 1923, and 1.258 in 1927), and two times by Ted Williams (1.288 in 1941 and 1.257 in 1957.) The numbers are extraordinary, and whatever you think of OPS as a measure of hitting skill or the personalities involved, Williams is among exceptional company.

And then there is the fact that Williams finished the 1941 season with a magic number that is famous everywhere in Red Sox Nation and much of the rest of the baseball world: a batting average of .406. No one has batted .400 or higher for a full season since Williams accomplished the feat in 1941.

And by the way, long before David "Big Papi" Ortiz was born, Williams was faced with an extreme defensive shift by many opposing teams. Beginning in 1941 and accelerating in 1946, a number of managers swung their fielders around to the right to attempt to reduce Williams' ability to pull the ball safely—at least as long as the ball stayed in the park. In most of the shifts the shortstop moved over to behind or to the right of second base, putting three infielders between first and second; the outfielders moved toward right field.

Can't really say it worked all that well, though: 1941 was the year Williams ended up with a .406 batting average, and in 1946 he was the MVP of the American League. And it was on June 9, 1946 that the Splendid Splinter hit one of the most famous home runs in Fenway history. Estimated to travel 502 feet, it landed in Section 42, Row 37, Seat 31, and according to reports of the day it struck the top of a spectator's straw hat. Today the seat that replaced the old bleacher spot at that location is painted red to commemorate the blast.

He had incredible eyesight and never swung at bad pitches. Even when they put the shift on him, it didn't bother him at all.

Back to 1941: That was also the year that the great Joe DiMaggio put together the amazing 56-game hitting streak, one of those records in baseball that may never be broken.

Williams approached the last day of the season—a doubleheader—with a batting average that had tailed off to .3995. Although he could have sat out the two games and allow baseball custom to round the number up to an even .400, that would not have been good enough for posterity—and certainly not good enough for Williams.

In the first game he hit a single, a home run, a single, another single, and then he reached base on an error. His batting average stood at .405. So now he could have sat out the second game but that was not his way: He recorded a single, a smash double, and finally a fly ball out. His average stood at .4057, which is in the record books (and on the walls of Fenway Park) rounded to .406.

Williams went on to put up nearly identical numbers for the 1942 season, with 186 hits, 36 homers, and 137 RBIs. His batting average was "only" .356 but he was the best hitter in baseball again, winning the Triple Crown. Any player would take that season.

And Williams could well have made another run at a .400 season except that after the 1942 season he put aside his baseball equipment and put on a military uniform. And this wasn't a publicity stunt, with a movie or sports star serving in a special unit entertaining the troops: Teddy Ballgame served as a Navy fighter pilot instructor, missing four seasons. (And in 1952 he was recalled to duty for the Korean War, where he flew 37 combat missions including a crash landing.)

Returned from his first stint in the Navy, Williams could still pound the ball. In 1947 he won his second Triple Crown, with 32 homers, 114 RBIs, and a .343 batting average. (The only other Boston Red Sox to ever win the Triple Crown was Williams' successor, Carl Yastrzemski, who took the title in 1967.)

On September 28, 1960 Ted Williams finally came to the end of the string. The Red Sox had stumbled through the latest in a series of uninspiring seasons, and his final years were not quite as spectacular as his early ones, but better than most any other ballplayer's would have been. And Ted was still being Ted: feuding with the "Knights of the Keyboard" in the press room and rarely acknowledging the fans.

Without a hit in the game, Williams came up to bat with one out in the eighth inning. The crowd gave him a long ovation; he spent the time working on his swing just outside of the batter's box. Finally, he came to bat. The first pitch from Baltimore's Jack Fischer was a ball, low and out of the zone. On the next pitch, Williams swung mightily . . . and missed. The third pitch was belt-high and over the plate and Williams did not miss. The ball came down over the fence just to the right of the triangle in centerfield. The Splendid Splinter's last hit was his 521st home run and the 2,654th hit of his long career. Williams ran the bases and went straight into the dugout without looking up. The small crowd of 10,454 fans cheered, but he did not tip his hat.

The Sox won the game in the ninth inning, scoring two runs for a walk-off. But Boston finished in seventh place, 32 games out of first place. (Yes, the Yankees with Mickey Mantle, Roger Maris, Yogi Berra, and other superstars were champions of the AL; New York, though, lost to the Pittsburgh Pirates in the World Series that year when Bill Mazeroski hit a home run in the bottom of the ninth inning of the seventh game.)

Now, I have concentrated here on the greatness of Ted Williams on the field. There have been more than enough books written about his personality, his spats with the press, and his difficult relationship with fans. He did tip his hat to the fans after a big hit or catch when he first started playing, but then he stopped.

He didn't tip his hat for two Triple Crown seasons, two MVP seasons, or six AL batting titles. And he didn't tip his hat in 1960 when, on his final at-bat as a professional ball player, he hit a home run. John Updike, writing about Williams' final at-bat, famously decided: "Gods do not answer letters."

Me, I'm much more interested in what happens on the field. As I've said before, my favorite time begins when the umpire says "play ball" and ends with the final out. Everything else is a distraction.

But for the record, on May 12, 1991 Ted Williams returned to Fenway Park for a special celebration of the 50th anniversary of his .406 season. Standing on the field, he reached into his pocket and pulled out a Red Sox cap and tipped it to the fans. (The hat was not his; he had borrowed it from Boston pitcher Jeff Reardon for the occasion.)

And then on July 13, 1999, Williams was back at Fenway as the superstar among superstars for an All-Star game that brought together one of the greatest collections of Hall of Famers ever on a field at the same time. Williams, 80 years old at the time and in failing health, was driven onto the field in a golf cart. Helped by Mark McGwire and Tony Gwynn, he threw out the ceremonial first pitch to Carlton Fisk.

Williams was surrounded by some of the all-time greats, including Willie Mays, Stan Musial, Hank Aaron, and Bob Feller. Stars of the day, including Nomar Garciaparra of the Red Sox as well as Sammy Sosa, Cal Ripken Jr., and Ken Griffey Jr., were also at his side. And he tipped his hat.

And finally, although I would never, ever want someone to compare my hitting style and results to those of Ted Williams, we did have a few connections.

In 1971, I was drafted out of high school by the Washington Senators, and if I had signed with them and things had been a little different he could have been my manager. (Williams managed the Senators from 1969 through 1971; I got called up to the majors in 1975.) To tell the truth, I am glad he wasn't my manager. That might have been tough. He was loud. He would always question you and put you on the spot. He was uncomfortable to be around because if he asked you a question and you didn't give him the right answer, or the one he expected to hear, he would give it to you in a loud way. He knew his reputation and he had no use for sportswriters, but he was bigger than life.

And though I never played for him on the Senators—I ended up signing with the California Angels—in 1978 there he was as an instructor at the Red Sox spring training camp after I had been traded to Boston during the off-season.

He certainly didn't lack confidence. He was down there as an instructor and he walked by a locker and stood in front of a mirror; he looked at himself and said, "This is the greatest hitter that ever played."

He loved talking baseball. He loved talking hitting. But sometimes it is hard for guys like him who were so great to relate to the average player.

As much as everybody loved him and wanted to pick his brain, I know on a lot of occasions sometimes you would see him coming and you would go the other direction because you didn't want to get into an argument with him. He was a loud guy and you knew he was around, no question about that.

"I'm impressed with this kid," Williams said . . . about me. "He really swings a bat. A left-handed hitter who hits to the opposite field as he does is going to help himself at Fenway Park. Some of those opposite-field fly balls will reach the screen or at least be off the wall."

Of course, he hated my style of hitting because he thought everybody should hit like Ted Williams. Well, there was only one Ted Williams.

My game was ground balls and line drives. His game was home runs. If he had been my hitting instructor, I don't think we would have meshed very well, because we had totally different styles. And for the record, of my seven career home runs, none came at Fenway Park.

Ted Williams

Year	Team	Age	G	AB	R	H	2B	3B	HR	RBI	BA	
1939	BOS (AL)	20	149	565	131	185	44	11	31	145	.327	
1940	BOS (AL)	21	144	561	134	193	43	14	23	113	.344	AS
1941	BOS (AL)	22	143	456	135	185	33	3	37	120	.406	AS

Year	Team	Age	G	AB	R	H	2B	3B	HR	RBI	BA	
1942	BOS (AL)	23	150	522	141	186	34	5	36	137	.356	AS
1946	BOS (AL)	27	150	514	142	176	37	8	38	123	.342	MVP, AS
1947	BOS (AL)	28	156	528	125	181	40	9	32	114	.343	AS
1948	BOS (AL)	29	137	509	124	188	44	3	25	127	.369	AS
1949	BOS (AL)	30	155	566	150	194	39	3	43	159	.343	MVP, AS
1950	BOS (AL)	31	89	334	82	106	24	1	28	97	.317	AS
1951	BOS (AL)	32	148	531	109	169	28	4	30	126	.318	AS
1952	BOS (AL)	33	6	10	2	4	0	1	1	3	.400	
1953	BOS (AL)	34	37	91	17	37	6	0	13	34	.407	AS
1954	BOS (AL)	35	117	386	93	133	23	1	29	89	.345	AS
1955	BOS (AL)	36	98	320	77	114	21	3	28	83	.356	AS
1956	BOS (AL)	37	136	400	71	138	28	2	24	82	.345	AS
1957	BOS (AL)	38	132	420	96	163	28	1	38	87	.388	AS
1958	BOS (AL)	39	129	411	81	135	23	2	26	85	.328	AS
1959	BOS (AL)	40	103	272	32	69	15	0	10	43	.254	AS
1960	BOS (AL)	41	113	310	56	98	15	0	29	72	.316	AS
Total			2292	7706	1798	2654	525	71	521	1839	.344	

Year	Team	OBP	SLG	OPS	BB	SO	TB	SB	CS	SH	SF	IBB	HBP	GDP
1939	BOS (AL)	.436	.609	1.045	107	64	344	2	1	3	#	#	2	10
1940	BOS (AL)	.442	.594	1.036	96	54	333	4	4	1	#	#	3	13
1941	BOS (AL)	.553	.735	1.288	147	27	335	2	4	0	#	#	3	10
1942	BOS (AL)	.499	.648	1.147	145	51	338	3	2	0	#	#	4	12
1946	BOS (AL)	.497	.667	1.164	156	44	343	0	0	0	#	#	2	12
1947	BOS (AL)	.499	.634	1.133	162	47	335	0	1	1	#	#	2	10
1948	BOS (AL)	.497	.615	1.112	126	41	313	4	0	0	#	#	3	10
1949	BOS (AL)	.490	.650	1.140	162	48	368	1	1	0	#	#	2	22
1950	BOS (AL)	.452	.647	1.099	82	21	216	3	0	0	#	#	0	12
1951	BOS (AL)	.464	.556	1.020	144	45	295	1	1	0	#	#	0	10
1952	BOS (AL)	.500	.900	1.400	2	2	9	0	0	0	#	#	0	0
1953	BOS (AL)	.509	.901	1.410	19	10	82	0	1	0	#	#	0	1
1954	BOS (AL)	.513	.635	1.148	136	32	245	0	0	0	3	#	1	10
1955	BOS (AL)	.496	.703	1.199	91	24	225	2	0	0	4	#	2	8
1956	BOS (AL)	.479	.605	1.084	102	39	242	0	0	0	0	11	1	13
1957	BOS (AL)	.526	.731	1.257	119	43	307	0	1	0	2	33	5	11
1958	BOS (AL)	.458	.584	1.042	98	49	240	1	0	0	4	12	4	19
1959	BOS (AL)	.372	.419	.791	52	27	114	0	0	0	5	6	2	7
1960	BOS (AL)	.451	.645	1.096	75	41	200	1	1	0	2	7	3	7
Total		.482	.634	1.116	2021	709	4884	24	17	5	20	86	39	197

*Not recorded

DICK RADATZ

Richard Raymond Radatz ("The Monster," "Moose")
(Boston 1962–1966; career 1962–1969)

Primary position: P	
Batted: R	
Threw: R	
Height: 6'5"	
Weight: 235 pounds	
First major league game: April 10, 1962	
Final major league game: August 15, 1969	
Born: April 2, 1937 in Detroit, Michigan	
Died: March 16, 2005 in Easton, Massachusetts	
Boston Red Sox Hall of Fame: 1997	

Dick Radatz was huge and intimidating, a wide-body who threw hard with a low sidearm delivery. He feared nothing.

Relievers in his day would take the mound in the fifth inning and finish the game. His career didn't last as long as most players' careers last today, because it was a totally different style of baseball at that time. Think about the kind of incredible numbers he might have had if he had been a closer today, with the way their work is structured.

Let's get one thing out of the way: Dick Radatz did not get his nickname, "the Monster," because of the wall over his right shoulder. His name comes from these statistics: 6 feet, 5 inches tall, at least 240 pounds, and big hands that could throw a baseball very hard. By some reports, the nickname was bestowed upon him by Mickey Mantle, one of the all-time greats. Mantle couldn't hit him. According to box scores, Mantle had 19 at-bats against Radatz in his career, and struck out 12 times; he had three hits, including a homer, but batted just .188 against the Monster.

Radatz threw what players call a "heavy ball," a late-breaking pitch that could flummox even the best of hitters. Radatz was a starting pitcher for Michigan State University, a teammate of Ron Perranoski. After being drafted as a starter, he pitched for the Seattle Rainiers, a AAA Pacific Coast League affiliate of the Red Sox in 1961; Johnny Pesky, manager of Seattle at the time, converted Radatz from

starter to reliever. In those days, that was considered a demotion for a pitcher, but Pesky convinced Radatz to take on the new role.

He was in Boston the next year, allowed only one run in his first 16 innings from the bullpen, and was named Relief Pitcher of the Year as he saved 24 games for the Red Sox. He credited Boston pitching coach Sal Maglie for improving his mechanics—a little thing like bending his back leg and taking better advantage of his power in pushing off the rubber as he threw—and launching his career.

I can't imagine what it would have been like to have been a right-handed batter facing someone like Radatz.

Dick Radatz

Year	Team	Age	W	L	G	GS	CG	SHO	GF	SV	WHIP	ERA	
1962	BOS (AL)	25	9	6	62	0	0	0	53	24	1.083	2.24	
1963	BOS (AL)	26	15	6	66	0	0	0	58	25	1.096	1.97	AS
1964	BOS (AL)	27	16	9	79	0	0	0	67	29	1.025	2.29	AS
1965	BOS (AL)	28	9	11	63	0	0	0	56	22	1.263	3.91	
1966	*Season*	*29*	*0*	*5*	*55*	*0*	*0*	*0*	*35*	*14*	*1.559*	*4.64*	
	BOS (AL)		0	2	16	0	0	0	10	4	1.842	4.74	
	CLE (AL)		0	3	39	0	0	0	25	10	1.465	4.61	
1967	*Season*	*30*	*1*	*0*	*23*	*0*	*0*	*0*	*11*	*5*	*1.633*	*6.49*	
	CLE (AL)		0	0	3	0	0	0	2	0	2.333	6.00	
	CHC (NL)		1	0	20	0	0	0	9	5	1.543	6.56	
1969	*Season*	*32*	*2*	*6*	*33*	*0*	*0*	*0*	*17*	*3*	*1.294*	*4.89*	
	DET (AL)		2	2	11	0	0	0	4	0	1.018	3.38	
	MON (NL)		0	4	22	0	0	0	13	3	1.442	5.71	
Total			**52**	**43**	**381**	**0**	**0**	**0**	**297**	**122**	**1.194**	**3.13**	
Boston			**49**	**34**	**286**	**0**	**0**	**0**	**244**	**104**	**1.136**	**2.65**	

Year	Team	IP	H	R	ER	HR	BB	SO	HBP	WP	IBB	BK
1962	BOS (AL)	124.7	95	32	31	9	40	144	4	4	2	0
1963	BOS (AL)	132.3	94	31	29	9	51	162	5	5	13	0
1964	BOS (AL)	157	103	44	40	13	58	181	7	1	9	0
1965	BOS (AL)	124.3	104	57	54	11	53	121	5	1	11	1
1966	*Season*	*75.7*	*73*	*43*	*39*	*9*	*45*	*68*	*3*	*5*	*8*	*0*
	BOS (AL)	19	24	10	10	3	11	19	0	0	2	0
	CLE (AL)	56.7	49	33	29	6	34	49	3	5	6	0
1967	*Season*	*26.3*	*17*	*23*	*19*	*5*	*26*	*19*	*5*	*9*	*2*	*0*
	CLE (AL)	3	5	2	2	1	2	1	0	0	0	0
	CHC (NL)	23.3	12	21	17	4	24	18	5	9	2	0
1969	*Season*	*53.3*	*46*	*30*	*29*	*9*	*23*	*50*	*1*	*0*	*1*	*0*
	DET (AL)	18.7	14	8	7	3	5	18	0	0	0	0
	MON (NL)	34.7	32	22	22	6	18	32	1	0	1	0
Total		**693.7**	**532**	**260**	**241**	**65**	**296**	**745**	**30**	**25**	**46**	**1**
Boston		**557.3**	**420**	**174**	**164**	**45**	**213**	**627**	**21**	**11**	**37**	**1**

RICO PETROCELLI
Americo Peter Petrocelli ("Rico")
(Boston 1963–1976)

Primary positions: 3B, SS

Batted: R

Threw: R

Height: 6'0"

Weight: 185 pounds

First major league game: September 21, 1963

Final major league game: September 14, 1976

Born: June 27, 1943 in Brooklyn, New York

Boston Red Sox Hall of Fame: 1997

Rico Petrocelli was a slick-fielding shortstop and third baseman who was a key member of the 1967 Impossible Dream team; in Game 6 of the World Series that year he hit two home runs against the St. Louis Cardinals to help force the deciding seventh game. He was always one of my favorites, a player I watched while I played high school ball in Somerset, Massachusetts.

A good Fenway hitter, he had power and could pull the ball. He also struck out a lot; I remember that when he struck out he just walked back to the dugout as fast as he could. It's weird sometimes how certain things stick out in your mind.

Petrocelli reached his hitting peak in the 1969 season when he batted .297 with 40 home runs. He played his entire career of 12 seasons for Boston.

In Game 6 of the 1967 World Series, Petrocelli was one of three Red Sox (along with Carl Yastrzemski and Reggie Smith) who set a postseason record of three home runs by a team in a single inning. This took place in the fourth inning; Rico had already hit a ball over the Green Monster in the second inning of the same game.

At the time, it was unusual to have an infielder with power. In 1969 he set an AL record for most home runs by a shortstop with 40 for the season and tied the record of the time for the fewest errors by a player at that position with 14. Alex Rodriguez eclipsed the home run record in 2002 with 57 for Texas; Cal Ripken (Baltimore, 1990)

Photo by the National Baseball Hall of Fame Library, Cooperstown, N.Y.

and Omar Vizquel (Cleveland, 2000) now hold the record for fewest errors with 3 for the season.

As a shortstop, he led the league in fielding percentage in 1968 and 1969; he switched to third base in 1971 when Luis Aparicio arrived in Boston. The change in position had little effect on him; in his first year at the corner he again led the league in fielding, making only 11 errors in 463 chances, and he hit 28 home runs and recorded 89 RBIs. A series of injuries reduced his playing time and his numbers in the following years, and he left the game at the end of the 1976 season with 210 home runs and 773 RBIs in the record books.

After retirement, Petrocelli worked in sports radio and as a pre-game analyst for Red Sox games; in 1992 he managed the Pawtucket Red Sox for a season.

I got to know him after his playing days were over; he is a good guy, very genuine for a tough guy from Brooklyn, New York.

Rico Petrocelli

Year	Team	Age	G	AB	R	H	2B	3B	HR	RBI	BA	
1963	BOS (AL)	20	1	4	0	1	1	0	0	1	.250	
1965	BOS (AL)	22	103	323	38	75	15	2	13	33	.232	
1966	BOS (AL)	23	139	522	58	124	20	1	18	59	.238	
1967	BOS (AL)	24	142	491	53	127	24	2	17	66	.259	AS
1968	BOS (AL)	25	123	406	41	95	17	2	12	46	.234	
1969	BOS (AL)	26	154	535	92	159	32	2	40	97	.297	AS
1970	BOS (AL)	27	157	583	82	152	31	3	29	103	.261	
1971	BOS (AL)	28	158	553	82	139	24	4	28	89	.251	
1972	BOS (AL)	29	147	521	62	125	15	2	15	75	.240	AS
1973	BOS (AL)	30	100	356	44	87	13	1	13	45	.244	
1974	BOS (AL)	31	129	454	53	121	23	1	15	76	.267	
1975	BOS (AL)	32	115	402	31	96	15	1	7	59	.239	
1976	BOS (AL)	33	85	240	17	51	7	1	3	24	.213	
Total			**1553**	**5390**	**653**	**1352**	**237**	**22**	**210**	**773**	**.251**	

Year	BOS (AL)	OBP	SLG	OPS	BB	SO	TB	SB	CS	SH	SF	IBB	HBP	GDP
1963	BOS (AL)	.250	.500	.750	0	1	2	0	0	0	0	0	0	0
1965	BOS (AL)	.309	.412	.721	36	71	133	0	2	1	2	4	1	6
1966	BOS (AL)	.295	.383	.678	41	99	200	1	1	2	4	2	3	8
1967	BOS (AL)	.330	.420	.750	49	93	206	2	4	8	3	9	5	4
1968	BOS (AL)	.292	.374	.666	31	73	152	0	1	6	4	2	4	7
1969	BOS (AL)	.403	.589	.992	98	68	315	3	5	3	6	13	1	12
1970	BOS (AL)	.334	.473	.807	67	82	276	1	1	2	10	6	2	16
1971	BOS (AL)	.354	.461	.815	91	108	255	2	0	6	9	5	2	20
1972	BOS (AL)	.339	.363	.702	78	91	189	0	1	2	4	9	2	8
1973	BOS (AL)	.333	.396	.729	47	64	141	0	0	1	2	3	1	10
1974	BOS (AL)	.336	.421	.757	48	74	191	1	0	0	5	4	2	11
1975	BOS (AL)	.310	.333	.643	41	66	134	0	2	3	5	1	3	16
1976	BOS (AL)	.307	.288	.595	34	36	69	0	5	2	3	3	0	9
Total		**.332**	**.420**	**.752**	**661**	**926**	**2263**	**10**	**22**	**36**	**57**	**61**	**26**	**127**

TONY CONIGLIARO

Anthony Richard Conigliaro ("Tony C," "Conig")
(Boston 1964–1970, 1975; career 1964–1975)

Primary position: RF	
Batted: R	
Threw: R	
Height: 6'3"	
Weight: 185 pounds	
First major league game: April 16, 1964	
Final major league game: June 12, 1975	
Born: January 7, 1945 in Revere, Massachusetts	
Died: February 24, 1990 in Salem, Massachusetts	
Boston Red Sox Hall of Fame: 1995	

Tony Conigliaro was like a shooting star, burning bright and all too quickly. He was a young kid coming to the big leagues with his hometown team. Good looking and a little bit brash, he had everything going for him.

He graduated from St. Mary's High School in Lynn in 1962. Two years later, at the age of 19, he appeared in the starting lineup of a not-too-great Red Sox team in 1964.

Conigliaro got a single in his third at-bat and helped the Red Sox beat the Yankees on opening day in New York. The next day the Sox opened at home against the Chicago White Sox and Tony C hit a home run in his first at-bat at Fenway.

For the first few years he was on an incredible pace, hitting 24 homers in his rookie year and batting .290 with 52 RBIs in 111 games. He broke his arm in late July and was out until September; otherwise he might have beaten out Tony Oliva for Rookie of the Year.

In 1965, he started off strongly again, but once again he went down in July, this time with a broken arm; despite missing 24 games he finished the season with 32 home runs. At age 20, he became the youngest home run champion in American League history.

In 1967, Conigliaro was having another fine year, batting .287 with 20 home runs and 67 RBIs; he had been named to the All-Star team and had played all 15 innings of that year's classic 2–1 pitcher's

duel in rightfield. On July 23 of that year, at the age of 22, he became the youngest player to ever reach 100 home runs—reaching the mark at a younger age than Alex Rodriguez would in 1998.

And then came August 18, 1967, the Red Sox against the Angels at Fenway Park. In the fourth inning of a scoreless game, a pitch from Jack Hamilton was up and in. I remember how he used to stand right on home plate, and of course guys like that always get pitched inside to try to get them off the plate.

The pitch hit him on his left cheek; it broke the bone and damaged the retina in his eye. There was no protective ear-flap on the helmet, and the sound at Fenway was baseball against bone. I can remember the photograph of him in the hospital with that eye blown up like a balloon.

It was one of the most gut-wrenching moments in Red Sox history, and it was the beginning of the end of a career that very well could have taken Conigliaro to the Hall of Fame. He missed the remainder of the year and all of the next season.

As it turned out, 1967 was one of the most exciting Red Sox seasons ever. Four teams were in the hunt for the AL pennant almost to the last day of the season, and Carl Yastrzemski won the Triple Crown—no one has done it since—and Boston's Impossible Dream team ended up in the World Series. The Red Sox lost to St. Louis.

As a ballplayer, do you go out there every day and wonder if today is the day you're going to get hit in the head, or blow out your knee? You don't think about those things, at least until they happen. You are thinking about playing the game. But when something bad happens it never really leaves your mind. I can't imagine what it would be like to step back there for the first time after something like that. Conigliaro was never the same after the beaning.

He returned to the lineup on April 8, 1969, hitting a two-run home run in the 10th inning and then scoring the eventual winning run in the 12th. It was a remarkable story and it seemed as if another impossible dream was going to be fulfilled. He hit 20 homers and drove in 82 runs and was named Comeback Player of the Year.

In 1970, he had the best year of his career, pounding 36 homers and 116 RBIs, but that would turn out to be his last hurrah. He was traded to the California Angels in the off-season, and his health problems returned. After an unhappy season batting just .222 in 74 games and hitting just 4 homers, he was out of baseball. In 1975, he attempted a comeback with Boston, but after 21 games and a batting average of .123 the star-crossed career of Tony C came to an end.

And then in 1982, Tony C suffered a serious heart attack and then a stroke; he had been in Boston to interview for a job as color analyst for the Red Sox television broadcasts, the job I took over in 1987. Conigliaro was severely disabled by his health problems and eventually passed away at the age of 45.

Today Major League Baseball bestows the Tony Conigliaro Award each year to the player who best overcomes obstacles and adversity.

In 2007, Red Sox pitcher Jon Lester was given the award after he came back from battling a rare form of cancer (non-Hodgkin's lymphoma) in 2006 and ended up clinching the 2007 World Series for Boston with a win in Game 4 against the Colorado Rockies.

Also in 2007, the Red Sox added a 200-seat bleacher section on the right field roof, naming the section "Conigliaro's Corner."

We'll never know if Tony C would have been as good a hitter as A-Rod throughout his career, for example, but I do know that Fenway Park was perfect for him. God knows what his career would have been like if not for the beaning. His story will always be remembered as an unfulfilled promise, a terrible loss of talent.

Tony Conigliaro

Year	Team	Age	G	AB	R	H	2B	3B	HR	RBI	BA	
1964	BOS (AL)	19	111	404	69	117	21	2	24	52	.290	
1965	BOS (AL)	20	138	521	82	140	21	5	32	82	.269	
1966	BOS (AL)	21	150	558	77	148	26	7	28	93	.265	
1967	BOS (AL)	22	95	349	59	100	11	5	20	67	.287	AS
1969	BOS (AL)	24	141	506	57	129	21	3	20	82	.255	
1970	BOS (AL)	25	146	560	89	149	20	1	36	116	.266	
1971	CAL (AL)	26	74	266	23	59	18	0	4	15	.222	
1975	BOS (AL)	30	21	57	8	7	1	0	2	9	.123	
Total			876	3221	464	849	139	23	166	516	.264	
Boston			802	2955	441	790	121	23	162	501	.267	

Year	Team	OBP	SLG	OPS	BB	SO	TB	SB	CS	SH	SF	IBB	HBP	GDP
1964	BOS (AL)	.354	.530	.884	35	78	214	2	4	0	0	1	5	11
1965	BOS (AL)	.338	.512	.850	51	116	267	4	2	6	3	6	5	9
1966	BOS (AL)	.330	.487	.817	52	112	272	0	2	6	7	8	5	6
1967	BOS (AL)	.341	.519	.860	27	58	181	4	6	2	6	2	5	3
1969	BOS (AL)	.321	.427	.748	48	111	216	2	4	3	5	6	4	11
1970	BOS (AL)	.324	.498	.822	43	93	279	4	2	0	6	4	8	11
1971	CAL (AL)	.285	.335	.620	23	52	89	3	3	1	1	1	1	10
1975	BOS (AL)	.221	.246	.467	8	9	14	1	0	1	3	0	0	2
Total		.327	.476	.803	287	629	1532	20	23	19	31	28	33	63
Boston		.331	.488	.819	264	577	1443	17	20	18	30	27	32	53

DAYS OF MY BASEBALL LIFE

CARL YASTRZEMSKI
Carl Michael Yastrzemski ("Yaz")
(Boston 1961–1983)

Primary position: LF	
Batted: L	
Threw: R	
Height: 5'11"	
Weight: 182 pounds	
First major league game: April 11, 1961	
Final major league game: October 2, 1983	
Born: August 22, 1939 in Southampton, New York	
Baseball Hall of Fame: 1989	
Boston Red Sox Hall of Fame: 1995	
Boston Red Sox Retired Uniform Number: 8	

It couldn't have been easy for Carl Yastrzemski to be the opening day leftfielder for Boston on April 11, 1961. Yaz singled to left in his first major league at-bat and his own legendary career was underway.

When Yaz took to the field that day, he was literally following in the footsteps of Ted Williams, who had retired at the end of the previous season. Williams had ended his career with a home run at Fenway in his last major league at-bat on September 28, 1960. Carroll Hardy finished out the last few games of that season in left, keeping the spot warm for Yaz.

Yastrzemski was one of my idols as a teenager. I'll never forget his 1967 season when he won the Triple Crown: number one in home runs, RBIs, and batting average. No one has done that since Yaz.

And then to get a chance to play with him was the thrill of my life. He was beginning to move from the outfield to first base and designated hitter by the time I arrived in Boston. Even late in his career, he was a very, very competitive guy, especially with his hitting. To the day he finished, you couldn't beat him on a fastball. He spent a ton of time working on his hitting. If he had a bad day, he would be out in the batting cage after the game. Most guys would be gone. He would still be there.

He wasn't someone who would be all over the clubhouse talking to everybody. He would pick and choose who he wanted to be around.

A lot of players who came over from the National League looked at him and said, "Gee, he is not that big at all." He was not a big guy, but he was strong. Overall, he was one of the most competitive hitters and hard workers that I have ever run into in the game of baseball.

At spring training in 1961, Carl Yastrzemski was promoted from the Red Sox AAA team in Minneapolis to the major league squad. He seemed like a sure lock to follow in the footsteps of the great Ted Williams; the only question for most sportswriters was how to spell his name. They eventually settled on a nickname of Yaz, and many fans probably never learned the rest of the letters. Yaz got off to a slow start in the season but finished with a solid if not spectacular rookie year. He steadily improved, and by 1963 at age 23 he batted .321 and was an All-Star.

He played 23 seasons for Boston, hitting 452 home runs. His best years were between 1967 and 1970. In the 1967 Impossible Dream season he was the American League's MVP, and put into the record book 44 home runs, a .326 batting average, and 121 RBI. His OPS that season was 1.040. (His OPS mark puts him in elite company. Boston Red Sox players who posted higher single-season records in that important hitting category are Ted Williams in 1953 at 1.410, Manny Ramirez in 2006 at 1.058, David Ortiz in 2006 at 1.049, and Wade Boggs in 1987 at 1.049. Yaz reached that level again in 1970, at 1.044.)

Yaz grew up on his family's potato farm on Long Island, and came oh-so-close to signing with the Yankees, but according to legend a scout for New York offended Carl's father with his negotiating stance and so Yaz crossed Long Island Sound to New England.

In the magical 1967 season, Yaz put on a display of intensity that has rarely been matched in baseball. The Sox won 8 of the last 12 games to win the pennant, with Yaz batting .523 in that stretch (including 5 home runs and 16 RBIs).

Carl Yastrzemski

Year	Team	Age	G	AB	R	H	2B	3B	HR	RBI	BA	
1961	BOS (AL)	21	148	583	71	155	31	6	11	80	.266	
1962	BOS (AL)	22	160	646	99	191	43	6	19	94	.296	
1963	BOS (AL)	23	151	570	91	183	40	3	14	68	.321	AS
1964	BOS (AL)	24	151	567	77	164	29	9	15	67	.289	
1965	BOS (AL)	25	133	494	78	154	45	3	20	72	.312	AS
1966	BOS (AL)	26	160	594	81	165	39	2	16	80	.278	AS
1967	BOS (AL)	27	161	579	112	189	31	4	44	121	.326	MVP, AS
1968	BOS (AL)	28	157	539	90	162	32	2	23	74	.301	AS
1969	BOS (AL)	29	162	603	96	154	28	2	40	111	.255	AS
1970	BOS (AL)	30	161	566	125	186	29	0	40	102	.329	AS
1971	BOS (AL)	31	148	508	75	129	21	2	15	70	.254	AS
1972	BOS (AL)	32	125	455	70	120	18	2	12	68	.264	AS

Year	Team	Age	G	AB	R	H	2B	3B	HR	RBI	BA	
1973	BOS (AL)	33	152	540	82	160	25	4	19	95	.296	AS
1974	BOS (AL)	34	148	515	93	155	25	2	15	79	.301	AS
1975	BOS (AL)	35	149	543	91	146	30	1	14	60	.269	AS
1976	BOS (AL)	36	155	546	71	146	23	2	21	102	.267	AS
1977	BOS (AL)	37	150	558	99	165	27	3	28	102	.296	AS
1978	BOS (AL)	38	144	523	70	145	21	2	17	81	.277	AS
1979	BOS (AL)	39	147	518	69	140	28	1	21	87	.270	AS
1980	BOS (AL)	40	105	364	49	100	21	1	15	50	.275	
1981	BOS (AL)	41	91	338	36	83	14	1	7	53	.246	
1982	BOS (AL)	42	131	459	53	126	22	1	16	72	.275	AS
1983	BOS (AL)	43	119	380	38	101	24	0	10	56	.266	AS
Totals			**3308**	**11988**	**1816**	**3419**	**646**	**59**	**452**	**1844**	**.285**	

Year	Team	OBP	SLG	OPS	BB	SO	TB	SB	CS	SH	SF	IBB	HBP	GDP
1961	BOS (AL)	.324	.396	.720	50	96	231	6	5	2	5	3	3	19
1962	BOS (AL)	.363	.469	.832	66	82	303	7	4	2	2	7	3	27
1963	BOS (AL)	.418	.475	.893	95	72	271	8	5	1	1	6	1	12
1964	BOS (AL)	.374	.451	.825	75	90	256	6	5	1	1	6	2	30
1965	BOS (AL)	.395	.536	.931	70	58	265	7	6	2	4	8	1	16
1966	BOS (AL)	.368	.431	.799	84	60	256	8	9	0	1	10	1	17
1967	BOS (AL)	.418	.622	1.040	91	69	360	10	8	1	5	11	4	5
1968	BOS (AL)	.426	.495	.921	119	90	267	13	6	0	4	13	2	12
1969	BOS (AL)	.362	.507	.869	101	91	306	15	7	0	2	9	1	14
1970	BOS (AL)	.452	.592	1.044	128	66	335	23	13	0	2	12	1	12
1971	BOS (AL)	.381	.392	.773	106	60	199	8	7	0	5	12	1	14
1972	BOS (AL)	.357	.391	.748	67	44	178	5	4	0	9	3	4	13
1973	BOS (AL)	.407	.463	.870	105	58	250	9	7	1	6	13	0	19
1974	BOS (AL)	.414	.445	.859	104	48	229	12	7	0	11	16	3	12
1975	BOS (AL)	.371	.405	.776	87	67	220	8	4	0	2	12	2	14
1976	BOS (AL)	.357	.432	.789	80	67	236	5	6	1	8	6	1	12
1977	BOS (AL)	.372	.505	.877	73	40	282	11	1	0	11	6	1	10
1978	BOS (AL)	.367	.423	.790	76	44	221	4	5	1	8	8	3	9
1979	BOS (AL)	.346	.450	.796	62	46	233	3	3	0	8	8	2	12
1980	BOS (AL)	.350	.462	.812	44	38	168	0	2	1	3	5	0	9
1981	BOS (AL)	.338	.355	.693	49	28	120	0	1	0	3	4	0	10
1982	BOS (AL)	.358	.431	.789	59	50	198	0	1	0	3	1	2	12
1983	BOS (AL)	.359	.408	.767	54	29	155	0	0	0	1	11	2	13
Total		**.379**	**.462**	**.841**	**1845**	**1393**	**5539**	**168**	**116**	**13**	**105**	**190**	**40**	**323**

JIM LONBORG

James Reynold Lonborg ("Gentleman Jim")
(Boston 1965–1971; career 1965–1979)

Primary position: P	
Batted: R	
Threw: R	
Height: 6'5"	
Weight: 210 pounds	
First major league game: April 23, 1965	
Final major league game: June 10, 1979	
Born: April 16, 1942 in Santa Maria, California	
Boston Red Sox Hall of Fame: 2002	

Gentleman Jim owned the inside of the plate for 15 years, including his spectacular 1967 season for the Red Sox.

Lonborg was nasty, throwing kind of a sidearm sinkerball. He had to make right-handed hitters uncomfortable; Lonborg had a hard fastball and was not afraid to throw it inside.

In 1967 he went 22–9 with a 3.16 ERA and won the Cy Young Award. I was a huge fan—I was 14 years old—and the 1967 team was my all-time favorite. That was what really hooked me on baseball and the Red Sox. As a member of the Impossible Dream team, Lonborg led the AL in wins, starts, and strikeouts that season.

More importantly, he won most—but not all—of the essential games that got the Red Sox into the World Series for the first time since 1946 and almost all the way to the Promised Land. Lonborg was the starting pitcher on October 1, 1967, as the Red Sox won the pennant on the last day of the season. He pitched all nine innings, besting Dean Chance and the Minnesota Twins 5–3. The Detroit Tigers were also in the hunt, but Lonborg's complete game punched Boston's ticket.

And then it was on to the World Series against St. Louis, with two of baseball's aces involved: Lonborg against Bob Gibson. Gibson won Game 1.

In Game 2 on October 5, pitching on three days of rest after the end of the season, Lonborg had a perfect game until he walked Curt

Photo by the National Baseball Hall of Fame Library, Cooperstown, N.Y.

Flood in the sixth inning; he held on to a no-hitter until there were two outs in the eighth inning and went on to win 5–0 for his second consecutive nine-inning complete game.

Lonborg came back to the mound for Game 5 on October 9, once again after just three days of rest, with the Sox against the wall down 3-1 in the Series. And Gentleman Jim did it again: a complete game three-hit 3–1 victory. Lonborg had gone 17 innings without giving up a run in the Series until Roger Maris homered in the ninth inning.

Back home at Fenway, the Red Sox came from behind twice in Game 6 to tie the Series and set up the fateful Game 7 that for the first time pitted Lonborg against Gibson. Lonborg was pitching on just two days rest now and it was finally too much, with the Cardinals winning 7–2 and extending Boston's long World Series drought.

Starting your ace on two day's rest? You wouldn't even think about that today. If only it had rained for a few days.

After the end of the Impossible Dream season of 1967, Jim Lonborg took his Cy Young–winning body to Lake Tahoe for a ski trip with actress Jill St. John. (The newspapers called it "cavorting," whatever that meant.) On Christmas Eve, Lonborg caught an edge of his ski and tore ligaments in his left knee.

I don't know exactly what the language is in today's contract, but I know when I signed my five-year deal with the Red Sox there were all kinds of clauses: you couldn't parachute, you couldn't ski. That might have started because of Lonborg. From a team's point of view, it makes sense that you don't want guys taking out-of-the-ordinary risks and ruining their career, especially with the money they are paying them.

The 1968 season saw his record drop from 22–9 in 39 games to 6–10 in 17 starts and 6 relief appearances. It was not until 1971 that Lonborg was able to approach his top form; in that year he started 26 games and posted a 10–7 record. We'll never know how many more Cy Young awards and how much greater of a career he could have had if he hadn't had that skiing accident.

Lonborg also played his part in the ongoing saga of the Red Sox and Yankees. On June 21, 1967 at Yankee Stadium, the star-crossed Tony Conigliaro had put Boston up by three runs with a first-inning homer; in the second inning Yankees pitcher Thad Tillotson threw a pitch up and in against Red Sox third baseman Joe Foy. The pitch missed Foy, but on the next throw Tillotson threw a fastball right at Foy's head, hitting him in the helmet.

In the bottom of the inning, Tillotson came up to bat against Lonborg and Gentleman Jim wasted no time in nailing the pitcher. The benches cleared and there was a five-minute pushing and shoving match on the field; neither pitcher was ejected from the game. Joe Pepitone hurt his wrist in the fight. Later in the game, just for good measure, Lonborg also hit pinch-hitter Dick Howser. Oh, and the Red Sox won 7–1.

He was mean on the mound, but gentle as he could be off the field. He is a really nice guy and very smart; he graduated from Stanford and after leaving baseball went on to be a dentist.

I'll talk a bit more about the 1967 Impossible Dream Team later on; the team has its own chapter in this book.

Jim Lonborg

Year	Team	Age	W	L	G	GS	CG	SHO	GF	SV	WHIP	ERA	
1965	BOS (AL)	23	9	17	32	31	7	1	0	0	1.392	4.47	
1966	BOS (AL)	24	10	10	45	23	3	1	7	2	1.255	3.86	
1967	BOS (AL)	25	22	9	39	39	15	2	0	0	1.138	3.16	CY, AS
1968	BOS (AL)	26	6	10	23	17	4	1	0	0	1.306	4.29	
1969	BOS (AL)	27	7	11	29	23	4	0	3	0	1.483	4.51	
1970	BOS (AL)	28	4	1	9	4	0	0	3	0	1.235	3.18	
1971	BOS (AL)	29	10	7	27	26	5	1	1	0	1.396	4.13	
1972	MIL (AL)	30	14	12	33	30	11	2	1	1	1.224	2.83	
1973	PHI (NL)	31	13	16	38	30	6	0	5	0	1.495	4.88	
1974	PHI (NL)	32	17	13	39	39	16	3	0	0	1.237	3.21	
1975	PHI (NL)	33	8	6	27	26	6	2	1	0	1.293	4.12	
1976	PHI (NL)	34	18	10	33	32	8	1	1	1	1.171	3.08	
1977	PHI (NL)	35	11	4	25	25	4	1	0	0	1.313	4.11	
1978	PHI (NL)	36	8	10	22	22	1	0	0	0	1.557	5.23	
1979	PHI (NL)	37	0	1	4	1	0	0	2	0	2.455	11.05	
Total			**157**	**137**	**425**	**368**	**90**	**15**	**24**	**4**	**1.308**	**3.86**	
Boston			**68**	**65**	**204**	**163**	**38**	**6**	**14**	**2**	**1.305**	**3.94**	

Year	Team	IP	H	R	ER	HR	BB	K	HBP	WP	IBB	BK
1965	BOS (AL)	185.3	193	112	92	20	65	113	3	8	3	1
1966	BOS (AL)	181.7	173	86	78	18	55	131	7	7	5	2
1967	BOS (AL)	273.3	228	102	96	23	83	246	19	12	5	1
1968	BOS (AL)	113.3	89	57	54	11	59	73	11	7	3	0
1969	BOS (AL)	143.7	148	78	72	15	65	100	7	8	3	0
1970	BOS (AL)	34	33	12	12	3	9	21	0	2	0	0
1971	BOS (AL)	167.7	167	86	77	15	67	100	14	3	6	0
1972	MIL (AL)	223	197	75	70	17	76	143	11	5	11	0

Year	Team	IP	H	R	ER	HR	BB	K	HBP	WP	IBB	BK
1973	PHI (NL)	199.3	218	124	108	25	80	106	9	1	7	0
1974	PHI (NL)	283	280	113	101	22	70	121	6	5	11	0
1975	PHI (NL)	159.3	161	84	73	12	45	72	5	3	7	2
1976	PHI (NL)	222	210	85	76	18	50	118	5	2	4	1
1977	PHI (NL)	157.7	157	77	72	15	50	76	5	6	5	2
1978	PHI (NL)	113.7	132	69	66	16	45	48	2	4	1	0
1979	PHI (NL)	7.3	14	10	9	3	4	7	1	0	0	0
Total		**2464.3**	**2400**	**1170**	**1056**	**233**	**823**	**1475**	**105**	**73**	**71**	**9**
Boston		**1099**	**1031**	**533**	**481**	**105**	**403**	**784**	**61**	**47**	**25**	**4**

GEORGE SCOTT

George Charles Scott Jr. ("Boomer")

(Boston 1966–1971, 1977–1979; career 1966–1979)

Primary position: 1B	
Batted: R	
Threw: R	
Height: 6'2"	
Weight: 215 pounds	
First major league game: April 12, 1966	
Final major league game: September 27, 1979	
Born: March 23, 1944 in Greenville, Mississippi	
Boston Red Sox Hall of Fame: 2006	

Scott was another one of the Red Sox homegrown stars. In 1965 he won the Triple Crown for the Pittsfield Red Sox of the AA Eastern League—predecessor of the Pawtucket Red Sox, now Boston's AAA team—and helped Pittsfield win the pennant. Scott was called up to Boston in 1966 and played in all 162 games that year. He was the starting first baseman for the American League All-Stars in his rookie year.

The Boomer hit more than 20 home runs in a season six times in his career. In the special Red Sox year of 1975 he tied Reggie Jackson in the American League with 36 homers, led the league with 109 RBIs, and took home a Gold Glove for defense at first base. Like many of the other great players on that team, he won just about everything but the World Series.

Defensively at first base he was unbelievable. He was a big guy, but he was as smooth as could be over there. He had great range and great hands; he saved so many errors for infielders by picking the ball out of the dirt. He played nearly all of his career at first base, although in 1969 he was the starting third baseman for Boston and occupied that position for two-thirds of the season.

I got to play with him toward the end of his career and he had slowed up a bit offensively, but certainly not defensively. Even though he was at a disadvantage as a right-hander at first base, he loved to make the play where he would go to his right, take the ball in front

of me at second base, and throw to the pitcher covering first. He was great at it. Every time he would make that play he would turn to me and say, "Call me off, call me off." I couldn't do that; he wanted to make that play. And anyway, no one could have stopped him once he got going.

George was sometimes hard to understand, with his thick Mississippi accent. Half the time you didn't know what he was saying, but he would be laughing his ass off with or without you.

At the end of his career George was heavy and was supposedly on a diet. So at the ballpark, all you would see him eat was salad. Then one night we were coming back to the hotel and we got on the elevator and there he was with a big tub of ribs that he had run out to get. He was dieting in the clubhouse but not off the field.

Scott suffered a series of injuries and his power numbers began to decline; he was traded to the Milwaukee Brewers in 1971 in one of the more complex deals I can recall. The Red Sox traded away Scott, Ken Brett, Jim Lonborg, Billy Conigliaro, Joe Lahoud, and Don Pavletitch in return for speedster Tommy Harper and pitchers Marty Pattin and Lew Krausse; there were a few minor leaguers involved as well.

The Boomer had a rebirth in Milwaukee, in 1975 returning to the All-Star team in a year in which he hit a career-high 36 homers, drove in 109 runs, and batted .285. And for the 1977 season, the Red Sox wanted him back. This time they traded Cecil Cooper to the Brewers for Scott and Bernie Carbo. Cooper went on to have a pretty good career in Milwaukee, while Scott delivered what amounted to one last hurrah in Boston: 33 homers and 96 RBIs. His numbers declined again in 1978, and by 1979 he was traded in mid-season to Kansas City; released by the Royals after a few months he played the final 16 games of his 14-year career as a Yankee. But we'll forgive him that; he was inducted into the Red Sox Hall of Fame in 2006. Scott finished his career with 271 home runs, which he appropriately called "taters."

George Scott

Year	Team	Age	G	AB	R	H	2B	3B	HR	RBI	BA	
1966	BOS (AL)	22	162	601	73	147	18	7	27	90	.245	AS
1967	BOS (AL)	23	159	565	74	171	21	7	19	82	.303	
1968	BOS (AL)	24	124	350	23	60	14	0	3	25	.171	
1969	BOS (AL)	25	152	549	63	139	14	5	16	52	.253	
1970	BOS (AL)	26	127	480	50	142	24	5	16	63	.296	
1971	BOS (AL)	27	146	537	72	141	16	4	24	78	.263	
1972	MIL (AL)	28	152	578	71	154	24	4	20	88	.266	
1973	MIL (AL)	29	158	604	98	185	30	4	24	107	.306	
1974	MIL (AL)	30	158	604	74	170	36	2	17	82	.281	
1975	MIL (AL)	31	158	617	86	176	26	4	36	109	.285	AS

Year	Team	Age	G	AB	R	H	2B	3B	HR	RBI	BA	
1976	MIL (AL)	32	156	606	73	166	21	5	18	77	.274	
1977	BOS (AL)	33	157	584	103	157	26	5	33	96	.269	AS
1978	BOS (AL)	34	120	412	51	96	16	4	12	54	.233	
1979	Season	35	105	346	46	88	20	4	6	49	.254	
	BOS (AL)		45	156	18	35	9	1	4	23	.224	
	KC (AL)		44	146	19	39	8	2	1	20	.267	
	NYY (AL)		16	44	9	14	3	1	1	6	.318	
Total			**2034**	**7433**	**957**	**1992**	**306**	**60**	**271**	**1051**	**.268**	
Boston			**1192**	**4234**	**527**	**1088**	**158**	**38**	**154**	**562**	**.257**	

Year	Team	OBP	SLG	OPS	BB	SO	TB	SB	CS	SH	SF	IBB	HBP	GDP
1966	BOS (AL)	.324	.433	.757	65	152	260	4	0	2	5	13	8	25
1967	BOS (AL)	.373	.465	.838	63	119	263	10	8	3	6	10	4	13
1968	BOS (AL)	.236	.237	.473	26	88	83	3	5	1	5	3	5	13
1969	BOS (AL)	.331	.384	.715	61	74	211	4	3	1	2	12	4	15
1970	BOS (AL)	.355	.467	.822	44	95	224	4	11	0	4	5	2	13
1971	BOS (AL)	.317	.441	.758	41	102	237	0	3	0	7	5	5	23
1972	MIL (AL)	.321	.426	.747	43	130	246	16	4	2	2	4	4	19
1973	MIL (AL)	.370	.488	.858	61	94	295	9	5	2	4	6	2	19
1974	MIL (AL)	.345	.432	.777	59	90	261	9	9	0	6	5	3	25
1975	MIL (AL)	.341	.515	.856	51	97	318	6	5	1	3	7	3	26
1976	MIL (AL)	.334	.414	.748	53	118	251	0	1	0	7	6	5	19
1977	BOS (AL)	.337	.500	.837	57	112	292	1	1	1	5	4	6	24
1978	BOS (AL)	.305	.379	.684	44	86	156	1	1	7	3	3	0	19
1979	Season	.317	.387	.704	31	61	134	2	1	2	3	2	2	24
	BOS (AL)	.299	.372	.671	17	22	58	0	0	1	1	1	0	12
	KC (AL)	.329	.370	.699	12	32	54	1	1	1	1	1	2	12
	NYY (AL)	.340	.500	.840	2	7	22	1	0	0	1	0	0	0
Total		**.333**	**.435**	**.768**	**699**	**1418**	**3231**	**69**	**57**	**22**	**62**	**85**	**53**	**277**
Boston		**.326**	**.421**	**.747**	**418**	**850**	**1784**	**27**	**32**	**16**	**38**	**56**	**34**	**157**

CARLTON FISK
Carlton Ernest Fisk ("Pudge")
(Boston 1969–1980; career 1969–1993)

Primary position: C	
Batted: R	
Threw: R	
Height: 6'2"	
Weight: 220 pounds	
First major league game: September 18, 1969	
Final major league game: June 22, 1993	
Born: December 26, 1947 in Bellows Falls, Vermont	
Baseball Hall of Fame: 2000	
Boston Red Sox Hall of Fame: 1997	
Boston Red Sox Retired Uniform Number: 27	

Carlton Fisk was the first guy to call me to welcome me to the team when I was traded to the Red Sox from the Angels. A few of my other former teammates had gone on to the Yankees. I will always remember one day when we were warming up before a game with New York, and Mickey Rivers came over to say "hi." Pudge came right up and said to me: "You don't talk to those guys." That's how serious the Yankee–Red Sox thing was in those days.

He was fiercely competitive, and that was probably most famously evident in the battle between him and Thurman Munson of the Yankees. They both wanted to be the best. One of the most famous incidents took place on August 1, 1973 at Fenway; the score was tied 2–2 in the top of the ninth inning when Munson tried to score on a missed bunt on a squeeze play. Munson slammed into Fisk and when the two squared off, there was a 10-minute bench-clearing brawl on the field. Munson was killed in a plane crash in 1979, the feud sadly unsettled.

I used to call Fisk "Magic" because his hands were so good for a big guy. But he also worked hard on his hitting. He had an uncanny ability to take balls that were down and in and somehow keep them fair down the leftfield line because his hands would come inside the baseball. He was also a great baserunner for a big guy.

Photo by the National Baseball Hall of Fame Library, Cooperstown, N.Y.

Just about any baseball fan will remember or has seen film of Fisk waving in the direction of a fly ball heading down the leftfield line at Fenway Park as if he could will it to stay fair. The moment came in the 12th inning of Game 6 of the 1975 World Series; Fisk hit the ball off Pat Darcy of the Cincinnati Reds, and when it finally hit the foul pole it gave the Red Sox a 7–6 win to force a seventh and deciding game. (Alas, the Red Sox lost the final game; it would be another 29 years before Boston reached the Promised Land.)

Fisk then went to the Chicago White Sox in 1981 and began working out with weights; he'd be still working out for hours after a game. I remember once when my knees were bad, and he invited me out to his house in Chicago to work with his trainer and a chiropractor to see if they could help me in any way. I went through a workout with him and I couldn't walk for three days later; that's how hard he worked.

It's hard enough to be a catcher; it's one of the most physically demanding positions in any sport. And it's harder still to be a consistently excellent hitter, handling the pitchers and the pitches on defense and then still having enough in the tank to be a serious threat at the plate.

That's why this is so impressive: Carlton Fisk played longer and caught more games than any other catcher in major league history: 2,226 games over 24 years. And he hit 351 of his 376 home runs as a catcher; in the history of baseball, only Mike Piazza had more with 396 as a catcher and 427 in total when he retired before the start of the 2008 season.

Fisk came up to the Red Sox in 1969 for a look-see, and again in 1971, but he announced himself to the baseball world in his first full year in 1972: He caught 131 games, batted .293, hit 22 home runs, and drove in 61 runs, and he was voted Rookie of the Year—the first unanimous winner in AL history—and was selected to his first of 11 All-Star teams.

Fisk put up solid numbers for each of the nine seasons he caught for Boston . . . and then management let him get away. A labor arbitrator declared Fisk a free agent in 1981, and the Red Sox were not willing to give him a serious raise from his $210,000 salary. It was a shame to see him leave the Red Sox. This is a guy who should have been in a Red Sox uniform his whole career—a local guy who became a Hall of Fame player. I think general manager Haywood Sullivan never really liked him and left him no other option but to go somewhere else.

Fisk went on to sign with the Chicago White Sox where he played for 13 more seasons. He retired in 1993 at age 45, after 24 seasons as a major leaguer. He was a friend, and he remains one.

In 2005, the Red Sox honored Fisk for his playing time at Fenway—and for the 1975 World Series home run—by naming the left-field foul pole as the "Fisk Pole." (The rightfield pole is known as the "Pesky Pole" for longtime player, manager, and coach Johnny Pesky.)

The Chicago White Sox also honored Fisk in the same year, putting up a life-sized bronze statue at U.S. Cellular Field.

His Red Sox number, 27, was retired in Boston in 2000. When he moved to Chicago he reversed the numbers on his jersey to 72, and that number was retired by the White Sox in 1997.

In 2008, Pudge came to Fenway and to the broadcast booth as part of the embarrassing—but very gratifying—Jerry Remy Day put on by the Red Sox. When I was speaking with him about what a shame it was that Boston had let him get away in 1981, he looked right into the camera and said, "It broke my heart, too." And on his Baseball Hall of Fame plaque he wears a Red Sox cap.

Carlton Fisk

Year	Team	Age	G	AB	R	H	2B	3B	HR	RBI	BA	
1969	BOS (AL)	21	2	5	0	0	0	0	0	0	.000	
1971	BOS (AL)	23	14	48	7	15	2	1	2	6	.313	
1972	BOS (AL)	24	131	457	74	134	28	9	22	61	.293	ROY, AS
1973	BOS (AL)	25	135	508	65	125	21	0	26	71	.246	AS
1974	BOS (AL)	26	52	187	36	56	12	1	11	26	.299	AS
1975	BOS (AL)	27	79	263	47	87	14	4	10	52	.331	
1976	BOS (AL)	28	134	487	76	124	17	5	17	58	.255	AS
1977	BOS (AL)	29	152	536	106	169	26	3	26	102	.315	AS
1978	BOS (AL)	30	157	571	94	162	39	5	20	88	.284	AS
1979	BOS (AL)	31	91	320	49	87	23	2	10	42	.272	
1980	BOS (AL)	32	131	478	73	138	25	3	18	62	.289	AS
1981	CHW (AL)	33	96	338	44	89	12	0	7	45	.263	AS, SS
1982	CHW (AL)	34	135	476	66	127	17	3	14	65	.267	AS
1983	CHW (AL)	35	138	488	85	141	26	4	26	86	.289	
1984	CHW (AL)	36	102	359	54	83	20	1	21	43	.231	
1985	CHW (AL)	37	153	543	85	129	23	1	37	107	.238	AS, SS
1986	CHW (AL)	38	125	457	42	101	11	0	14	63	.221	
1987	CHW (AL)	39	135	454	68	116	22	1	23	71	.256	
1988	CHW (AL)	40	76	253	37	70	8	1	19	50	.277	SS
1989	CHW (AL)	41	103	375	47	110	25	2	13	68	.293	
1990	CHW (AL)	42	137	452	65	129	21	0	18	65	.285	
1991	CHW (AL)	43	134	460	42	111	25	0	18	74	.241	AS
1992	CHW (AL)	44	62	188	12	43	4	1	3	21	.229	
1993	CHW (AL)	45	25	53	2	10	0	0	1	4	.189	
Total			**2499**	**8756**	**1276**	**2356**	**421**	**47**	**376**	**1330**	**.269**	
Boston			**1078**	**3860**	**627**	**1097**	**207**	**33**	**162**	**568**	**.284**	

Year	Team	OBP	SLG	OPS	BB	SO	TB	SB	CS	SH	SF	IBB	HBP	GDP
1969	BOS (AL)	.000	.000	.000	0	2	0	0	0	0	0	0	0	0
1971	BOS (AL)	.327	.521	.848	1	10	25	0	0	0	0	0	0	1
1972	BOS (AL)	.370	.538	.908	52	83	246	5	2	1	0	6	4	11
1973	BOS (AL)	.309	.441	.750	37	99	224	7	2	1	2	2	10	11
1974	BOS (AL)	.383	.551	.934	24	23	103	5	1	2	1	2	2	5
1975	BOS (AL)	.395	.529	.924	27	32	139	4	3	0	2	4	2	7
1976	BOS (AL)	.336	.415	.751	56	71	202	12	5	3	5	3	6	11
1977	BOS (AL)	.402	.521	.923	75	85	279	7	6	2	10	3	9	9
1978	BOS (AL)	.366	.475	.841	71	83	271	7	2	3	6	6	7	10
1979	BOS (AL)	.304	.450	.754	10	38	144	3	0	1	3	0	6	9
1980	BOS (AL)	.353	.467	.820	36	62	223	11	5	0	3	6	13	12
1981	CHW (AL)	.354	.361	.715	38	37	122	3	2	1	5	3	12	9
1982	CHW (AL)	.336	.403	.739	46	60	192	17	2	4	4	7	6	12
1983	CHW (AL)	.355	.518	.873	46	88	253	9	6	2	3	3	6	8
1984	CHW (AL)	.289	.468	.757	26	60	168	6	0	1	4	4	5	7
1985	CHW (AL)	.320	.488	.808	52	81	265	17	9	2	6	12	17	9
1986	CHW (AL)	.263	.337	.600	22	92	154	2	4	0	6	2	6	10
1987	CHW (AL)	.321	.460	.781	39	72	209	1	4	1	6	8	8	9
1988	CHW (AL)	.377	.542	.919	37	40	137	0	0	1	2	9	5	6
1989	CHW (AL)	.356	.475	.831	36	60	178	1	0	0	5	8	3	15
1990	CHW (AL)	.378	.451	.829	61	73	204	7	2	0	1	8	7	12
1991	CHW (AL)	.299	.413	.712	32	86	190	1	2	0	2	4	7	19
1992	CHW (AL)	.313	.309	.622	23	38	58	3	0	0	2	5	1	2
1993	CHW (AL)	.228	.245	.473	2	11	13	0	1	1	1	0	1	0
Total		.341	.457	.798	849	1386	3999	128	58	26	79	105	143	204
Boston		.356	.481	.837	389	588	1856	61	26	13	32	32	59	86

LUIS TIANT
Luis Clemente (Vega) Tiant ("El Tiante")
(Boston 1971–1978; career 1964–1982)

Primary position: P	
Batted: R	
Threw: R	
Height: 5'11"	
Weight: 190 pounds	
First major league game: July 19, 1964	
Final major league game: September 4, 1982	
Born: November 23, 1940 in Marianao, Cuba	
Boston Red Sox Hall of Fame: 2007	

In his prime he was unbelievable, and even when he pitched with us at the end of his career he was still good. He wanted the ball and he wanted to throw nine innings. He didn't want anybody to screw it up for him. He wanted nine innings.

Luis Tiant was, to some baseball people, a washed-up superstar by the time he arrived in Boston in 1971. He had been in the majors for seven years; in 1968 in Cleveland he posted a 21–9 record and his 1.60 ERA was the lowest in the American League since Walter Johnson's 1.49 in the dead-ball era in 1919. Of his wins that year, nine were shutouts.

But he was injured in 1969, and again in 1970 after he had been traded to the Minnesota Twins. And his first year with Boston was not all that promising either: In 1971 he was just 1–7 with an ERA of 4.85, which did not look very promising for a 30-year-old man, if you believed that was his actual age.

But El Tiante began to thrive again at Fenway Park. In 1972 he put up a 15–6 record with a league-leading ERA of 1.91. The next year he won 20 games, and in 1974 he posted a career-high win total of 22.

In the 1975 season, when almost everything went right for the Red Sox, Tiant won 18 games even though he was suffering from back problems. In the playoffs he beat the Oakland Athletics (winner of the past three World Series) with a three-hit complete game. Then he was the Game 1 pitcher as the Red Sox took on the Cincinnati Reds in the

Series, throwing a five-hit shutout; Tiant led off the seventh inning with a single and scored the first (and winning) run for Boston.

El Tiante also defeated the Reds in Game 4, and then had a no-decision in the famous Game 6 that ended with Carlton Fisk's walk-off homer in the 12th inning.

One of the keys to El Tiante's success was his unusual windup, something he developed after coming to the major leagues; he would turn away from the plate, looking out at second base before rotating and throwing the pitch. The extra hesitation threw off the timing of many batters.

I remember facing him when I was with the Angels, and there was always this jingling and jangling coming from the mound. I don't know if it was jewelry or keys in his pants.

Luis was one of the funniest guys I ever met in the game. He was great to have on the team; even when things were as bad as they could possibly be, you could count on something funny coming out of his mouth. He and Yaz used to go at it.

He had a tremendous fear of flying and every time we would take off, all you could hear him yelling from the back of the plane was "Get up, get up!"

But aside from the crazy stuff, he was a real professional. He never blamed you for making a mistake behind him. He would always pat you on the back.

I also remember guys hitting home runs off him. They would sometimes hit the ball so far that before it would get out of the park you could hear him yelling "Oh my God!"

But then he would also give it to other guys. When another Red Sox pitcher would give up a home run he would walk right up to them when they got back to the dugout and go "How do you hold that pitch?"

You couldn't have a bad day because somewhere along the line he would crack everybody up. Sometimes you didn't know what the hell he was saying but you would laugh anyway.

Luis Tiant

Year	Team	Age	W	L	G	GS	CG	SHO	GF	SV	WHIP	ERA	
1964	CLE (AL)	23	10	4	19	16	9	3	3	1	1.110	2.83	
1965	CLE (AL)	24	11	11	41	30	10	2	4	1	1.182	3.53	
1966	CLE (AL)	25	12	11	46	16	7	5	22	8	1.103	2.79	
1967	CLE (AL)	26	12	9	33	29	9	1	4	2	1.142	2.74	
1968	CLE (AL)	27	21	9	34	32	19	9	0	0	0.871	1.60	AS
1969	CLE (AL)	28	9	20	38	37	9	1	0	0	1.434	3.71	
1970	MIN (AL)	29	7	3	18	17	2	1	1	0	1.349	3.40	
1971	BOS (AL)	30	1	7	21	10	1	0	4	0	1.452	4.85	
1972	BOS (AL)	31	15	6	43	19	12	6	12	3	1.078	1.91	
1973	BOS (AL)	32	20	13	35	35	23	0	0	0	1.085	3.34	

Year	Team	Age	W	L	G	GS	CG	SHO	GF	SV	WHIP	ERA	
1974	BOS (AL)	33	22	13	38	38	25	7	0	0	1.166	2.92	AS
1975	BOS (AL)	34	18	14	35	35	18	2	0	0	1.285	4.02	
1976	BOS (AL)	35	21	12	38	38	19	3	0	0	1.211	3.06	AS
1977	BOS (AL)	36	12	8	32	32	3	3	0	0	1.383	4.53	
1978	BOS (AL)	37	13	8	32	31	12	5	1	0	1.140	3.31	
1979	NYY (AL)	38	13	8	30	30	5	1	0	0	1.242	3.91	
1980	NYY (AL)	39	8	9	25	25	3	0	0	0	1.386	4.89	
1981	PIT (NL)	40	2	5	9	9	1	0	0	0	1.273	3.92	
1982	CAL (AL)	41	2	2	6	5	0	0	0	0	1.584	5.76	
Total			**229**	**172**	**573**	**484**	**187**	**49**	**51**	**15**	**1.199**	**3.30**	
Boston			**122**	**81**	**274**	**238**	**113**	**26**	**17**	**3**	**1.201**	**3.36**	

Year	Team	IP	H	R	ER	HR	BB	SO	HBP	WP	IBB	BK
1964	CLE (AL)	127	94	41	40	13	47	105	2	4	2	0
1965	CLE (AL)	196	166	88	77	20	66	152	3	2	3	0
1966	CLE (AL)	155	121	50	48	16	50	145	2	3	4	0
1967	CLE (AL)	214	177	76	65	24	67	219	1	1	2	1
1968	CLE (AL)	258	152	53	46	16	73	264	4	3	4	0
1969	CLE (AL)	250	229	123	103	37	129	156	8	0	11	1
1970	MIN (AL)	92.7	84	36	35	12	41	50	2	2	0	0
1971	BOS (AL)	72.3	73	42	39	8	32	59	1	4	1	0
1972	BOS (AL)	179	128	45	38	7	65	123	0	0	5	0
1973	BOS (AL)	272	217	105	101	32	78	206	7	2	3	0
1974	BOS (AL)	311	281	106	101	21	82	176	4	1	3	0
1975	BOS (AL)	260	262	126	116	25	72	142	4	2	0	0
1976	BOS (AL)	279	274	107	95	25	64	131	3	1	2	0
1977	BOS (AL)	189	210	98	95	26	51	124	2	0	3	0
1978	BOS (AL)	212	185	80	78	26	57	114	5	0	4	2
1979	NYY (AL)	196	190	94	85	22	53	104	0	0	1	0
1980	NYY (AL)	136	139	79	74	10	50	84	1	2	3	0
1981	PIT (NL)	57.3	54	31	25	3	19	32	0	0	2	0
1982	CAL (AL)	29.7	39	20	19	3	8	30	0	0	0	0
Total		**3486**	**3075**	**1400**	**1280**	**346**	**1104**	**2416**	**49**	**27**	**53**	**4**
Boston		**1775**	**1630**	**709**	**663**	**170**	**501**	**1075**	**26**	**10**	**21**	**2**

RICK BURLESON
Richard Paul Burleson ("Rooster")
(Boston 1974–1980; career 1974–1987)

Primary position: SS	
Batted: R	
Threw: R	
Height: 5'10"	
Weight: 165 pounds	
First major league game: May 4, 1974	
Final major league game: July 8, 1987	
Born: April 29, 1951 in Lynwood, California	
Boston Red Sox Hall of Fame: 2002	

Rick was about as intense a player as you could imagine.

He was a very good shortstop with good but not great range. Playing second base next to him you always had to be on your toes. He wouldn't let you take a minute off.

Rick was just one of those guys who got the very most out of the ability that he had. He was very, very competitive and pissed off all the time. He was always mad about something; it was like his game face.

He would walk into the clubhouse and he was pissed. He was pissed during the game, and he was pissed after the game. That is just the way he played the game. That had to be the way he would go about things to be the type of player he was.

But yet we were friends off the field, and it wasn't an act. I wouldn't call him mild mannered, but I would say he was nowhere near as intense off the field as he was on the field.

The Rooster was one of the best defensive shortstops to ever play for the Red Sox, and I know that from first-hand experience: he was my partner across the Boston infield from 1978 through 1980.

He wasn't stylish and he didn't have the greatest range, but he had a great throwing arm, one of the best I've ever seen. I remember going out to warm up with him before a game, and the first throw he would make was like a mid-game throw. He couldn't throw the ball softly.

Photo by the National Baseball Hall of Fame Library, Cooperstown, N.Y.

When you play second and your shortstop has a rifle for an arm, you have to be a little bit more aware on balls that are hit to his right, because there would be a little extra zip on the throws. But when he was coming toward the bag on routine plays, it was all touch and feel. You learn the style of your partner in the infield very quickly. In 1980, he was involved in 147 double plays, a Red Sox record that still stands.

Before the 1981 season, Burleson was traded to the California Angels along with Butch Hobson in return for Carney Lansford, Rick Miller, and Mark Clear. He was injured for most of the 1982, 1983, and 1984 seasons and then missed the entire 1985 season with a torn rotator cuff—a not-unexpected injury for a guy who threw so hard. He returned to the Angels for the 1986 season at age 35 and regained his intensity, winning the Comeback Player of the Year award as a utility infielder and DH. Burleson finished his career with a 1987 season in Baltimore.

Rick Burleson

Year	Team	Age	G	AB	R	H	2B	3B	HR	RBI	BA	
1974	BOS (AL)	23	114	384	36	109	22	0	4	44	.284	
1975	BOS (AL)	24	158	580	66	146	25	1	6	62	.252	
1976	BOS (AL)	25	152	540	75	157	27	1	7	42	.291	
1977	BOS (AL)	26	154	663	80	194	36	7	3	52	.293	AS
1978	BOS (AL)	27	145	626	75	155	32	5	5	49	.248	AS
1979	BOS (AL)	28	153	627	93	174	32	5	5	60	.278	AS
1980	BOS (AL)	29	155	644	89	179	29	2	8	51	.278	
1981	CAL (AL)	30	109	430	53	126	17	1	5	33	.293	SS, AS
1982	CAL (AL)	31	11	45	4	7	1	0	0	2	.156	
1983	CAL (AL)	32	33	119	22	34	7	0	0	11	.286	
1984	CAL (AL)	33	7	4	2	0	0	0	0	0	.000	
1986	CAL (AL)	35	93	271	35	77	14	0	5	29	.284	
1987	BAL (AL)	36	62	206	26	43	14	1	2	14	.209	
Total			**1346**	**5139**	**656**	**1401**	**256**	**23**	**50**	**449**	**.273**	
Boston			**1031**	**4064**	**514**	**1114**	**203**	**21**	**38**	**360**	**.274**	

Year	Team	OBP	SLG	OPS	BB	SO	TB	SB	CS	SH	SF	IBB	HBP	GDP
1974	BOS (AL)	.320	.372	.692	21	34	143	3	3	3	5	0	2	13
1975	BOS (AL)	.305	.329	.634	45	44	191	8	5	17	9	1	3	18
1976	BOS (AL)	.365	.383	.748	60	37	207	14	9	8	3	2	5	15
1977	BOS (AL)	.338	.382	.720	47	69	253	13	12	3	6	1	2	15
1978	BOS (AL)	.295	.339	.634	40	71	212	8	8	10	5	2	4	16
1979	BOS (AL)	.315	.368	.683	35	54	231	9	5	9	8	0	3	13
1980	BOS (AL)	.341	.366	.707	62	51	236	12	13	6	4	0	2	24
1981	CAL (AL)	.357	.372	.729	42	38	160	4	6	11	4	2	3	8

Year	Team	OBP	SLG	OPS	BB	SO	TB	SB	CS	SH	SF	IBB	HBP	GDP
1982	CAL (AL)	.255	.178	.433	6	3	8	0	0	2	0	2	0	2
1983	CAL (AL)	.348	.345	.693	12	12	41	0	2	2	1	0	0	5
1984	CAL (AL)	.000	.000	.000	0	2	0	0	0	1	0	0	0	0
1986	CAL (AL)	.363	.391	.754	33	32	106	1	3	6	1	1	1	2
1987	BAL (AL)	.279	.316	.595	17	30	65	0	2	6	0	0	3	7
Total		**.328**	**.361**	**.689**	**420**	**477**	**1853**	**72**	**68**	**84**	**46**	**11**	**28**	**138**
Boston		**.326**	**.362**	**.688**	**310**	**360**	**1473**	**67**	**55**	**56**	**40**	**6**	**21**	**114**

DWIGHT EVANS
Dwight Michael Evans ("Dewey")
(Boston 1972–1990; career 1972–1991)

Primary position: RF	
Batted: R	
Threw: R	
Height: 6'2"	
Weight: 205 pounds	
First major league game: September 16, 1972	
Final major league game: October 6, 1991	
Born: November 3, 1951 in Santa Monica, California	
Boston Red Sox Hall of Fame: 2000	

Dwight Evans was one of the best—probably the best I can recall—at playing right field at Fenway. He won eight Gold Gloves for Boston, which is quite impressive when you think about how tough it is to play that corner of Fenway Park, where the ball can bounce around like it's inside a pinball machine. Fenway's right field is one of the toughest places to play in the majors. There are lots of goofy angles and you get a lot of sun during the day.

It's appropriate that one of the enduring images of Evans is the great play he made at Fenway in the 11th inning of Game 6 of the 1975 World Series to rob Joe Morgan of a home run, doubling Ken Griffey Sr. off of first base with a strong throw. Although Boston went on to win that game in the 12th, Cincinnati won the seventh game the next day . . . but it was a ray of hope in a long dry spell between trophies.

He wasn't the fastest of guys, but he covered a lot of ground out there in that big outfield. If you were playing against him you didn't think about going to second base on most hits to right. If you got to second, you stopped because he could spin around on a dime and throw you out easily. He was part of the great Red Sox outfield of Jim Rice in left, and Fred Lynn and later Tony Armas in center.

As a hitter, Dewey was always experimenting with different stances; some wags called him the Man of a Thousand Stances. He finally connected up with Walt Hriniak—a great hitting coach who was my best friend in baseball—and Walt told him he was going to

Photo by the National Baseball Hall of Fame Library, Cooperstown, N.Y.

stick with one stance and one swing every day and it made him a good hitter.

The setup that they came up with was unusual. As the pitcher prepared to throw, Evans would curl himself up almost into a ball with his bat draped lightly on his back. But as the pitcher went into motion, Evans would unwind his body and raise his bat and swing from what amounted to his own personal center of balance.

Whatever it was, it worked. Evans recorded 2,446 hits in his career and was in the Top 10 in voting for MVP four times. In 1981—one of his better years—he was an All-Star, won a Gold Glove, and led the league in walks, total bases, and home runs.

He ended up with 379 home runs; from 1981 to 1990 he hit 251 homers, the most of any American League player in that period. He made the All-Star team three times.

Evans played 19 seasons for the Red Sox, and ended up in second place in total games played for Boston with 2,505; only Carl Yastrzemski has been in a Boston lineup more times, 3,308 games. Evans is in Boston's top five in all of these categories: games played, RBIs, at-bats, runs scored, hits, doubles, extra base hits, total bases, and walks.

Dwight Evans

Year	Team	Age	G	AB	R	H	2B	3B	HR	RBI	BA	
1972	BOS (AL)	20	18	57	2	15	3	1	1	6	.263	
1973	BOS (AL)	21	119	282	46	63	13	1	10	32	.223	
1974	BOS (AL)	22	133	463	60	130	19	8	10	70	.281	
1975	BOS (AL)	23	128	412	61	113	24	6	13	56	.274	
1976	BOS (AL)	24	146	501	61	121	34	5	17	62	.242	
1977	BOS (AL)	25	73	230	39	66	9	2	14	36	.287	
1978	BOS (AL)	26	147	497	75	123	24	2	24	63	.247	AS
1979	BOS (AL)	27	152	489	69	134	24	1	21	58	.274	
1980	BOS (AL)	28	148	463	72	123	37	5	18	60	.266	
1981	BOS (AL)	29	108	412	84	122	19	4	22	71	.296	AS, SS
1982	BOS (AL)	30	162	609	122	178	37	7	32	98	.292	
1983	BOS (AL)	31	126	470	74	112	19	4	22	58	.238	
1984	BOS (AL)	32	162	630	121	186	37	8	32	104	.295	
1985	BOS (AL)	33	159	617	110	162	29	1	29	78	.263	
1986	BOS (AL)	34	152	529	86	137	33	2	26	97	.259	
1987	BOS (AL)	35	154	541	109	165	37	2	34	123	.305	AS, SS
1988	BOS (AL)	36	149	559	96	164	31	7	21	111	.293	
1989	BOS (AL)	37	146	520	82	148	27	3	20	100	.285	
1990	BOS (AL)	38	123	445	66	111	18	3	13	63	.249	
1991	BAL (AL)	39	101	270	35	73	9	1	6	38	.270	
Total			2606	8996	1470	2446	483	73	385	1384	.272	
Boston			2505	8726	1435	2373	474	72	379	1346	.272	

Year	Team	OBP	SLG	OPS	BB	SO	TB	SB	CS	SH	SF	IBB	HBP	GDP
1972	BOS (AL)	.344	.404	.748	7	13	23	0	0	0	0	0	0	2
1973	BOS (AL)	.320	.383	.703	40	52	108	5	0	3	2	2	1	8
1974	BOS (AL)	.335	.421	.756	38	77	195	4	4	6	5	2	2	9
1975	BOS (AL)	.353	.456	.809	47	60	188	3	4	5	2	3	4	10
1976	BOS (AL)	.324	.431	.755	57	92	216	6	7	3	4	4	6	11
1977	BOS (AL)	.363	.526	.889	28	58	121	4	2	6	1	0	0	3
1978	BOS (AL)	.336	.449	.785	65	119	223	8	5	6	2	2	2	15
1979	BOS (AL)	.364	.456	.820	69	76	223	6	9	3	1	7	1	14
1980	BOS (AL)	.358	.484	.842	64	98	224	3	1	6	4	6	5	5
1981	BOS (AL)	.415	.522	.937	85	85	215	3	2	3	3	1	1	8
1982	BOS (AL)	.402	.534	.936	112	125	325	3	2	3	2	1	1	17
1983	BOS (AL)	.338	.436	.774	70	97	205	3	0	0	2	5	2	12
1984	BOS (AL)	.388	.532	.920	96	115	335	3	1	1	7	2	4	19
1985	BOS (AL)	.378	.454	.832	114	105	280	7	2	1	7	4	5	16
1986	BOS (AL)	.376	.476	.852	97	117	252	3	3	2	6	4	6	11
1987	BOS (AL)	.417	.569	.986	106	98	308	4	6	0	7	6	3	10
1988	BOS (AL)	.375	.487	.862	76	99	272	5	1	2	7	3	1	16
1989	BOS (AL)	.397	.463	.860	99	84	241	3	3	1	7	1	3	16
1990	BOS (AL)	.349	.391	.740	67	73	174	3	4	0	6	5	4	18
1991	BAL (AL)	.393	.378	.771	54	54	102	2	3	1	2	2	2	7
Total		**.370**	**.470**	**.840**	**1391**	**1697**	**4230**	**78**	**59**	**52**	**77**	**60**	**53**	**227**
Boston		**.369**	**.473**	**.842**	**1337**	**1643**	**4128**	**76**	**56**	**51**	**75**	**58**	**51**	**220**

FRED LYNN
Frederic Michael Lynn
(Boston 1974–1980; career 1974–1990)

Primary positions: CF, OF	
Batted: L	
Threw: L	
Height: 6'1"	
Weight: 190 pounds	
First major league game: September 5, 1974	
Final major league game: October 3, 1990	
Born: February 3, 1952 in Chicago, Illinois	
Boston Red Sox Hall of Fame: 2002	

At age 23, Fred Lynn was the opening day centerfielder for the 1975 Red Sox. By the end of that special season, he became the first player in history to win both the Rookie of the Year and MVP awards, an achievement since equaled only by Mariners outfielder Ichiro Suzuki, whose rookie status was questioned by some because of his professional career in Japan. Lynn hit .331 with 21 home runs and 105 RBIs, and led the league with 103 runs and 47 doubles. Oh, and he also picked up a Gold Glove for his debut year. By the third day of the season, Lynn was joined in the outfield by Jim Rice in left and Boston's "Gold Dust Twins" were in place.

If he had played his whole career in Boston I think Lynn would have been a Hall of Famer. We played together in 1979 and 1980, and he had one of the prettiest swings I have ever seen, as well as being a great outfielder and a good baserunner. Those were MVP-caliber seasons.

He was kind of a laid back California guy (he was born in Chicago and originally drafted by the Yankees), but he chose to go to school at the University of Southern California before turning pro. He was a great player but he was able to leave the game at the park. He was one of those guys who could get off a flight at eight in the morning and go fishing. He knew how to relax.

If you talk to many players who have left Boston, they will tell you that as hard as it is to play here, it probably brought the best out of them. I think playing in Boston pushed him to be great.

Photo by the National Baseball Hall of Fame Library, Cooperstown, N.Y.

He earned selection to the All-Star team for each of his first nine years, but he was hampered by injuries—some of them caused by his fearlessness as a fielder and a baserunner. He broke a rib crashing into an outfield wall and hurt his knee breaking up a double play. He was a fine player throughout his career, but he could not sustain the level he achieved in his rookie year.

After the 1980 season, he was traded with Rick Burleson to the California Angels, and though he continued to hit for power, being away from left-hander–friendly Fenway brought down his batting average.

In 1983 in his ninth consecutive year as an All-Star, he became the first player to hit a grand slam in that special game.

Fred Lynn

Year	Team	Age	G	AB	R	H	2B	3B	HR	RBI	BA	
1974	BOS (AL)	22	15	43	5	18	2	2	2	10	.419	
1975	BOS (AL)	23	145	528	103	175	47	7	21	105	.331	MVP, ROY, AS
1976	BOS (AL)	24	132	507	76	159	32	8	10	65	.314	AS
1977	BOS (AL)	25	129	497	81	129	29	5	18	76	.260	AS
1978	BOS (AL)	26	150	541	75	161	33	3	22	82	.298	AS
1979	BOS (AL)	27	147	531	116	177	42	1	39	122	.333	AS
1980	BOS (AL)	28	110	415	67	125	32	3	12	61	.301	AS
1981	CAL (AL)	29	76	256	28	56	8	1	5	31	.219	AS
1982	CAL (AL)	30	138	472	89	141	38	1	21	86	.299	AS
1983	CAL (AL)	31	117	437	56	119	20	3	22	74	.272	AS
1984	CAL (AL)	32	142	517	84	140	28	4	23	79	.271	
1985	BAL (AL)	33	124	448	59	118	12	1	23	68	.263	
1986	BAL (AL)	34	112	397	67	114	13	1	23	67	.287	
1987	BAL (AL)	35	111	396	49	100	24	0	23	60	.253	
1988	*Season*	36	*114*	*391*	*46*	*96*	*14*	*1*	*25*	*56*	*.246*	
	BAL (AL)		87	301	37	76	13	1	18	37	.252	
	DET (AL)		27	90	9	20	1	0	7	19	.222	
1989	DET (AL)	37	117	353	44	85	11	1	11	46	.241	
1990	SDP (NL)	38	90	196	18	47	3	1	6	23	.240	
Total			**1969**	**6925**	**1063**	**1960**	**388**	**43**	**306**	**1111**	**.283**	
Boston			**828**	**3062**	**523**	**944**	**217**	**29**	**124**	**521**	**.308**	

Year	Team	OBP	SLG	OPS	BB	SO	TB	SB	CS	SH	SF	IBB	HBP	GDP
1974	BOS (AL)	.490	.698	1.188	6	6	30	0	0	0	1	2	1	0
1975	BOS (AL)	.401	.566	.967	62	90	299	10	5	6	6	10	3	11
1976	BOS (AL)	.367	.467	.834	48	67	237	14	9	0	10	2	1	9
1977	BOS (AL)	.327	.447	.774	51	63	222	2	3	5	8	2	3	14
1978	BOS (AL)	.380	.492	.872	75	50	266	3	6	4	6	11	1	9
1979	BOS (AL)	.423	.637	1.060	82	79	338	2	2	0	5	4	4	9
1980	BOS (AL)	.383	.480	.863	58	39	199	12	0	0	5	3	0	10
1981	CAL (AL)	.322	.316	.638	38	42	81	1	2	1	4	4	3	7

Year	Team	OBP	SLG	OPS	BB	SO	TB	SB	CS	SH	SF	IBB	HBP	GDP
1982	CAL (AL)	.374	.517	.891	58	72	244	7	8	5	7	4	3	9
1983	CAL (AL)	.352	.483	.835	55	83	211	2	2	0	6	10	2	7
1984	CAL (AL)	.366	.474	.840	77	97	245	2	2	2	2	8	2	14
1985	BAL (AL)	.339	.449	.788	53	100	201	7	3	0	6	6	1	7
1986	BAL (AL)	.371	.499	.870	53	59	198	2	2	0	4	1	2	20
1987	BAL (AL)	.320	.487	.807	39	72	193	3	7	0	2	6	1	8
1988	*Season*	*.302*	*.478*	*.780*	*33*	*82*	*187*	*2*	*2*	*1*	*6*	*1*	*1*	*9*
	BAL (AL)	.312	.482	.794	28	66	145	2	2	1	4	1	0	7
	DET (AL)	.265	.467	.732	5	16	42	0	0	0	2	0	1	2
1989	DET (AL)	.328	.371	.699	47	71	131	1	1	0	5	1	1	5
1990	SDP (NL)	.315	.357	.672	22	44	70	2	0	1	3	2	1	1
Total		**.360**	**.484**	**.844**	**857**	**1116**	**3539**	**72**	**54**	**26**	**92**	**78**	**31**	**158**
Boston		**.383**	**.520**	**.902**	**382**	**394**	**1591**	**43**	**25**	**15**	**41**	**34**	**13**	**62**

JIM RICE
James Edward Rice
(Boston 1974–1989)

Primary position: LF	
Batted: R	
Threw: R	
Height: 6'2"	
Weight: 205 pounds	
First major league game: August 19, 1974	
Final major league game: August 3, 1989	
Born: March 8, 1983 in Anderson, South Carolina	
Baseball Hall of Fame: 2009	
Boston Red Sox Hall of Fame: 1995	

From 1975 to 1986, Jim Rice was the most feared and most dominant hitter in baseball; in that time he had eight seasons with 100 or more RBIs, seven seasons when he finished with a batting average of .300 or better, four 200-hit seasons, and he was the American League home run leader three times.

Just look at his 1978 numbers: 46 home runs, 139 RBIs, 213 hits, and a .315 batting average. And he took home the trophy as Most Valuable Player. This is a guy who hit with power as well as for average. Looking back you may remember the home run he hit, but you forget the three other hits he had in the game. And those 46 home runs and all of those hits were in a time when most of us agree that neither the ball nor the players were juiced. They were for real. This is a guy who should have been elected to the Baseball Hall of Fame a long time ago.

All he wanted to do was play, and as he says, let his numbers speak for themselves. I think he came off as a bad guy to the media, but that wasn't him. I don't think he had a particular fondness for the media, but mostly he just liked to be left alone. And he could be a little snarly. I always felt that he was just not comfortable in that atmosphere.

He made himself into a good left fielder. He played all the time, playing hurt. Unfortunately for Rice, it ended a little prematurely. Had he been able to tack on a couple more decent years I don't think Rice would still be waiting for his place in Cooperstown.

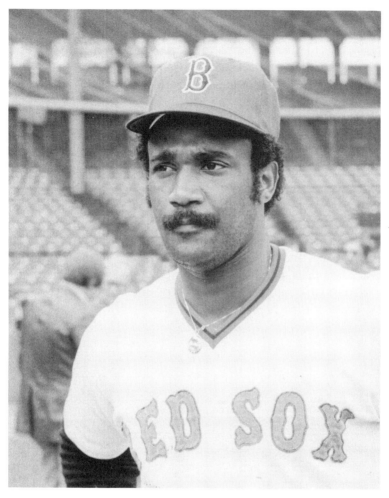

Photo by the National Baseball Hall of Fame Library, Cooperstown, N.Y.

Jim came up to the Red Sox in 1975, a year after collecting nearly all of the hardware available in the AAA minor leagues; the year before, playing for the Pawtucket Red Sox, he had been the International League Rookie of the Year, the Most Valuable Player, and also recorded a Triple Crown: most home runs, most RBIs, and highest batting average.

Rice joined the team the same year as another one of my Red Sox Heroes: Fred Lynn. Together, the two were known as the "Gold Dust Twins." In that great season, the Red Sox made it all the way to the postseason, but Rice hurt his wrist during the last week of the regular season. He tried his best to get back into the lineup, but management shut him down . . . and the Sox lost the World Series four games to three to the Cincinnati Reds.

In 1986, the Red Sox were once again in the postseason and Rice was on a tear: He had 14 hits and scored 14 runs in 14 games, but this time Boston fell victim to the New York Mets.

Throughout his career, Rice wanted to be judged on his numbers—not on his personality, not on his relationships with baseball writers. Unfortunately, though his numbers were very, very good, it is almost certainly his off-the-field demeanor that has kept him out of the Hall of Fame. That's where he belongs, and I hope he gets there some day.

For many years now, Jim has worked as a hitting instructor for the Red Sox and has helped with the development of many recent stars for the team. And he has been opening up more and more in recent years; ironically, after all of his years trying to avoid the media, he has become a baseball commentator. He's part of the NESN team and very good at what he does.

Jim Rice

Year	Team	Age	G	AB	R	H	2B	3B	HR	RBI	BA	
1974	BOS (AL)	21	24	67	6	18	2	1	1	13	.269	
1975	BOS (AL)	22	144	564	92	174	29	4	22	102	.309	
1976	BOS (AL)	23	153	581	75	164	25	8	25	85	.282	
1977	BOS (AL)	24	160	644	104	206	29	15	39	114	.320	AS
1978	BOS (AL)	25	163	677	121	213	25	15	46	139	.315	MVP, AS
1979	BOS (AL)	26	158	619	117	201	39	6	39	130	.325	AS
1980	BOS (AL)	27	124	504	81	148	22	6	24	86	.294	AS
1981	BOS (AL)	28	108	451	51	128	18	1	17	62	.284	
1982	BOS (AL)	29	145	573	86	177	24	5	24	97	.309	
1983	BOS (AL)	30	155	626	90	191	34	1	39	126	.305	SS, AS
1984	BOS (AL)	31	159	657	98	184	25	7	28	122	.280	SS, AS
1985	BOS (AL)	32	140	546	85	159	20	3	27	103	.291	AS
1986	BOS (AL)	33	157	618	98	200	39	2	20	110	.324	AS
1987	BOS (AL)	34	108	404	66	112	14	0	13	62	.277	
1988	BOS (AL)	35	135	485	57	128	18	3	15	72	.264	
1989	BOS (AL)	36	56	209	22	49	10	2	3	28	.234	
Total			2089	8225	1249	2452	373	79	382	1451	.298	

Year	Team	OBP	SLG	OPS	BB	SO	TB	SB	CS	SH	SF	IBB	HBP	GDP
1974	BOS (AL)	.307	.373	.680	4	12	25	0	0	0	3	0	1	2
1975	BOS (AL)	.350	.491	.841	36	122	277	10	5	1	8	7	4	19
1976	BOS (AL)	.315	.482	.797	28	123	280	8	5	2	9	2	4	18
1977	BOS (AL)	.376	.593	.969	53	120	382	5	4	0	5	10	8	21
1978	BOS (AL)	.370	.600	.970	58	126	406	7	5	1	5	7	5	15
1979	BOS (AL)	.381	.596	.977	57	97	369	9	4	0	8	4	4	16
1980	BOS (AL)	.336	.504	.840	30	87	254	8	3	1	3	5	4	16
1981	BOS (AL)	.333	.441	.774	34	76	199	2	2	0	7	3	3	14
1982	BOS (AL)	.375	.494	.869	55	98	283	0	1	0	3	6	7	29
1983	BOS (AL)	.361	.550	.911	52	102	344	0	2	0	5	10	6	31
1984	BOS (AL)	.323	.467	.790	44	102	307	4	0	0	6	8	1	36
1985	BOS (AL)	.349	.487	.836	51	75	266	2	0	0	9	5	2	35
1986	BOS (AL)	.384	.490	.874	62	78	303	0	1	0	9	5	4	19
1987	BOS (AL)	.357	.408	.765	45	77	165	1	1	0	3	3	7	22
1988	BOS (AL)	.330	.406	.736	48	89	197	1	1	0	6	2	3	18
1989	BOS (AL)	.276	.344	.620	13	39	72	1	0	0	5	0	1	4
Total		**.352**	**.502**	**.854**	**670**	**1423**	**4129**	**58**	**34**	**5**	**94**	**77**	**64**	**315**

BOB STANLEY
Robert William Stanley ("Stanley Steamer")
(Boston 1977–1989)

Primary position: P	
Batted: R	
Threw: R	
Height: 6'4"	
Weight: 215 pounds	
First major league game: April 16, 1977	
Final major league game: September 5, 1989	
Born: November 10, 1954 in Portland, Maine	
Boston Red Sox Hall of Fame: 2000	

Bob Stanley doesn't get all the credit he deserves, probably because he did everything. He was one of the most versatile pitchers I have seen. He started. He closed. He was available for middle relief.

He was a first-round pick for the Red Sox in 1974; by 1977 he was up in Boston as a starter and reliever at age 22. In 1979, when they needed him in the rotation, he started 30 times and he posted a record of 16–12 with 9 complete games. Throughout his career they could count on him in any role.

We went back and looked at his career stats and found at least four times when he pitched in both halves of a doubleheader. One I remember was July 29, 1988 against Milwaukee at Fenway. In the first game he came in to pitch the seventh and eighth innings, giving up just one hit and setting up Lee Smith to get the save. Then later that day he was brought in to pitch the ninth inning of the second game and earned a save on his own.

Stanley still leads the Red Sox in a number of categories. He threw 168.1 innings in relief in 1982. He holds the overall record for saves with 132, and relief wins with 85. And he also set the Red Sox record for saves in a month, with 12 in August of 1980.

(Until the arrival of Jonathan Papelbon as a closer, the Steamer also had the team record for saves in a season with 33 in 1983. In Papelbon's first three seasons, from 2006 through 2008, he notched 35, 37, and then 41 saves, setting a new team record each year. If

Photo by the National Baseball Hall of Fame Library, Cooperstown, N.Y.

Papelbon stays healthy, stays in the bullpen, and stays with the Red Sox he would seem almost certain to take over both the season and career records and have a shot at the monthly title as well.)

Stanley was a stalwart of the Red Sox pitching staff for 13 seasons, from 1977 to 1989, which includes my entire career in Boston. In the period from 1982 to 1984 he was an effective closer, saving 69 games across those three seasons. His best year came in 1983 when he appeared in 64 games, finished 53 of them, and notched 33 saves with an ERA of 2.85.

He threw a sinker-slider-type pitch, a pitch that dropped low or out of the strike zone at the last fraction of a second. As an infielder that would cause me to play some guys differently. For example, with a left-handed hitter, even if he was a pull hitter, I wouldn't expect the batter to pull much because Stanley's ball ran so hard down away from the batter. So, instead I would shade them up the middle a little bit more.

I remember one time he moved me, as pitchers commonly do, and wouldn't you know it but the ball went right where I had been before. He said: "I will never move you again."

He went through a rough stretch at Fenway toward the end of his career. Some fans were booing him, which was awfully hard for him to take. And it got to the point where sometimes they wouldn't pitch him at home and only bring him into games on the road. I felt so bad because he was a great guy, one of my best friends and it was painful to see that.

He reminded me a lot of Derek Lowe. They both had an effective sinker-slider pitch, both could start, relieve, and close, and their excellent statistics were sometimes overlooked.

In 1986, Stanley was an important player on the team that almost broke the Curse, coming within one out of winning the World Series against the New York Mets. Boston had gone ahead 5-3 in the top of the ninth on a Dave Henderson home run and a Marty Barrett RBI.

Calvin Schiraldi, who had posted an excellent record for the season as a setup man and closer (9 saves and a 1.41 ERA), was brought in to shut down the Mets and bring home the trophy. After getting the first two outs, he allowed consecutive singles to Gary Carter, Kevin Mitchell, and Ray Knight. Schiraldi was replaced by Bob Stanley, who threw a wild pitch beyond the reach of catcher Rich Gedman that allowed Kevin Mitchell to score the tying run. And then came the moment that haunted Red Sox fans for 18 years; Mets outfielder Mookie Wilson hit a weak ground ball up the first base line that went below the glove of Bill Buckner. Ray Knight scored and the Mets lived to play (and win) the seventh game.

Wes Gardner was the closer for the Red Sox in 1987, and Stanley returned to the starting rotation; he started 20 games and posted a record of 4-15 with a 5.01 ERA. When Stanley retired at the end of the 1989 season he did so with a record of 115 wins and 97 losses, 693 strikeouts, and a 3.64 ERA spread across 1,707 innings and 637 games.

His nickname, by the way, may not make sense to younger fans and perhaps even some not-so-young fans. The Stanley Motor Carriage Company of Newton, Massachusetts, was one of the first car makers in America, building and selling its first steam-powered vehicle in 1897. The last Steamer was built in the mid 1920s. The name Stanley Steamer is buried in the cultural DNA of Red Sox Nation, probably a bit deeper with each generation.

Bob Stanley

Year	Team	Age	W	L	G	GS	CG	SHO	GF	SV	WHIP	ERA	
1977	BOS (AL)	22	8	7	41	13	3	1	13	3	1.450	3.99	
1978	BOS (AL)	23	15	2	52	3	0	0	35	10	1.242	2.60	
1979	BOS (AL)	24	16	12	40	30	9	4	7	1	1.357	3.99	AS
1980	BOS (AL)	25	10	8	52	17	5	1	25	14	1.360	3.39	
1981	BOS (AL)	26	10	8	35	1	0	0	14	0	1.499	3.83	
1982	BOS (AL)	27	12	7	48	0	0	0	33	14	1.254	3.10	
1983	BOS (AL)	28	8	10	64	0	0	0	53	33	1.259	2.85	AS
1984	BOS (AL)	29	9	10	57	0	0	0	47	22	1.275	3.54	
1985	BOS (AL)	30	6	6	48	0	0	0	41	10	1.209	2.87	
1986	BOS (AL)	31	6	6	66	1	0	0	50	16	1.592	4.37	
1987	BOS (AL)	32	4	15	34	20	4	1	5	0	1.572	5.01	
1988	BOS (AL)	33	6	4	57	0	0	0	31	5	1.170	3.19	
1989	BOS (AL)	34	5	2	43	0	0	0	22	4	1.614	4.88	
Total			**115**	**97**	**637**	**85**	**21**	**7**	**376**	**132**	**1.364**	**3.64**	

Year	Team	IP	H	R	ER	HR	BB	SO	HBP	WP	IBB	BK
1977	BOS (AL)	151.0	176	74	67	10	43	44	3	2	5	1
1978	BOS (AL)	141.7	142	50	41	5	34	38	1	0	5	0
1979	BOS (AL)	216.7	250	110	96	14	44	56	4	0	4	0
1980	BOS (AL)	175.0	186	75	66	11	52	71	7	1	8	0
1981	BOS (AL)	98.7	110	46	42	3	38	28	6	1	4	0
1982	BOS (AL)	168.3	161	60	58	11	50	83	4	2	6	0
1983	BOS (AL)	145.3	145	56	46	7	38	65	3	4	12	0
1984	BOS (AL)	106.7	113	57	42	9	23	52	2	1	9	0
1985	BOS (AL)	87.7	76	30	28	7	30	46	2	1	10	0
1986	BOS (AL)	82.3	109	48	40	9	22	54	0	1	8	0
1987	BOS (AL)	152.7	198	96	85	17	42	67	1	3	7	0
1988	BOS (AL)	101.7	90	41	36	6	29	57	7	5	7	1
1989	BOS (AL)	79.3	102	54	43	4	26	32	1	1	2	0
Total		**1707**	**1858**	**797**	**690**	**113**	**471**	**693**	**41**	**22**	**87**	**2**

DENNIS ECKERSLEY
Dennis Lee Eckersley ("Eck")
(Boston 1978–1984, 1998; career 1975–1998)

Primary position: P	
Batted: R	
Threw: R	
Height: 6'2"	
Weight: 190 pounds	
First major league game: April 12, 1975	
Final major league game: September 26, 1998	
Born: October 3, 1954 in Oakland, California	
Boston Red Sox Hall of Fame: 2004	
Baseball Hall of Fame: 2004	

I faced Dennis Eckersley in the first half of his two-part Hall of Fame career, when he was one of the most dominating starting pitchers in the league. I particularly remember May 30, 1977, when I was in the lineup for the California Angels as he threw a lights-out no-hitter for the Cleveland Indians.

In that game Eckersley was really dealing. He struck out 12 batters—he got me twice—and gave up only one walk, which came in the first inning. The only other baserunner was Bobby Bonds, who struck out in the eighth but made it to first on a wild pitch; he was erased on a double play.

Centerfielder Gil Flores came up to bat with two outs in the ninth. Eckersley had been jabbering with our pitcher, Frank Tanana (who was nearly as brilliant, giving up one run—in the first inning—and just five hits in a complete game loss).

From about the seventh inning on, each time Eckersley got an out he would point to the on-deck circle like he was saying "Next!" We were just dying to get a hit off him. But obviously we didn't.

Eck later told a newspaper near his hometown of Oakland, the *Contra Costa Times*, about yelling at Flores. "I was ready, but Gil kept on stepping out of the [batter's box]," the paper reported. "I pointed at him, 'Get in there. They're not here to take your picture. You're the last out. Get in there.' I was pretty cocky back then."

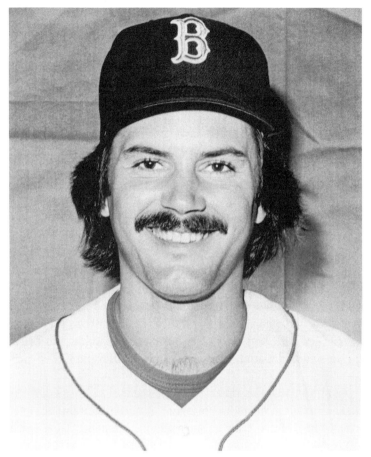

When he got the last out—a strikeout—I was standing in the on-deck circle.

And then the Red Sox got him at the end of spring training in 1978, which was also my first year with Boston. That was a huge boost for us.

He was, as he said, very cocky and confident on the mound. But what you saw on the mound wasn't really how he felt about himself. He was always afraid that the sky was going to fall on him. He didn't walk around thinking he was the greatest thing in the world. He would piss off the opponents with the way he acted, but that really wasn't him.

His first season with the Red Sox, in 1978, was the best of his career as a starting pitcher. He had a 20–8 record with a 2.99 ERA, and he was amazing down the stretch as Boston won ten of twelve games to end in a tie with the Yankees and force the one-game play-off for the league championship. Eck won all four of his starts at the end of the season, including three complete games; he gave up a total of three earned runs over 33 innings.

Alas, the Yankees won that final game; it was the best ball game I was ever a part of, except for the score. And it was that season that earns him a spot as one of the Red Sox Heroes.

Eck put up a 17–10 season the next year, but then his numbers began to slide toward the middle of the pack. The Red Sox traded Eck to Chicago on May 25, 1984, where he contributed to the first post-season appearance by the Cubs since 1945, a loss to the San Diego Padres.

In return for Eckersley, the Red Sox received first baseman Bill Buckner, who performed well at the plate and was a pretty good fielder; unfortunately, Buckner is best remembered by some for his error in the sixth game of the 1986 World Series that opened the door to a New York Mets win. After Boston finally won it all in 2004, many in Red Sox Nation welcomed Buckner back into their good graces.

Before the 1987 season Eckersley was traded once again, to the Oakland Athletics, where his role was at first uncertain. Athletics manager Tony LaRussa took a chance on him, intending to use him as a setup man and occasional starter, but because of an injury to Jay Howell all of a sudden Eckersley was the team's closer and on the way to the Baseball Hall of Fame. He could always throw strikes, and that is one thing that made him very effective as a closer.

Eck saved 16 games in 1987, and then settled in to a remarkable streak of years as one of the best closers ever; he notched 45 saves in the 1988 regular season plus saves in each of the four games the A's won as they swept the Red Sox in the AL Championship Series that year.

In 1989 he got the win in Game 2 of the World Series and the save in the fourth and final game as the A's swept the San Francisco Giants.

From 1988 to 1992, Eckersley saved 220 games over five seasons. He yielded only five earned runs for the entire 1990 season, finishing with an ERA of 0.61. He set a record as the only reliever in history to have more saves than baserunners allowed (48 saves against 41 hits and 4 walks for the season).

In 1992, Eckersley became the first pitcher in baseball history to have both 20 wins in a season as a starter (20–8 for Boston in 1978) and a 50-save season as a closer (51 saves for Oakland in 1992.) In that amazing 1992 season he took home the MVP and Cy Young awards. (In 2002, John Smoltz of the Atlanta Braves became the second pitcher to record separate seasons of 20 wins and 50 saves.)

After following LaRussa to St. Louis in 1995, Eckersley played his final year in 1998 in a return appearance with the Red Sox. He was still effective as a situational reliever, posting a 4–1 record from the bullpen; he also picked up one save, the last of his great career.

One more footnote to history: Eckersley was the lights-out closer for the Oakland A's who was called on to finish off the Los Angeles Dodgers in the ninth inning of Game 1 of the 1988 World Series. The Dodgers were trailing 4–3, and they were playing without one of their big boppers, Kirk Gibson; he would be named MVP of the National League that season. He had injured his leg from ankle to hamstring and everything in between and spent most of the game in the clubhouse—he was too hurt to even come out on the field during the pregame introductions.

But as the ninth inning approached, Gibson began working out in the batting cage, and he sent word to Dodger manager Tommy Lasorda that he would be ready to pinch hit. Eckersley got an easy infield popup and then a strikeout for the first two batters. Mike Davis, who had a terrible season that year at the plate, came up as a pinch-hitter; it should have been an easy out, but Davis disrupted Eckersley's rhythm by repeatedly stepping out of the box. He earned a walk.

And then from the dugout came Gibson, hobbling like a man on crutches, only without the crutches. Everyone knew Gibson was hurt, and Eck started him off with hard stuff. But Gibson managed to foul off the strikes and worked the count full. And then Gibson remembered what the Dodger scouting report said about Eckersley: Watch for a backdoor slider on a 3-2 count. And that's just what he got, and somehow—using only his wrists—Gibson found the pitch and hit it over the fence for a 5–4 Dodgers win. It doesn't get much more dramatic than that.

Why is that story in this book? Because Eckersley spoke the truth when he was asked about what happened. "It was a dumb pitch," he said. "It was the one pitch he could pull for power. I threw him the only pitch he could hit out."

Eckersley played his career scared to death, always convinced that disaster was around the corner. But he managed to channel that into the competitive fire that you saw on the mound.

And Eck is still among us. He was inducted into the Baseball Hall of Fame in 2004, and he does some great work as an analyst on pregame and postgame Red Sox broadcasts; just as you would expect, he has absolutely no fear of calling it as he sees it.

Dennis Eckersley

Year	Team	Age	W	L	G	GS	CG	SHO	GF	SV	WHIP	ERA	
1975	CLE (AL)	20	13	7	34	24	6	2	5	2	1.270	2.60	
1976	CLE (AL)	21	13	12	36	30	9	3	3	1	1.169	3.43	
1977	CLE (AL)	22	14	13	33	33	12	3	0	0	1.084	3.53	AS
1978	BOS (AL)	23	20	8	35	35	16	3	0	0	1.226	2.99	
1979	BOS (AL)	24	17	10	33	33	17	2	0	0	1.188	2.99	
1980	BOS (AL)	25	12	14	30	30	8	0	0	0	1.174	4.28	
1981	BOS (AL)	26	9	8	23	23	8	2	0	0	1.266	4.27	
1982	BOS (AL)	27	13	13	33	33	11	3	0	0	1.208	3.73	AS
1983	BOS (AL)	28	9	13	28	28	2	0	0	0	1.486	5.61	
1984	*Season*	*29*	*14*	*12*	*33*	*33*	*4*	*0*	*0*	*0*	*1.209*	*3.60*	
	BOS (AL)		4	4	9	9	2	0	0	0	1.299	5.01	
	CHC (NL)		10	8	24	24	2	0	0	0	1.173	3.03	
1985	CHC (NL)	30	11	7	25	25	6	2	0	0	0.969	3.08	
1986	CHC (NL)	31	6	11	33	32	1	0	0	0	1.338	4.57	
1987	OAK (AL)	32	6	8	54	2	0	0	33	16	1.003	3.03	
1988	OAK (AL)	33	4	2	60	0	0	0	53	45	0.867	2.35	AS
1989	OAK (AL)	34	4	0	51	0	0	0	46	33	0.607	1.56	
1990	OAK (AL)	35	4	2	63	0	0	0	61	48	0.614	0.61	AS
1991	OAK (AL)	36	5	4	67	0	0	0	59	43	0.908	2.96	AS
1992	OAK (AL)	37	7	1	69	0	0	0	65	51	0.913	1.91	MVP, CY, AS
1993	OAK (AL)	38	2	4	64	0	0	0	52	36	1.194	4.16	
1994	OAK (AL)	39	5	4	45	0	0	0	39	19	1.398	4.26	
1995	OAK (AL)	40	4	6	52	0	0	0	48	29	1.272	4.83	
1996	STL (NL)	41	0	6	63	0	0	0	53	30	1.183	3.30	

Year	Team	Age	W	L	G	GS	CG	SHO	GF	SV	WHIP	ERA
1997	STL (NL)	42	1	5	57	0	0	0	47	36	1.075	3.91
1998	BOS (AL)	43	4	1	50	0	0	0	13	1	1.361	4.76
Total			**197**	**171**	**1071**	**361**	**100**	**20**	**577**	**390**	**1.161**	**3.50**
Boston			**88**	**71**	**241**	**191**	**64**	**10**	**13**	**1**	**1.250**	**3.92**

Year	Team	IP	H	R	ER	HR	BB	SO	HBP	WP	IBB	BK
1975	CLE (AL)	186.7	147	61	54	16	90	152	7	4	8	2
1976	CLE (AL)	199.3	155	82	76	13	78	200	5	6	2	1
1977	CLE (AL)	247.3	214	100	97	31	54	191	7	3	11	0
1978	BOS (AL)	268.3	258	99	89	30	71	162	7	3	8	0
1979	BOS (AL)	246.7	234	89	82	29	59	150	6	1	4	1
1980	BOS (AL)	197.7	188	101	94	25	44	121	2	0	7	0
1981	BOS (AL)	154	160	82	73	9	35	79	3	0	2	0
1982	BOS (AL)	224.3	228	101	93	31	43	127	2	1	3	0
1983	BOS (AL)	176.3	223	119	110	27	39	77	6	1	4	0
1984	*Season*	*225*	*223*	*97*	*90*	*21*	*49*	*114*	*5*	*3*	*9*	*2*
	BOS (AL)	64.7	71	38	36	10	13	33	1	2	2	0
	CHC (NL)	160.3	152	59	54	11	36	81	4	1	7	2
1985	CHC (NL)	169.3	145	61	58	15	19	117	3	0	4	3
1986	CHC (NL)	201	226	109	102	21	43	137	3	2	3	5
1987	OAK (AL)	115.7	99	41	39	11	17	113	3	1	3	0
1988	OAK (AL)	72.7	52	20	19	5	11	70	1	0	2	2
1989	OAK (AL)	57.7	32	10	10	5	3	55	1	0	0	0
1990	OAK (AL)	73.3	41	9	5	2	4	73	0	0	1	0
1991	OAK (AL)	76	60	26	25	11	9	87	1	1	3	0
1992	OAK (AL)	80	62	17	17	5	11	93	1	0	6	0
1993	OAK (AL)	67	67	32	31	7	13	80	2	0	4	0
1994	OAK (AL)	44.3	49	26	21	5	13	47	1	0	2	0
1995	OAK (AL)	50.3	53	29	27	5	11	40	1	0	0	0
1996	STL (NL)	60	65	26	22	8	6	49	4	0	2	0
1997	STL (NL)	53	49	24	23	9	8	45	2	2	0	0
1998	BOS (AL)	39.7	46	21	21	6	8	22	2	0	3	0
Total		**3285.6**	**3076**	**1382**	**1278**	**347**	**738**	**2401**	**75**	**28**	**91**	**16**
Boston		**1371.6**	**1408**	**650**	**598**	**167**	**312**	**771**	**29**	**8**	**33**	**1**

WADE BOGGS
Wade Anthony Boggs ("Chicken Man")
(Boston 1982–1992; career 1982–1999)

Primary position: 3B	
Batted: L	
Threw: R	
Height: 6'2"	
Weight: 197 pounds	
First major league game: April 10, 1982	
Final major league game: August 27, 1999	
Born: June 15, 1958 in Omaha, Nebraska	
Baseball Hall of Fame: 2005	
Boston Red Sox Hall of Fame: 2004	

Wade Boggs spent six full seasons working his way up through the minors, playing at Elmira, Winston-Salem, Bristol, and Pawtucket. And even when he finally came up to the Red Sox in 1982, the organization wasn't sure he had what it takes to be a major leaguer. Boy, were they wrong. About 3,010 hits wrong.

I remember watching him hit in 1982, and we all thought that sooner or later other teams would figure a way to get this guy out. They never did, and he had a fantastic career as a batter. Across 11 seasons in Boston, he had a combined batting average of .338, second only to Ted Williams at .344.

He won five batting titles with the Red Sox, including four seasons in a row from 1985 to 1988, and had at least 200 hits in seven straight seasons in Boston. Looking back, we can wonder why he was down in the minors for so long; imagine what his numbers might have been if he had come up two or three years earlier. He finished his career with 3,010 hits in the majors; if you add in the 724 he collected in the minor leagues, he is in the top ten for all of professional baseball.

He wanted to be the best; there was no question about that. Sometimes he wore his emotions on his sleeve, which didn't go over well with his own team. But he was a determined guy who wanted to do well in the big leagues.

Photo by the National Baseball Hall of Fame Library, Cooperstown, N.Y.

He was probably the best two-strike hitter I have ever seen. Boggs seemed like he could foul off the pitch any time he wanted to keep the at-bat alive. He had great hand-eye coordination. He knew the strike zone, and he didn't swing at very many bad pitches. When he was down two strikes, he was like Ichiro is today; obviously they have different hitting styles, but they share great bat control.

He was also a guy who probably could have hit 25 home runs a year if he wanted to. (He did reach 24 in 1987, but for his career he averaged 8 per season.) He used to put on a tremendous exhibition in batting practice. But he preferred maintaining a high batting average, which certainly got him into the Hall of Fame. He led the league in batting five times, with his best percentage at .368 in 1985. He finished with a career batting average of .328.

The first-string lineup for the Red Sox when the 1982 season began had Carl Yastrzemski or Dave Stapleton at first, a guy named Jerry Remy at second, Glenn Hoffman at shortstop, and Carney Lansford at third. In the outfield we had big Jim Rice in left, Rick Miller or Reid Nichols in center, and Dwight Evans in right. Rich Gedman and Gary Allenson split time behind the plate. Our opening day pitcher was Dennis Eckersley, who pitched a six-hit shutout.

The man holding Wade Boggs back was Lansford, who was the American League batting champion in 1981, finishing with a .336 average. And so even when Boggs made the team in 1982, he was there as an extra man, coming in for occasional appearances late in the game or as a pinch-hitter.

History changed on June 22, 1982. Boston was playing against Detroit at Fenway, and Lansford started at third base while Boggs watched from the bench. With the Red Sox behind 4–2 in the bottom of the ninth inning, Boggs was sent in to pinch hit for shortstop Glenn Hoffman; he grounded out. Then after Rick Miller singled and Tony Perez pinch hit for me . . . and struck out . . . Dwight Evans hit a homer to tie the game. Boggs took over at first base.

In the bottom of the eleventh inning, Boggs came up to bat again. This time he hit it in the air: a game-winning, walk-off home run. The next day, he was back on the bench with Lansford playing third. But in the third inning, Lansford injured his ankle when he tried to stretch a triple into an inside-the-park home run, and by the sixth inning, Boggs was in the game. He ended up batting .349 for the season in 338 at-bats. During the off-season, the Red Sox traded Lansford to the Oakland Athletics for outfielder Tony Armas Sr. and catcher Jeff Newman, and Wade Boggs was the starting third baseman for Boston.

Boggs' best years with Boston included 1985, when he batted .368 for the season; playing at Fenway he batted .418. Again he was just behind the record set by Ted Williams, who hit .428 at home in 1941 en route to his .406 season.

Throughout his career, Boggs would almost always take the first pitch—the opposite of another fine hitter, Nomar Garciaparra. But every once in a while he would let it fly, especially if the pitcher believed too much in the scouting report and threw a batting-practice fastball to open the at-bat.

He shared another trait with Garciaparra; he was a bit obsessed. I don't think I ever met anybody in the game who was as structured as he was. He used to go out and run his sprints at 7:17 before a 7:30 game, not a minute earlier and not a minute later. He would take 150 grounders in infield practice, not 149 or 151. And he would eat chicken for lunch every day; Jim Rice gave him his unofficial nickname of Chicken Man.

What impressed me most about Boggs was how hard he worked to become a good defensive third baseman: He was probably only an average fielder when he came to the majors. He spent as much time and effort on making himself a better third baseman as he did on hitting. I give him a lot of credit for that because most guys just want to hit. He got to the point where he won two Gold Gloves.

The Red Sox finished in first place three times while Boggs was on the team and came within one strike of winning the World Series against the New York Mets in 1986. Boggs moved over to the Yankees in 1993, and finished playing in Tampa Bay. And in a perfect moment that capped his career, his 3,000th hit was a home run; he finished in 1999 with 3,010 hits. And though he didn't get much credit for it during his career, by today's way of measurement he would be an on-base superstar; his sharp eye at the plate earned him 1,412 walks. In his 1988 season for the Red Sox, he had a batting average of .366, an on-base percentage of .476, and an OPS of .966.

Wade Boggs

Year	Team	Age	G	AB	R	H	2B	3B	HR	RBI	BA		
1982	BOS (AL)	24	104	338	51	118	14	1	5	44	.349		
1983	BOS (AL)	25	153	582	100	210	44	7	5	74	.361	SS	
1984	BOS (AL)	26	158	625	109	203	31	4	6	55	.325		
1985	BOS (AL)	27	161	653	107	240	42	3	8	78	.368	AS	
1986	BOS (AL)	28	149	580	107	207	47	2	8	71	.357	SS,	AS
1987	BOS (AL)	29	147	551	108	200	40	6	24	89	.363	SS,	AS
1988	BOS (AL)	30	155	584	128	214	45	6	5	58	.366	SS,	AS
1989	BOS (AL)	31	156	621	113	205	51	7	3	54	.330	SS,	AS
1990	BOS (AL)	32	155	619	89	187	44	5	6	63	.302	AS	
1991	BOS (AL)	33	144	546	93	181	42	2	8	51	.332	SS,	AS

Year	Team	Age	G	AB	R	H	2B	3B	HR	RBI	BA		
1992	BOS (AL)	34	143	514	62	133	22	4	7	50	.259	AS	
1993	NYY (AL)	35	143	560	83	169	26	1	2	59	.302	SS,	AS
1994	NYY (AL)	36	97	366	61	125	19	1	11	55	.342	SS,	AS
1995	NYY (AL)	37	126	460	76	149	22	4	5	63	.324	AS	
1996	NYY (AL)	38	132	501	80	156	29	2	2	41	.311	AS	
1997	NYY (AL)	39	103	353	55	103	23	1	4	28	.292		
1998	TAMPA (AL)	40	123	435	51	122	23	4	7	52	.280		
1999	TAMPA (AL)	41	90	292	40	88	14	1	2	29	.301		
Total			**2439**	**9180**	**1513**	**3010**	**578**	**61**	**118**	**1014**	**.328**		
Boston			**1625**	**6213**	**1067**	**2098**	**422**	**47**	**85**	**687**	**.338**		

Year	Team	OBP	SLG	OPS	BB	SO	TB	SB	CS	SH	SF	IBB	HBP	GDP
1982	BOS (AL)	.406	.441	.847	35	21	149	1	0	4	4	4	0	9
1983	BOS (AL)	.444	.486	.930	92	36	283	3	3	3	7	2	1	15
1984	BOS (AL)	.407	.416	.823	89	44	260	3	2	8	4	6	0	13
1985	BOS (AL)	.450	.478	.928	96	61	312	2	1	3	2	5	4	20
1986	BOS (AL)	.453	.486	.939	105	44	282	0	4	4	4	14	0	11
1987	BOS (AL)	.461	.588	1.049	105	48	324	1	3	1	8	19	2	13
1988	BOS (AL)	.476	.490	.966	125	34	286	2	3	0	7	18	3	23
1989	BOS (AL)	.430	.449	.879	107	51	279	2	6	0	7	19	7	19
1990	BOS (AL)	.386	.418	.804	87	68	259	0	0	0	6	19	1	14
1991	BOS (AL)	.421	.460	.881	89	32	251	1	2	0	6	25	0	16
1992	BOS (AL)	.353	.358	.711	74	31	184	1	3	0	6	19	4	10
1993	NYY (AL)	.378	.363	.741	74	49	203	0	1	1	9	4	0	10
1994	NYY (AL)	.433	.489	.922	61	29	179	2	1	2	4	3	1	10
1995	NYY (AL)	.412	.422	.834	74	50	194	1	1	0	7	5	0	13
1996	NYY (AL)	.389	.389	.778	67	32	195	1	2	1	5	7	0	10
1997	NYY (AL)	.373	.397	.770	48	38	140	0	1	2	4	3	0	3
1998	TAMPA (AL)	.348	.400	.748	46	54	174	3	2	0	2	6	0	13
1999	TAMPA (AL)	.377	.377	.754	38	23	110	1	0	0	4	2	0	14
Total		**.415**	**.433**	**.848**	**1412**	**745**	**4064**	**24**	**35**	**29**	**96**	**180**	**23**	**236**
Boston		**.428**	**.462**	**.890**	**1004**	**470**	**2869**	**16**	**27**	**23**	**61**	**150**	**22**	**163**

MO VAUGHN
Maurice Samuel Vaughn ("Hit Dog")
(Boston 1991–1998; career 1991–2003)

Primary position: 1B	
Batted: L	
Threw: R	
Height: 6'1"	
Weight: 230 pounds	
First major league game: June 27, 1991	
Final major league game: May 2, 2003	
Born: December 15, 1967 in Norwalk, Connecticut	
Boston Red Sox Hall of Fame: 2008	

For the period of time he was with the Red Sox, Mo Vaughn was the most feared hitter in the lineup. The Hit Dog was the American League MVP in the 1995 season, shortened by 18 games because of the hangover from the strike the season before. He had an even better year in 1996 but came in fifth in MVP voting behind four pretty impressive rising stars: winner Juan Gonzalez, Alex Rodriguez, Albert Belle, and Ken Griffey Jr.

As a left-handed batter, he was mostly a pull hitter, but he could also use Fenway Park to his advantage and go the other way and use the wall. He crowded the plate, leaning into the strike zone. He was not bad as a first baseman, and very tough.

In 1988, Mo Vaughn was a star of the Seton Hall college baseball team; that summer he played first base for the Wareham Gatemen of the Cape Cod League. His teammates for the Gatemen included future Red Sox infielder John Valentin as well as Chuck Knoblauch and Craig Biggio.

Vaughn was drafted by the Red Sox in the first round in 1989 and by June of 1991 he was the starting first baseman (and occasional DH) in Boston.

By the end of 1993, he was batting cleanup for the Red Sox; that year he batted .297 with 29 home runs and 101 RBIs. His best years for Boston came in 1995 (Most Valuable Player, .300, 39 home runs, and 126 RBIs in a strike-shortened season) and 1996 when he recorded a .326 batting average, 44 home runs, and 143 RBIs.

Photo by the National Baseball Hall of Fame Library, Cooperstown, N.Y.

In 1998, Vaughn's final year with the Red Sox, the middle of the lineup included Nomar Garciaparra; the two combined for 75 home runs for the season.

Vaughn left after the 1998 season for Anaheim, during a period when bitterness and verbal sniping marked the relationship between players and management in Boston. It was the Dan Duquette era; he did not have a good relationship with his players, and he sometimes said things that perhaps he shouldn't have.

Mo Vaughn

Year	Team	Age	G	AB	R	H	2B	3B	HR	RBI	BA	
1991	BOS (AL)	23	74	219	21	57	12	0	4	32	.260	
1992	BOS (AL)	24	113	355	42	83	16	2	13	57	.234	
1993	BOS (AL)	25	152	539	86	160	34	1	29	101	.297	
1994	BOS (AL)	26	111	394	65	122	25	1	26	82	.310	
1995	BOS (AL)	27	140	550	98	165	28	3	39	126	.300	MVP, AS, SS
1996	BOS (AL)	28	161	635	118	207	29	1	44	143	.326	AS
1997	BOS (AL)	29	141	527	91	166	24	0	35	96	.315	
1998	BOS (AL)	30	154	609	107	205	31	2	40	115	.337	AS
1999	ANA (AL)	31	139	524	63	147	20	0	33	108	.281	
2000	ANA (AL)	32	161	614	93	167	31	0	36	117	.272	
2002	NYM (NL)	34	139	487	67	126	18	0	26	72	.259	
2003	NYM (NL)	35	27	79	10	15	2	0	3	15	.190	
Total			1512	5532	861	1620	270	10	328	1064	.293	
Boston			1046	3828	628	1165	199	10	230	752	.304	

Year	Team	OBP	SLG	OPS	BB	SO	TB	SB	CS	SH	SF	IBB	HBP	GDP
1991	BOS (AL)	.339	.370	.709	26	43	81	2	1	0	4	2	2	7
1992	BOS (AL)	.326	.400	.726	47	67	142	3	3	0	3	7	3	8
1993	BOS (AL)	.390	.525	.915	79	130	283	4	3	0	7	23	8	14
1994	BOS (AL)	.408	.576	.984	57	112	227	4	4	0	2	20	10	7
1995	BOS (AL)	.388	.575	.963	68	150	316	11	4	0	4	17	14	17
1996	BOS (AL)	.420	.583	1.003	95	154	370	2	0	0	8	19	14	17
1997	BOS (AL)	.420	.560	.980	86	154	295	2	2	0	3	17	12	10
1998	BOS (AL)	.402	.591	.993	61	144	360	0	0	0	3	13	8	13
1999	ANA (AL)	.358	.508	.866	54	127	266	0	0	0	3	7	11	11
2000	ANA (AL)	.365	.498	.863	79	181	306	2	0	0	5	11	14	14
2002	NYM (NL)	.349	.456	.805	59	145	222	0	1	0	2	6	10	15
2003	NYM (NL)	.323	.329	.652	14	22	26	0	0	0	1	2	2	2
Total		.383	.523	.906	725	1429	2894	30	18	0	45	144	108	135
Boston		.394	.542	.936	519	954	2074	28	17	0	34	118	71	93

MODERN TIMES

ROGER CLEMENS
William Roger Clemens ("The Rocket")
(Boston 1984–1996; career 1984–2007)

Primary position: P	
Batted: R	
Threw: R	
Height: 6'4"	
Weight: 220 pounds	
First major league game: May 15, 1984	
Final major league game: October 7, 2007	
Born: August 4, 1962 in Dayton, Ohio	

When certain guys come up to the majors, players might say "this guy is going to be good," but they never know how good. On May 15, 1984, Roger Clemens made his debut as a rookie pitcher for the Red Sox. We could see right away that he had extraordinary ability. The fastball was there; all the raw talent was there.

It turned out not to be the greatest game—for him or for me. We were in Cleveland, and Clemens started and gave up eleven hits in five and two-thirds innings, also allowing five runs and six stolen bases. Rookie stuff . . . but he did record the first four strikeouts of his career, and he got off the hook because the Sox came back to tie the game before eventually losing.

I was hurting, and my appearance in the game was as a pinch-hitter; I drew a walk, and then they sent in Glenn Hoffman to pinch run for me. My final game came three days later: another pinch-hitting appearance, this time resulting in a fly ball out to left field.

But back to The Rocket: His next appearance came on May 20, 1984, and it was a winning effort. He led the Red Sox to a 5–4 win over Minnesota, striking out seven in seven innings. It was the start of one of the greatest pitching careers in baseball history.

When the clock stopped at the end of the 2007 season, Clemens had 354 wins against 184 losses. He had amassed an amazing 4,672 strikeouts, and posted a career ERA of 3.12. The hardware on his shelf includes seven Cy Young Awards, the Most Valuable Player award in 1986, and two Triple Crowns (lowest ERA, most wins, and most strikeouts for the season).

Photo by the National Baseball Hall of Fame Library, Cooperstown, N.Y.

As of the start of the 2009 season, he was in ninth place in major league baseball history with 354 wins. He was passed in 2008 by Greg Maddux, who reached 355 in his last start of the season.

Clemens is number three on the list of career strikeouts with an amazing 4,626. This was another instance of slippage in 2008; he was passed by Randy Johnson, who moved into second place. I don't think there are any other active players who are likely to come anywhere near Clemens or Johnson (or Nolan Ryan, who sits at the top of the list with 5,714 whiffs).

Clemens pitched for four teams in the majors, but his numbers for the Red Sox alone would be considered a fabulous career. In 13 seasons with the Red Sox, he posted a 192–111 record with 2,590 strikeouts.

The next eleven seasons—for Toronto, the Yankees, Houston, and back to the Yankees—were just as dominating: 157–70 with 2,036 more Ks.

But let's consider him as a Red Sox Hero. Clemens was a home-grown product, by way of Texas. He had been the Red Sox first pick in the 1983 free-agent draft out of the University of Texas, the 19th pick overall that year.

He did not linger long in the minors: He started four games for Winter Haven in Single-A, going 3–1 and posting a 1.24 ERA; then he was promoted to Double-A New Britain where he started seven games for a 4–1 record and a 1.38 ERA. Although he performed well at spring training in 1984 (at the age of 22), he was sent to Pawtucket for a bit of AAA seasoning. Pitching for the Pawsox his numbers were better than his won-lost record: 2–3 in 7 games, but an ERA of just 1.93 and 50 strikeouts in 46 innings.

By May, he was called up to the big club (bumping "Oil Can" Boyd back down to Pawtucket for a while), and in 21 games he posted a 9–4 record.

The 1985 season was mostly forgettable, but 1986 was not. With the Red Sox on their way to a league pennant and the World Series, Roger Clemens suddenly blossomed.

Early in the 1986 season, Clemens made himself known to anyone who hadn't noticed him before: On April 29 at Fenway against the Seattle Mariners he struck out 20 batters, something that had never before been accomplished in the majors. (Clemens did it again against Detroit in 1996; Kerry Wood of the Cubs equaled the record in one game in 1998.)

And he kept on winning, going 14–0 before finally dropping a pair in July. By the end of the season, Clemens had won 24 games—the most he ever recorded in a season—and lost just 4. After the season he was voted the American League's Most Valuable Player and the winner of the Cy Young Award. (Everything but a World Championship ring, alas.)

He picked up Cy Youngs again in 1987, 1991, and 1997 for the Red Sox. And in 1998, after moving on to Toronto, he did it again. In 2001 he brought the pitching trophy to the New York Yankees, and then in 2004 he earned a Cy Young as a pitcher for the Houston Astros in the National League. The total of seven Cy Young Awards is two more than any other pitcher has ever accumulated.

As he developed, it was more than just his fastball that made him special; he also had a great splitter. If you want to point to a shortcoming, you could say he never had an excellent breaking ball.

But like all great pitchers, a good part of his success was due to his determination and the fact that he would not be intimidated by anybody. He was willing to back a player off the plate. He was the boss; he knew it and he made sure you knew it, too.

Anybody who knew Roger knew that he was totally driven to be the best. He had a very different style than another Red Sox great, Pedro Martinez; Clemens was the big Texan, bigger and stronger. He had a mean, mean streak through him, but that's because the game was very personal to him and he didn't want to be beat.

In his prime, every time he went out there you knew you had a chance to see a no-hitter. It was that way with Nolan Ryan, who had seven of them in his career. You felt that way about Pedro Martinez at times, and you felt that way about Roger. As luck would have it, neither Clemens nor Martinez ever managed to throw a no-hitter. Luck, of course, plays a big role in the difference between a one- or two-hitter and a no-no.

An awful lot was made about the fact that Clemens left the Red Sox in 1997 to go to the Toronto Blue Jays. I actually think it was the right time to leave Boston because I think he was getting a little stale here; it was the kick in the ass that he needed to continue his great career.

Boston's general manager at the time, Dan Duquette, was quoted as saying Clemens was in the "twilight of his career" after four unexceptional seasons from 1993 to 1996. Clemens left town with the attitude that he was going to show us—and Duquette— that he was far from done. He was going to show everyone the kind of guy he was.

He certainly did that up in Toronto, winning Cy Young Awards in 1997 and again in 1998, and then in 2001 for the Yankees and in 2005 for the Houston Astros. Sometimes change is good for people.

In 2003, as a Yankee, he reached two milestones in one game: his 300th win and his 4,000th strikeout. As this is written, only four pitchers in the history of baseball have crossed that strikeout marker: Nolan Ryan in first place, Randy Johnson, and Steve Carlton.

What may have been Clemens's final major league game took place on October 7, 2007 when he started for the Yankees against the Cleveland Indians in the AL Division Series. Clemens lasted only 2.1 innings, leaving with a strained left hamstring; he gave up 4 hits and 3 runs, but New York rallied behind youngster Phil Hughes to win that game. That would be the only ALDS game the Yankees would win that year; the Red Sox, meanwhile, cleaned out the Los Angeles Angels in a sweep and then squeaked by the Cleveland Indians on their way to winning the World Series.

Perhaps fittingly, his last regular season start had come a few weeks earlier at Fenway Park in a matchup against Boston's Curt Schilling. Clemens left after six innings, with the teams tied 1–1; Schilling gave up three runs on a home run by Derek Jeter in the eighth inning and the Yankees held on to win 4–3.

And then in 2008 Clemens got caught up in the backward-looking investigation by Major League Baseball about use of performance-enhancing drugs, including steroids. I don't know if the allegations are true or not.

How many games did he win because of steroids? How many Cy Young Awards did he win because of steroids? Who knows? The same goes for Barry Bonds. I don't know how you could possibly make a judgment with what we know now.

It is a shame that a career like the one posted by Clemens has been tainted. This much is certain: When Clemens left the Red Sox in 1996, the record book showed him tied with Cy Young (the great pitcher, not the award) for the Boston record of 192 wins. He went on to pitch for 11 more seasons and win four more engraved Cy Young plaques for Toronto, that AL team in New York, and Houston.

The question is, are the charges going to hurt his chances to be elected to the Hall of Fame? I'm glad I don't have to vote on it; how do you say "no" to a guy with his record?

He's a Red Sox hero, but his great career came to a sad ending with his reputation in ruins.

Roger Clemens

Year	Team	Age	W	L	G	GS	CG	SHO	GF	SV	WHIP	ERA	
1984	BOS (AL)	21	9	4	21	20	5	1	0	0	1.313	4.32	
1985	BOS (AL)	22	7	5	15	15	3	1	0	0	1.220	3.29	
1986	BOS (AL)	23	24	4	33	33	10	1	0	0	0.969	2.48	
1987	BOS (AL)	24	20	9	36	36	18	7	0	0	1.175	2.97	MVP, CY, AS
1988	BOS (AL)	25	18	12	35	35	14	8	0	0	1.057	2.93	CY
1989	BOS (AL)	26	17	11	35	35	8	3	0	0	1.216	3.13	AS
1990	BOS (AL)	27	21	6	31	31	7	4	0	0	1.082	1.93	
1991	BOS (AL)	28	18	10	35	35	13	4	0	0	1.047	2.62	AS
1992	BOS (AL)	29	18	11	32	32	11	5	0	0	1.074	2.41	CY, AS
1993	BOS (AL)	30	11	14	29	29	2	1	0	0	1.263	4.46	AS
1994	BOS (AL)	31	9	7	24	24	3	1	0	0	1.143	2.85	
1995	BOS (AL)	32	10	5	23	23	0	0	0	0	1.436	4.18	
1996	BOS (AL)	33	10	13	34	34	6	2	0	0	1.327	3.63	
1997	TOR (AL)	34	21	7	34	34	9	3	0	0	1.030	2.05	
1998	TOR (AL)	35	20	6	33	33	5	3	0	0	1.095	2.65	CY, AS
1999	NYY (AL)	36	14	10	30	30	1	1	0	0	1.465	4.60	CY, AS
2000	NYY (AL)	37	13	8	32	32	1	0	0	0	1.312	3.70	
2001	NYY (AL)	38	20	3	33	33	0	0	0	0	1.257	3.51	
2002	NYY (AL)	39	13	6	29	29	0	0	0	0	1.306	4.35	CY, AS
2003	NYY (AL)	40	17	9	33	33	1	1	0	0	1.214	3.91	
2004	HOU (NL)	41	18	4	33	33	0	0	0	0	1.157	2.98	AS
2005	HOU (NL)	42	13	8	32	32	1	0	0	0	1.008	1.87	CY, AS
2006	HOU (NL)	43	7	6	19	19	0	0	0	0	1.041	2.30	AS
2007	NYY (AL)	44	6	6	18	17	0	0	0	0	1.313	4.18	
Total			354	184	709	707	118	46	0	0	1.173	3.12	
Boston			192	111	383	382	100	38	0	0	1.158	3.06	

Year	Team	IP	H	R	ER	HR	BB	SO	HBP	WP	IBB	BK
1984	BOS (AL)	133.3	146	67	64	13	29	126	2	4	3	0
1985	BOS (AL)	98.3	83	38	36	5	37	74	3	1	0	3
1986	BOS (AL)	254.0	179	77	70	21	67	238	4	11	0	3
1987	BOS (AL)	281.7	248	100	93	19	83	256	9	4	4	3
1988	BOS (AL)	264.0	217	93	86	17	62	291	6	4	4	7
1989	BOS (AL)	253.3	215	101	88	20	93	230	8	7	5	0
1990	BOS (AL)	228.3	193	59	49	7	54	209	7	8	3	0
1991	BOS (AL)	271.3	219	93	79	15	65	241	5	6	12	0

Year	Team	IP	H	R	ER	HR	BB	SO	HBP	WP	IBB	BK
1992	BOS (AL)	246.7	203	80	66	11	62	208	9	3	5	0
1993	BOS (AL)	191.7	175	99	95	17	67	160	11	3	4	1
1994	BOS (AL)	170.7	124	62	54	15	71	168	4	4	1	0
1995	BOS (AL)	140.0	141	70	65	15	60	132	14	9	0	0
1996	BOS (AL)	242.7	216	106	98	19	106	257	4	8	2	1
1997	TOR (AL)	264.0	204	65	60	9	68	292	12	4	1	0
1998	TOR (AL)	234.7	169	78	69	11	88	271	7	6	0	0
1999	NYY (AL)	187.7	185	101	96	20	90	163	9	8	0	0
2000	NYY (AL)	204.3	184	96	84	26	84	188	10	2	0	1
2001	NYY (AL)	220.3	205	94	86	19	72	213	5	14	1	0
2002	NYY (AL)	180.0	172	94	87	18	63	192	7	14	6	0
2003	NYY (AL)	211.7	199	99	92	24	58	190	5	5	1	0
2004	HOU (NL)	214.2	169	76	71	15	79	218	6	5	5	0
2005	HOU (NL)	211.3	151	51	44	11	62	185	3	3	5	1
2006	HOU (NL)	113.3	89	34	29	7	29	102	4	3	1	0
2007	NYY (AL)	99.0	99	52	46	9	31	68	5	7	0	0
Total		**4916.7**	**4185**	**1885**	**1707**	**363**	**1580**	**4672**	**159**	**143**	**63**	**20**
Boston		**2776**	**2359**	**1045**	**943**	**194**	**856**	**2590**	**86**	**72**	**43**	**18**

TIM WAKEFIELD
Timothy Stephen Wakefield ("Wake")
(Boston 1995–2008; career 1992–2008,
active through 2008)

Primary position: P	
Bats: R	
Throws: R	
Height: 6'2"	
Weight: 204 pounds	
First major league game: July 31, 1992	
Born: August 2, 1966 in Melbourne, Florida	

Tim Wakefield is a master of an almost uncontrollable and sometimes unhittable pitch. When his knuckleball is knuckling in or near the strike zone he is a very effective pitcher. He has been a major contributor to Red Sox success for fourteen seasons and counting.

As this book goes to press at the start of the 2009 season, Wakefield is the senior member of the team in years wearing a Boston uniform. His name is scattered about in the Boston Red Sox record book in and among some of the greatest names in baseball history.

With 164 wins, he has the second highest number of victories in Red Sox history, behind only Roger Clemens and Cy Young who are tied with 192. He's in third place behind Clemens and Young for the most innings pitched; he's likely to surpass them both if he pitches at least one more full season. He's in second place behind Clemens for the number of games started, and in 2007 he climbed past Pedro Martinez into second place behind Clemens for the most strikeouts recorded by a Red Sox pitcher.

And of course, he's also in possession of some other records that accrue to a pitcher who has been around for a long time, and especially to one who throws a tricky pitch like the knuckleball. He is the team leader in career losses, ahead of Clemens and Young. And he also has given up the most walks of any Red Sox pitcher in history.

Finally, in company with about twenty other pitchers in baseball history, he is in the record books for striking out four batters in one inning. For Wakefield, it happened on August 10, 1999 against the

Kansas City Royals. That one inning showed the thrills and dangers of being a knuckleball pitcher.

Here's the story of that inning: Wakefield came into the game to start the ninth inning as a relief pitcher with the Sox up 5–3. Catcher Chad Kreuter was called out on strikes, and pinch-hitter Scott Pose swung and missed a third strike. With two outs and the win within reach, Johnny Damon struck out . . . but he reached first on a passed ball. And then catcher Jason Varitek allowed another passed ball, with Damon moving to second. Royals second baseman Carlos Febles, not known as a long-ball threat, managed to hit a two-run homer to tie the game. And then, finally, Carlos Beltrán—a guy with real power—whiffed for the fourth strikeout of the inning.

In the top of the tenth, Boston pinch-hitter Butch Huskey started a rally with a single. Varitek got a bunt single, and before the inning was over the Red Sox had scored four runs to go out in front 9–5. They shut down the Royals in the bottom of the inning, and Wakefield picked up the victory.

That's the sort of thing that happens when you throw that pitch—they don't always end up in the catcher's mitt. Sometimes there are passed balls or wild pitches, sometimes there are moon shots, and in Tim Wakefield's career often there are great successes.

Tim Wakefield had a remarkable pitching debut with the Pittsburgh Pirates in 1992, coming up from the minors and going 8–1 down the stretch. And then he seemed to lose his touch and was sent back down to the minors in 1993 and stayed there in 1994. Before the start of the 1995 season, the Pirates released him and he might well have been done.

Instead, Boston took a chance on him. He made his Red Sox debut on May 27, 1995 against the Angels and gave up just one run and five hits in seven innings, earning the win. He went on to reel off four consecutive wins, finishing the season 16–8 with a strong ERA of 2.95.

Over the years, we have come to count on an extraordinary number of innings from Wakefield. He has had a few injuries in recent years, but basically he has been healthy for the majority of his career. He has been successful as a starter, a reliever, and a closer, and over the course of some seasons he has done all three jobs. And he's also a pretty good fielder; he started in the minors as an infielder, and his pitch takes so long to get to the plate that he can get into good position to make a play if a ball comes back at him.

Wakefield is a very good athlete and makes himself a better pitcher by fielding his position well. But his success is mostly about throwing the knuckleball. It is totally different than anything else seen by batters.

He gives hitters something they really can't practice against. Why would you want to go up and swing at a knuckleball in batting practice? All that does is get you out of your regular routine.

It's not just that he throws a freak pitch; he can throw it for strikes. And he also has a fastball and a curveball that he can throw into the mix, or use if he is not getting his knuckleball over the plate. They are not exceptional, but if the knuckleball has gotten into the hitter's head, he may be equally flummoxed by a 78-mile-per-hour fastball or a slow curve.

I don't think managers are particularly crazy about managing knuckleball pitchers because things can change so quickly. He can be cruising along and then walk a batter, the catcher can allow a passed ball, runners can steal bases pretty easily, and "boom," all of a sudden you're down four runs.

A manager or a pitching coach can watch from the dugout and see that any other pitcher is getting tired, having an off night, or making mistakes. How do you do that with a knuckleball pitcher?

For the record, Wakefield's knuckleball comes in somewhere between about 55 and 68 miles per hour. By comparison, his fastball can seem pretty zippy at about 75 to 78-mile-per-hour. And he can surprise with a slow curve at 60 to 65-mile-per-hour. Can you understand why he can be so confusing to batters who are used to timing their swing to hit a 90+-mile-per-hour fastball?

If he's healthy, he may be able to pitch for quite a while. He'd like to stay in Boston, and the Red Sox want to hold on to him. Charlie Hough pitched 25 seasons in the majors, retiring in 1994 at age 46. And Phil Niekro made it to the Hall of Fame with 318 wins across 24 seasons, retiring at age 48 in 1987.

If there was any doubt about the respect Red Sox fans have for Wakefield, consider the rollercoaster ride of the 2003 and 2004 ALCS. In 2003, Wakefield was one of Boston's most effective pitchers against the Yankees, giving up only three runs in 13 innings; he started the first and fourth game, and the Red Sox won both.

And then in the seventh and final game, after the Yankees tied the score and sent the contest into extra innings, it was Wakefield the Red Sox called on. He retired the side in order in the 10th inning, but on the first pitch of the 11th he gave up a heartbreaking game-winning home run to Aaron Boone.

Wakefield apologized to Red Sox fans after the game, and then he had to spend the entire off-season replaying that pitch in his mind.

But when Boston opened its season in 2004, the fans gave him a huge ovation when he was introduced.

Fast-forward to the 2004 ALCS and this time the Red Sox were in deep trouble, on their way to losing the first three games of the series. Boston's bullpen was shot and the Yankees were winning in a blowout; Wakefield volunteered to come in as a reliever, giving up his scheduled start in Game 4 the next day. He soaked up the innings, allowing Derek Lowe to start Game 4, which began the incredible comeback for the Red Sox.

And then Wakefield got the win in Game 5, fluttering three shut-out innings against the Yankees in a 14-inning 5–4 win.

In 2007, he had a shoulder injury and asked to be left off the World Series roster. But he was with the team, and he watched as Beckett, Schilling, Matsuzaka, and Lester swept the Colorado Rockies for Boston's second crown in four seasons. They probably could not have done it without him.

Wakefield had a decent season in 2008, winning 10 games and losing 11. Actually, his record could have been much better. At the age of 41, he put up some very impressive numbers: Opposing batters hit only .228 against him, the third-best record in the American League, behind only Detroit rookie Armando Galarraga at .226 and Boston's Daisuke Matsuzaka at .211. And Wakefield also held batters to a slim on-base percentage of .302 in 2008. Both of those numbers are well below his career average.

Some of his starts in 2008 were short and ugly and some were full-length works of art. On May 6 he held the Detroit Tigers to two hits and no runs across eight innings; he also gave up just two hits in seven-inning wins over the Arizona Diamondbacks on June 25 and against the Baltimore Orioles on July 12. And then in the ALCS against the Tampa Bay Rays, he was shelled and knocked out after just 2.2 innings, yielding six hits and five earned runs in Boston's third loss, a 13–4 thumping at Fenway.

Wakefield is still capable of making the best hitters look pitiful; alas, when one of his magic pitches flattens out or rises up sometimes the result is not pretty. But he is a hero for 14-plus seasons of heart. Days after the end of the 2008 season, the Red Sox picked up their 2009 option on Wakefield.

Tim Wakefield

Year	Team	Age	W	L	G	GS	CG	SHO	GF	SV	WHIP	ERA
1992	PIT (NL)	25	8	1	13	13	4	1	0	0	1.207	2.15
1993	PIT (NL)	26	6	11	24	20	3	2	1	0	1.714	5.61
1995	BOS (AL)	28	16	8	27	27	6	1	0	0	1.183	2.95
1996	BOS (AL)	29	14	13	32	32	6	0	0	0	1.550	5.14
1997	BOS (AL)	30	12	15	35	29	4	2	2	0	1.391	4.25
1998	BOS (AL)	31	17	8	36	33	2	0	1	0	1.343	4.58
1999	BOS (AL)	32	6	11	49	17	0	0	28	15	1.557	5.08
2000	BOS (AL)	33	6	10	51	17	0	0	13	0	1.475	5.48
2001	BOS (AL)	34	9	12	45	17	0	0	5	3	1.358	3.90
2002	BOS (AL)	35	11	5	45	15	0	0	10	3	1.053	2.81
2003	BOS (AL)	36	11	7	35	33	0	0	2	1	1.305	4.09
2004	BOS (AL)	37	12	10	32	30	0	0	0	0	1.381	4.87
2005	BOS (AL)	38	16	12	33	33	3	0	0	0	1.234	4.15
2006	BOS (AL)	39	7	11	23	23	1	0	0	0	1.329	4.63
2007	BOS (AL)	40	17	12	31	31	0	0	0	0	1.349	4.76
2008	BOS (AL)	41	10	11	30	30	1	0	0	0	1.182	4.13
Total			**178**	**157**	**541**	**400**	**30**	**6**	**62**	**22**	**1.346**	**4.32**
Boston			**164**	**145**	**504**	**367**	**23**	**3**	**61**	**22**	**1.333**	**4.33**

Year	Team	IP	H	R	ER	HR	BB	K	HBP	WP	IBB	BK
1992	PIT (NL)	92.0	76	26	22	3	35	51	1	3	1	1
1993	PIT (NL)	128.3	145	83	80	14	75	59	9	6	2	0
1995	BOS (AL)	195.3	163	76	64	22	68	119	9	11	0	0
1996	BOS (AL)	211.6	238	151	121	38	90	140	12	4	0	1
1997	BOS (AL)	201.3	193	109	95	24	87	151	16	6	5	0
1998	BOS (AL)	216.0	211	123	110	30	79	146	14	6	1	1
1999	BOS (AL)	140.0	146	93	79	19	72	104	5	1	2	0
2000	BOS (AL)	159.3	170	107	97	31	65	102	4	4	3	0
2001	BOS (AL)	168.7	156	84	73	13	73	148	18	5	5	1
2002	BOS (AL)	163.3	121	57	51	15	51	134	9	5	2	2
2003	BOS (AL)	202.3	193	106	92	23	71	169	12	8	0	0
2004	BOS (AL)	188.3	197	121	102	29	63	116	16	9	3	0
2005	BOS (AL)	225.3	210	113	104	35	68	151	11	8	4	0
2006	BOS (AL)	140.0	135	80	72	19	51	90	10	6	0	0
2007	BOS (AL)	189.0	191	104	100	22	64	110	4	10	1	0
2008	BOS (AL)	181.0	154	89	83	25	60	117	13	12	0	0
Total		**2802.0**	**2699**	**1522**	**1345**	**362**	**1072**	**1907**	**163**	**104**	**29**	**6**
Boston		**2581.3**	**2478**	**1413**	**1243**	**345**	**962**	**1797**	**153**	**95**	**26**	**5**

TROT NIXON
Christopher Trotman Nixon
(Boston 1996–2006; career 1996–2008,
active through 2008)

Primary position: RF	
Bats: L	
Throws: L	
Height: 6'1"	
Weight: 195 pounds	
First major league game: September 21, 1996	
Final major league game: Active player	
Born: April 11, 1974 in Durham, North Carolina	

Trot Nixon was the original Dirt Dog. He threw himself into the game 100 percent every day in everything he did. People loved him because he was a lunch bucket type of guy they could identify with.

Unfortunately for him, he had trouble with injuries, and as good as he was, I don't think he ever became the player that many thought he might be. His injuries kept him from being one of the top echelon outfielders in the game.

But the injuries came because of the way he played the game. There was no wall he would not try to run through. That was his personality. Guys like Trot are infectious on a team, because when you see guys playing as hard as they do day-in and day-out, you feel like you've got to do the same thing too.

He was a first-round pick for Boston in 1993 (seventh overall in the draft); he came up for a look-see from the minors for parts of the 1996 and 1998 seasons before becoming a Red Sox regular in 1999. He patrolled rightfield for much of eight seasons before going to Cleveland for 2007.

In his native North Carolina, Nixon was an accomplished high school athlete. As a senior, he was Player of the Year in both football and baseball; he broke passing records held by former NFL quarterbacks Sonny Jurgensen and Roman Gabriel. And also as a senior, he was picked as *Baseball America* magazine's high school player of the year; he led his team to a title with a .512 batting average and 12

Photo by Brita Meng Outzen

home runs, and also recorded a pitching record of 12–0 and an ERA of 0.40.

As a member of the Red Sox, his best year was 2003, when he batted .306 with 28 home runs and 87 RBIs. In Game 3 of the AL Division Series against Oakland, with the Red Sox facing elimination, Nixon came up as a pinch-hitter in the bottom of the 11th inning against right-handed reliever Rich Harden and put a ball over the centerfield wall for a walk-off win.

Nixon missed several months of the 2004 season because of injuries including a herniated disc in his back; he played in only 48 games. But when it came to the fourth and winning game of the 2004 World Series, it was Nixon who hit a two-run double with two outs in the third inning to give Boston a 3–0 lead. Derek Lowe combined with the bullpen to shut out the St. Louis Cardinals to end the 86-year drought and bring the Series trophy home to Boston.

Nixon was such a fan favorite in Red Sox Nation. As 2006 came to a close, manager Terry Francona replaced him with two outs in the fifth inning of the last game of the season, allowing him to trot into the dugout in front of a standing ovation from the Fenway Faithful.

He was a part-timer for the Cleveland Indians in 2007, and in mid-season 2008 he was brought up from the minors as a role player for the New York Mets. Alas, after working himself into playing shape for his chance to return to the majors, he made it into only 11 games before he was once again injured. He finished out the 2008 season on the disabled list, and as this book goes to press we don't know if he will get to show his stuff again.

If he does indeed retire, consider that his final game and his final at-bat was against the Yankees, wearing a New York Mets uniform. He was sent up as a pinch-hitter in the ninth inning with two outs and the Mets trailing 3–2; unfortunately, he was up against Mariano Rivera, and mighty Nixon struck out.

True Red Sox fans will root for him wherever he plays or whatever he does.

Trot Nixon

Year	Age	Team	G	AB	R	H	2B	3B	HR	RBI	BA
1996	22	BOS (AL)	2	4	2	2	1	0	0	0	.500
1998	24	BOS (AL)	13	27	3	7	1	0	0	0	.259
1999	25	BOS (AL)	124	381	67	103	22	5	15	52	.270
2000	26	BOS (AL)	123	427	66	118	27	8	12	60	.276
2001	27	BOS (AL)	148	535	100	150	31	4	27	88	.280
2002	28	BOS (AL)	152	532	81	136	36	3	24	94	.256
2003	29	BOS (AL)	134	441	81	135	24	6	28	87	.306
2004	30	BOS (AL)	48	149	24	47	9	1	6	23	.315
2005	31	BOS (AL)	124	408	64	112	29	1	13	67	.275
2006	32	BOS (AL)	114	381	59	102	24	0	8	52	.268
2007	33	CLE (AL)	99	307	30	77	17	0	3	31	.251
2008	34	NYM (NL)	11	35	2	6	1	0	1	1	.171
Total			**1092**	**3627**	**579**	**995**	**222**	**28**	**137**	**555**	**.274**
Boston			**982**	**3285**	**547**	**912**	**204**	**28**	**133**	**523**	**.278**

Year	Team	OBP	SLG	OPS	BB	SO	TB	SB	CS	SH	SF	IBB	HBP	GDP
1996	BOS (AL)	.500	.750	1.250	0	1	3	1	0	0	0	0	0	0
1998	BOS (AL)	.286	.296	.582	1	3	8	0	0	0	0	0	0	0
1999	BOS (AL)	.357	.472	.830	53	75	180	3	1	2	8	1	3	7
2000	BOS (AL)	.368	.461	.830	63	85	197	8	1	5	5	2	2	11
2001	BOS (AL)	.376	.505	.881	79	113	270	7	4	6	6	1	7	8
2002	BOS (AL)	.338	.470	.808	65	109	250	4	2	3	7	2	5	7
2003	BOS (AL)	.396	.578	.975	65	96	255	4	2	1	3	4	3	3
2004	BOS (AL)	.377	.510	.887	15	24	76	0	0	0	2	1	1	3
2005	BOS (AL)	.357	.446	.804	53	59	182	2	1	0	6	3	3	7
2006	BOS (AL)	.373	.394	.767	60	56	150	0	2	0	5	1	7	10
2007	CLE (AL)	.342	.336	.677	44	59	103	0	0	0	3	7	0	9
2008	NYM (NL)	.293	.286	.579	6	9	10	1	0	0	0	1	0	0
Total		**.364**	**.464**	**.828**	**504**	**689**	**1684**	**30**	**13**	**17**	**45**	**23**	**31**	**65**
Boston		**.366**	**.478**	**.845**	**454**	**621**	**1571**	**29**	**13**	**17**	**42**	**15**	**31**	**56**

NOMAR GARCIAPARRA

Anthony Nomar Garciaparra
(Boston 1996–2004; career 1996–2008,
active through 2008)

Primary position: SS, 1B, 3B	
Bats: R	
Throws: R	
Height: 6'0"	
Weight: 165 pounds	
First major league game: August 31, 1996	
Final major league game: Active player	
Born: July 23, 1973 in Whittier, California	

Nomar's light shone bright and fierce for a four-year stretch from 1997 to 2000.

He was a talented athlete, lettering in baseball, football, and soccer in high school in California. At Georgia Tech, he and his college teammate Jason Varitek helped the Yellow Jackets reach the College World Series in 1994. He was selected by Boston as their first round draft pick that year and he quickly moved through the Red Sox minors.

After coming up for a look-see at the end of the 1996 season, he was the Red Sox starting shortstop the next year. It was a heck of a debut: he won Rookie of the Year, the Silver Slugger, and was selected for the All-Star team. Right from the start, he was the golden child. Fans absolutely loved him in Boston.

And in 2000 his batting average of .372 set the Red Sox record for a right-handed hitter. (Ted Williams, of course, holds the team record, batting .406 from the left side in 1941.)

His hands were almost always in a good hitting position and he rarely was jammed; he almost never broke a bat. But he never got started in 2001; he showed up for spring training with a wrist injury and ended up having surgery on Opening Day. His first game of the season that year came on July 30. Fans were thrilled when he hit a home run and a two-run single to lead the Red Sox to a 4–3 victory over the White Sox at Fenway. But though he had very good seasons

Photo by the National Baseball Hall of Fame Library, Cooperstown, N.Y.

in 2002 and 2003, his defense and some of his offensive numbers began to slip. He went into a slump at the end of the 2003 season that extended into the unsuccessful playoff series that year.

Ted Williams and Johnny Pesky both said that they thought Nomar had the best chance to be the next batter to finish the season with an average of .400 or better. Obviously that didn't happen; I'm not sure anyone is ever going to hit that high.

Nomar would almost always swing at the first pitch and didn't walk very much, which would make it difficult to hit .400. He came awfully close, though.

Another one of my heroes, Wade Boggs, almost never swung at the first pitch; Nomar almost never missed the opportunity to poke at almost anything that was remotely near the strike zone. In his early years, he was one of the best first-ball hitters in baseball, in the company of players like Paul Molitor and Kirby Puckett. He went up to the plate looking for a particular pitch in a certain place; if he got it, he swung. At his peak, it would have been crazy for a hitting coach to try to change his attitude.

He won the American League batting championship in 1999 and 2000, the first right-hander to do that since Joe DiMaggio in 1939 and 1940. Left-handed hitter Wade Boggs grabbed four trophies in a row from 1985 to 1988 as a Red Sox.

In the field, Nomar was not what I would call "smooth." He attacked the ball and he did everything on the run. He seemed to be more comfortable charging than staying back on the ball. When he attacked the ball, he made it look easy . . . at least for him.

There were some plays he made better than anybody else. I can picture in my mind Garciaparra charging to his right, a play that for him appeared to be as easy as it would be for another player fielding a ball hit right at him. He would grab the ball on the run and continue toward third base, and then without planting his feet make an off-balance throw. No Little League coach would ever advise someone to play like Garciaparra.

In any case I always felt his best position might have been third base, but for the Red Sox he was a good, not great, shortstop. Red Sox second basemen used to get blamed for not making double plays, but a lot of times it was because they weren't getting good feeds from him.

But by 2004, when the Red Sox were battling to get into the playoffs, Garciaparra's star was dimming in Boston. As good as he was, he never seemed comfortable in the Boston environment. I think the intensity of the fans and sports talk shows and reporters, which can be pretty negative, bothered him a lot.

And then all of a sudden he was gone. He was dealt to the Chicago Cubs on the July 31st trading deadline for shortstop Orlando Cabrera and first baseman Doug Mientkiewicz. There was shock, and then there was celebration, because the Red Sox played well enough to make the playoffs and then launched their miraculous comeback in the ALCS against the Yankees and beat the Cardinals to end the Curse. Quick as can be, it was, "Nomar Who?"

He went on from Chicago to the Los Angeles Dodgers, but he has been dogged by injuries. He was on the Dodgers playoff roster in 2008 as a reserve infielder. He didn't get into a game in the NLDS but was given his shot in the League Championship Series; in seven at-bats spread over one start and three pinch-hit or late-game insertions he picked up three hits and an RBI. And then he had the dubious distinction of making the final out for the Dodgers in their fifth and final game against the Phillies: a popup to the catcher in foul territory.

I can't let Nomar go by without thinking back to his rituals at the plate. He would tug on his batting gloves over and over, tap his helmet, and then settle in for a pitch. If he didn't get a pitch to hit, he'd do it all over again. I wonder what he's like when he's off the field puttering around the house.

In any case, let's not forget his contributions when he was at the top of his game here in Boston. He was an exciting offensive player with great hand-eye coordination, and he was a very good baserunner. For those first four seasons, he was one of the best players ever to be in the Red Sox lineup.

Nomar Garciaparra

Year	Team	Age	G	AB	R	H	2B	3B	HR	RBI	BA	
1996	BOS (AL)	22	24	87	11	21	2	3	4	16	.241	
1997	BOS (AL)	23	153	684	122	209	44	11	30	98	.306	ROY, SS, AS
1998	BOS (AL)	24	143	604	111	195	37	8	35	122	.323	
1999	BOS (AL)	25	135	532	103	190	42	4	27	104	.357	AS
2000	BOS (AL)	26	140	529	104	197	51	3	21	96	.372	AS
2001	BOS (AL)	27	21	83	13	24	3	0	4	8	.289	AS
2002	BOS (AL)	28	156	635	101	197	56	5	24	120	.310	AS
2003	BOS (AL)	29	156	658	120	198	37	13	28	105	.301	AS
2004	*Season*	*30*	*81*	*321*	*52*	*99*	*21*	*3*	*9*	*41*	*.308*	
	BOS (AL)		38	156	24	50	7	3	5	21	.321	
	CHC (NL)		43	165	28	49	14	0	4	20	.297	
2005	CHC (NL)	31	62	230	28	65	12	0	9	30	.283	
2006	LAD (NL)	32	122	469	82	142	31	2	20	93	.303	AS
2007	LAD (NL)	33	121	431	39	122	17	0	7	59	.283	
2008	LAD (NL)	34	55	163	24	43	9	0	8	28	.264	
Total			**1369**	**5426**	**910**	**1702**	**362**	**52**	**226**	**920**	**.314**	
Boston			**966**	**3968**	**709**	**1281**	**279**	**50**	**178**	**690**	**.323**	

Year	Team	OBP	SLG	OPS	BB	K	TB	SB	CS	SH	SF	IBB	HBP	GDP
1996	BOS (AL)	.272	.471	.743	4	14	41	5	0	1	1	0	0	0
1997	BOS (AL)	.342	.534	.876	35	92	365	22	9	2	7	2	6	9
1998	BOS (AL)	.362	.584	.946	33	62	353	12	6	0	7	1	8	20
1999	BOS (AL)	.418	.603	1.021	51	39	321	14	3	0	4	7	8	11
2000	BOS (AL)	.434	.599	1.033	61	50	317	5	2	0	7	20	2	8
2001	BOS (AL)	.352	.470	.822	7	9	39	0	1	0	0	0	1	1
2002	BOS (AL)	.352	.528	.880	41	63	335	5	2	0	11	4	6	17
2003	BOS (AL)	.345	.524	.869	39	61	345	19	5	1	10	1	11	10
2004	*Season*	*.365*	*.477*	*.842*	*24*	*30*	*153*	*4*	*1*	*1*	*2*	*2*	*6*	*10*
	BOS (AL)	.367	.500	.867	8	16	78	2	0	0	1	2	4	4
	CHC (NL)	.364	.455	.819	16	14	75	2	1	1	1	0	2	6
2005	CHC (NL)	.320	.452	.772	12	24	104	0	0	0	3	0	2	6
2006	LAD (NL)	.367	.505	.872	42	30	237	3	0	0	4	9	8	15
2007	LAD (NL)	.328	.371	.699	31	41	160	3	1	0	4	5	0	6
2008	LAD (NL)	.326	.466	.792	15	11	10	1	1	0	2	2	1	12
Total		**.363**	**.525**	**.887**	**395**	**526**	**2780**	**93**	**31**	**5**	**62**	**53**	**59**	**125**
Boston		**.370**	**.553**	**.923**	**279**	**406**	**2194**	**84**	**28**	**4**	**48**	**37**	**46**	**80**

DEREK LOWE

Derek Christopher Lowe ("D-Lowe")
(Boston 1997–2004; career 1997–2008,
active through 2008)

Primary position: P	
Bats: R	
Throws: R	
Height: 6'7"	
Weight: 170 pounds	
First major league game: April 26, 1997	
Final major league game: Active player	
Born: June 1, 1973 in Dearborn, Michigan	

Derek Lowe has had his ups and downs on and off the field. But when he was good, he was very good. And he came through in the 2004 postseason, something that will forever endear him to Red Sox Nation.

When he first came to the Red Sox in a trade from Seattle, he was tried out in several different roles. He had a good year as Boston's closer in 2000, leading the American League with 42 saves—although not all of them were pretty.

And then in 2001 he had a pretty unpleasant experience as a closer. You could see it on his face and in his body language; he was crushed. He began the season as the closer, but at the trading deadline Boston obtained the fiery Ugueth Urbina from the Montreal Expos and Lowe was relegated to a setup role.

But he was given the opportunity to get in a few starts at the end of that miserable season, and that sent him home on a high note. When he came back in 2002 he was in the starting rotation and early in the season, on April 27, he pitched a no-hitter against Tampa Bay, the first no-no at Fenway since Dave Morehead threw one in 1965. He built on that for the season, posting a 21–8 record and a 2.58 ERA, finishing third in the Cy Young Award voting.

His specialty pitch with the Red Sox was a two-seam fastball, a pitch that takes a sharp dip and moves down and in toward a right-handed hitter or down and away against a lefty. If a batter makes contact, he feels like he's hit a shotput.

Photo by the National Baseball Hall of Fame Library, Cooperstown, N.Y.

Lowe had a less spectacular 2003 season, but still had 17 wins against 7 losses, buoyed by Boston's strong offense. He seemed to be sliding again in 2004, despite the Red Sox run toward the postseason; he finished 14–12 with a 5.42 ERA, starting 33 games.

When the 2004 postseason began, Boston had Curt Schilling, Pedro Martinez, and Bronson Arroyo set up for their first three starters. Lowe was on the roster, but assigned to the bullpen for the division series.

He came in as a reliever in the top of the tenth inning in Game 3 of the ALDS against Anaheim. Bronson Arroyo had started the game and four Boston relievers had followed. Lowe earned the win when David Ortiz hit a two-run walk-off home run to win the series.

Then in the fabulous AL Championship Series against New York, Lowe pitched two critical games. He was the starter of the fourth game after Boston had lost the first three to the Yankees. And though he didn't figure in the final result (Mike Timlin was charged with a blown save), this was the contest that turned the series around. This game included both The Steal by Dave Roberts and the second walk-off home run of the postseason by Ortiz. The Red Sox were still alive, with their first win.

And then Lowe was the starter of the seventh and final game of the ALCS. He threw six solid innings of one-hit ball, giving up a single run, and won the game as the rejuvenated Red Sox pounded the staggering Yankees 10–3.

Finally, he was the winning pitcher in the fourth game of the World Series against St. Louis. He pitched seven innings, giving up no runs and just three hits, and then watched as Arroyo, Alan Embree, and Keith Foulke held the Cardinals scoreless for a 3–0 victory and the first World Series championship for Boston since 1918.

So, Lowe was the winner of the final game of all three postseason series in 2004—the first and only pitcher in baseball history with that particular record.

Lowe had come to the Red Sox in 1997 as part of one of the more productive deals in Boston history: uneven reliever Heathcliff Slocumb for Lowe and catcher Jason Varitek. Together, along with a few friends, they broke the Curse.

D-Lowe cashed in after the 2004 season, accepting the high bid from the Los Angeles Dodgers. But he did come back to Fenway and put on a Red Sox uniform top to accept his World Series ring with his former teammates on April 11, 2005. In October of 2008 it looked possible that Lowe (and a few other expatriates like Nomar Garcia-parra and Manny Ramirez) might be coming to Boston for a World Series matchup, but that was not to be.

On the West Coast, Lowe has continued to pitch well, posting a 54–48 record in four seasons. Lowe started three games in the 2008 postseason for the Dodgers. He helped Los Angeles beat the Chicago Cubs in the opening game of the NLDS, giving up two runs across six games. He then started Game 1 of the League Championship Series against the Philadelphia Phillies and lost a tight 3–2 game. He pitched well in the fourth game, leaving with a lead, but the Dodgers coughed it up and lost the game; the next night Los Angeles had to endure losing the series before their own fans.

Derek Lowe

Year	Team	Age	W	L	G	GS	CG	SHO	GF	SV	WHIP	ERA
1997	*Season*	*24*	*2*	*6*	*20*	*9*	*0*	*0*	*1*	*0*	*1.406*	*6.13*
	SEA (AL)		2	4	12	9	0	0	1	0	1.491	6.96
	BOS (AL)		0	2	8	0	0	0	0	0	1.125	3.38
1998	BOS (AL)	25	3	9	63	10	0	0	8	4	1.366	4.02
1999	BOS (AL)	26	6	3	74	0	0	0	32	15	0.997	2.63
2000	BOS (AL)	27	4	4	74	0	0	0	64	42	1.226	2.56
2001	BOS (AL)	28	5	10	67	3	0	0	50	24	1.440	3.53
2002	BOS (AL)	29	21	8	32	32	1	1	0	0	0.974	2.58
2003	BOS (AL)	30	17	7	33	33	1	0	0	0	1.416	4.47
2004	BOS (AL)	31	14	12	33	33	0	0	0	0	1.615	5.42
2005	LAD (NL)	32	12	15	35	35	2	2	0	0	1.252	3.61
2006	LAD (NL)	33	16	8	35	34	1	0	1	0	1.266	3.63
2007	LAD (NL)	34	12	14	33	32	3	0	0	0	1.269	3.88
2008	LAD (NL)	35	14	11	34	34	1	0	0	0	1.133	3.24
Total			**126**	**107**	**533**	**255**	**9**	**3**	**156**	**85**	**1.268**	**3.75**
Boston			**70**	**55**	**384**	**111**	**2**	**1**	**154**	**85**	**1.288**	**3.72**

Year	Team	IP	H	R	ER	HR	BB	SO	HBP	WP	IBB	BK
1997	*Season*	*69*	*74*	*49*	*47*	*11*	*23*	*52*	*4*	*2*	*3*	*0*
	SEA (AL)	53	59	43	41	11	20	39	2	2	2	0
	BOS (AL)	16	15	6	6	0	3	13	2	0	1	0
1998	BOS (AL)	123	126	65	55	5	42	77	4	8	5	0
1999	BOS (AL)	109.3	84	35	32	7	25	80	4	1	1	0
2000	BOS (AL)	91.3	90	27	26	6	22	79	2	1	5	1 AS
2001	BOS (AL)	91.7	103	39	36	7	29	82	5	4	9	0
2002	BOS (AL)	219.7	166	65	63	12	48	127	12	5	0	0 AS
2003	BOS (AL)	203.3	216	113	101	17	72	110	11	3	4	0
2004	BOS (AL)	182.7	224	138	110	15	71	105	8	3	2	0
2005	LAD (NL)	222	223	113	89	28	55	146	5	3	1	2
2006	LAD (NL)	218	221	97	88	14	55	123	5	3	2	2
2007	LAD (NL)	199.3	194	100	86	20	59	147	1	3	2	1
2008	LAD (NL)	211	194	84	76	14	45	147	1	2	7	0
Total		**1940.3**	**1915**	**925**	**809**	**156**	**546**	**1275**	**62**	**38**	**41**	**6**
Boston		**1037**	**1024**	**488**	**429**	**69**	**312**	**673**	**48**	**25**	**27**	**1**

JASON VARITEK
Jason Andrew Varitek ("Tek")
(Boston 1997–2008, active through 2008)

Primary position: C	
Bats: Both	
Throws: R	
Height: 6'2"	
Weight: 210 pounds	
First major league game: September 24, 1997	
Final major league game: Active player	
Born: April 11, 1972 in Rochester, Michigan	

Consider the job of a major league catcher. First of all, he has to field his position, which is one of the most demanding assignments on the team—catch the pitched ball wherever it ends up, make plays on popups and bunts, throw to the bases to try to stop steals, and sometimes put his body in the way of an oncoming runner attempting to score a run.

The catcher also has to understand and work with the abilities and mentalities of the entire pitching staff, and he has to work with the coaching staff to come up with a plan to neutralize the hitters on the other team. And then four or five times each game he has to put all of that aside and come up to bat as a hitter.

In the history of the game, there have been relatively few catchers who have excelled in all facets of the game. In this book, we salute Red Sox Heroes like Rick Ferrell (who was way before my time but whose numbers speak volumes) and Carlton Fisk (with whom I played from 1978 to 1980). They are both in the Hall of Fame.

In the modern era of the Red Sox, a team that has been to the postseason seven times since 1998 and won two World Series in that span, one of the bedrocks of the team has been catcher Jason Varitek. He is without a doubt one of the best-prepared catchers in baseball. He takes great pride in his game, planning and studying all of the scouting reports and information available about the opposing team.

And he is very good at making adjustments during the game. He can recognize a pitcher's strengths or weaknesses on a particular

Photo by the National Baseball Hall of Fame Library, Cooperstown, N.Y.

day. He watches the way hitters move in the batter's box and adjusts the pitch location or type. He knows that his most important job is managing the pitching staff. When the pitchers know they have a guy like that behind the plate it makes their job easier. It takes a lot of the head work out of it for them.

Consider someone like Daisuke Matsuzaka, who spoke virtually no English when he joined the team in 2007. He had to rely totally on Varitek to call the game because he didn't know any of the hitters. As Daisuke's career goes on he will have memories of guys he has faced and he will choose more of his pitches himself. That is a balancing act that pitchers and catchers always have to go through.

And then sometimes a veteran pitcher, like Curt Schilling, might feel differently about a particular matchup. In 2007, Schilling shook off Varitek's call with two outs in the ninth inning and lost his chance for a no-hitter. That act of willfulness will most likely stick with Schilling the rest of his life.

The other way to think about Varitek's skill in working with pitchers is this: On May 19, 2008, he set a major league record as he caught the fourth no-hitter of his career. In the history of baseball, that has never happened before. Varitek was behind the plate that night for Jon Lester. Before that there had been the 2007 gem by Clay Buchholz, the 2002 no-hitter by Derek Lowe, and the 2001 no-no by Hideo Nomo.

Varitek said he was just "lucky," but there's more to it than that. When Varitek took that record, he broke a tie that included three Hall of Famers (Roy Campanella and Ray Schalk had three in regular season games, and Yogi Berra caught two during the season plus a perfect game in the World Series). When you're in that sort of company, more than luck is involved.

And then he has to come up to bat. Everybody loves to hit, but on top of everything else, he is a switch hitter so he has to be ready on either side of the plate. I am sure that hitting is important in his book, but it doesn't take away from what he has to do defensively, which he realizes is his most vital job.

Varitek has been at the top of his game for most of his life. In 1984, at age 12, he played in the championship game of the Little League World Series. In high school, as a third baseman and catcher, his team from Altamonte, Florida won the state championship. He went on to college at the Georgia Institute of Technology, and in 1992 he was National Collegiate Player of the Year and a member of the 1992 U.S. Olympic team in baseball.

In 1994 he helped lead the Yellow Jackets to the College World Series; his teammates included Nomar Garciaparra and Jay Payton. He graduated with a degree in management, not an inappropriate specialty for someone who plays his position in major league baseball.

Varitek was taken by the Seattle Mariners in the first round of the 1994 amateur draft, the 14th pick overall. As an experienced college and Olympics player, he bypassed the Rookie and Single-A minor league levels and went straight to Double-A for two seasons. He was promoted to Triple-A in 1997, and he was playing there when the Mariners made what was probably one of worst trades in baseball history, a good one for Boston but not so great for Seattle. The Red Sox unloaded reliever Heathcliff Slocumb for a pair of talented young players who would make major contributions for the club: Jason Varitek and Derek Lowe.

Varitek finished 1997 with the Pawtucket Red Sox, coming up to Boston for a one-game look-see at the end of the season. He joined the regular roster in 1998, as backup catcher to Scott Hatteberg. By the end of the season, the two players were splitting time behind the plate and in 1999 he moved ahead to become the first-string catcher for the Red Sox.

Through his years in Boston, Varitek has been consistent as a hitter, averaging about .267 with close to 15 home runs per year. With knuckleball pitcher Tim Wakefield on the staff, Varitek has typically caught four out of five starts in each season in recent years with a backup catcher (Doug Mirabelli and in 2008 Kevin Cash) assigned the tough job of knocking down Wakefield's dancing pitches.

Tek had one of his best years in baseball in 2004, batting .296 for the season and hitting 18 home runs. Most importantly, he managed the Red Sox pitching staff to the postseason and all the way through to victory in the World Series. In doing so he became the first and only player to have participated in the Little League World Series, the College World Series, the Olympics, and World Series.

As a free agent at the end of the triumphant season, Varitek signed a four-year deal for big money . . . and the Red Sox added a symbolic recognition of his importance to the team: He was named captain. He became only the third Red Sox captain in the modern era, following in the footsteps of Jim Rice (who served from 1986 to 1989) and Carl Yastrzemski (1969–1983).

On July 18, 2006, Varitek played his 991st game behind the plate for Boston, breaking Carlton Fisk's club record of 990. By the end of the 2008 season, he had gone past 1,300 games behind the plate and also held the team record for career putouts at 8,962.

In recent years, his offensive numbers have begun to drop; he had his least-productive year in 2008 when he batted only .220 for the season and drove in only 43 runs. But included in those totals were more than a few key hits over the season.

And consider, just as one example, the fourth and deciding game of the American League Division Series against the Los Angeles Angels in 2008. In that game, he caught all nine innings, handling a superb outing by Jon Lester followed by relief appearances by Hideki Okajima, Justin Masterson, and Manny Delcarmen.

In the fifth inning of that tense, scoreless game he came up to bat with Mark Kotsay on first base; after falling in the hole down two strikes, he took a ball in the dirt, fouled off a curveball, took two more balls, and then with a full count he hit a tough curveball from pitcher John Lackey into rightfield for a single. Kotsay scored on a groundout, and then Varitek came home on a double by Dustin Pedroia.

And then in the top of the ninth inning, with the playoff game tied 2–2, the Angels had a runner on third base with one out. Knowing the situation and knowing manager Mike Scioscia, I was fully expecting an attempt at a suicide squeeze. Varitek and pitcher Manny Delcarmen expected it too, and on a 2-0 count Erick Aybar tried to bunt while runner Reggie Willits took off from third. Aybar missed the pitch, which was a 96-mile-per-hour fastball inside at Aybar's knees, and Varitek chased down Willits and made a diving tag a few feet away from third base. That was the last chance the Angels had, as the Red Sox scored a walk-off win in the bottom of the ninth. And it was all in a day for a major league catcher.

And then in the ALCS, mired in a terrible slump, Varitek came through with a home run in the sixth inning of the sixth game to put Boston ahead and set the stage for the ultimate seventh game against the Tampa Bay Rays. Alas, the final game did not end well.

In today's game, being named captain is almost entirely an honorary position. In 2008, there were only three major league teams with captains: Derek Jeter of the Yankees, Paul Konerko of the Chicago White Sox, and Jason Varitek of the Boston Red Sox. That's good company and high praise.

Jason Varitek

Year	Team	Age	G	AB	R	H	2B	3B	HR	RBI	BA	
1997	BOS (AL)	25	1	1	0	1	0	0	0	0	1.000	
1998	BOS (AL)	26	86	221	31	56	13	0	7	33	.253	
1999	BOS (AL)	27	144	483	70	130	39	2	20	76	.269	
2000	BOS (AL)	28	139	448	55	111	31	1	10	65	.248	
2001	BOS (AL)	29	51	174	19	51	11	1	7	25	.293	
2002	BOS (AL)	30	132	467	58	124	27	1	10	61	.266	
2003	BOS (AL)	31	142	451	63	123	31	1	25	85	.273	AS
2004	BOS (AL)	32	137	463	67	137	30	1	18	73	.296	
2005	BOS (AL)	33	133	470	70	132	30	1	22	70	.281	SS, AS
2006	BOS (AL)	34	103	365	46	87	19	2	12	55	.238	
2007	BOS (AL)	35	131	435	57	111	15	3	17	68	.255	
2008	BOS (AL)	36	131	423	37	93	20	0	13	43	.220	
Total			**1330**	**4401**	**573**	**1156**	**266**	**13**	**161**	**654**	**.263**	

Year	Team	OBP	SLG	OPS	BB	K	TB	SB	CS	SH	SF	IBB	HBP	GDP
1997	BOS (AL)	1.000	1.000	2.000	0	0	1	0	0	0	0	0	0	0
1998	BOS (AL)	.309	.407	.716	17	45	90	2	2	4	3	1	2	8
1999	BOS (AL)	.330	.482	.812	46	85	233	1	2	5	8	2	2	12
2000	BOS (AL)	.342	.388	.730	60	84	174	1	1	1	4	3	6	16
2001	BOS (AL)	.371	.489	.860	21	35	85	0	0	1	1	3	1	6
2002	BOS (AL)	.332	.392	.724	41	95	183	4	3	1	3	3	7	13
2003	BOS (AL)	.351	.512	.863	51	106	231	3	2	5	7	8	7	10
2004	BOS (AL)	.390	.482	.872	62	126	223	10	3	0	1	9	10	11
2005	BOS (AL)	.366	.489	.855	62	117	230	2	0	1	3	3	3	10
2006	BOS (AL)	.325	.400	.725	46	87	146	1	2	1	2	7	2	10
2007	BOS (AL)	.367	.421	.788	71	122	183	1	2	0	4	9	8	9
2008	BOS (AL)	.313	.359	.672	52	122	152	0	1	0	2	3	6	13
Total		**.346**	**.439**	**.785**	**529**	**1024**	**1931**	**25**	**18**	**19**	**38**	**51**	**54**	**118**

PEDRO MARTINEZ
Pedro Jaime Martinez
(Boston 1998–2004; career 1992–2008,
active through 2008)

Primary position: P

Bats: R

Throws: R

Height: 5'11"

Weight: 170 pounds

First major league game: September 24, 1992

Born: October 25, 1971 in Manoguayabo, Dominican Republic

Pedro was my all-time favorite pitcher. I faced a lot of great ones in my career and I have seen many other fine pitchers from my seat in the broadcast booth, but I have never seen a guy dominate the American League the way he did at his peak.

His numbers are just incredible. To me it was an event every time he pitched; it was like a heavyweight fight. I couldn't wait for his turn in the rotation.

When he was with the Red Sox he was listed at about 180 pounds and 5-foot-11, but he was probably a bit smaller than that. He could throw a fastball at 97 mph and had a decent curveball, but he had the best changeup I have ever seen in my life.

Though at his peak he could do it, Pedro didn't have to throw 97 or 98 mph to win, because he was so smart. His ability to put the ball where wanted was excellent, and so even at 80 mph he could win.

Remember that when he was with the Red Sox he pitched in a league with the designated hitter and during what was—for some hitters—the age of steroids. For most of the time he was with Boston there was no one close to him.

Regardless of whether he had his best stuff or not on any particular day, he was not intimidated by anybody. It was mano-a-mano every time he threw a pitch and he wanted to be the winner. He wasn't afraid to drill someone if he had to.

I think the best game I ever saw him throw was September 10, 1999 at Yankee Stadium. Chili Davis got to Martinez for a home run

in the second inning, and that was it. One hit, one run, no walks, and 17 strikeouts; Pedro got the complete game 3–1 win.

Other than Davis's hit, Martinez made the Yankees look like fools. I have played on the winning side of no-hitters and I have been on the losing side of no-hitters. But I have never seen a game pitched like that. That was better than a no-hitter.

Another of the most dominating performances I have seen came earlier that year during the All-Star Game at Fenway. Martinez was the starting and winning pitcher for the American League and he faced six batters in two innings. In the first, he struck out Barry Larkin,

Larry Walker, and Sammy Sosa. In the second, he struck out Mark McGwire; after Matt Williams reached on an error by second baseman Roberto Alomar, he struck out Jeff Bagwell while Williams was caught stealing. Five strikeouts in two innings tied an All-Star record; he added the All-Star MVP award to his collection of hardware.

He has the highest winning percentage among any pitcher in the history of baseball with more than 110 wins; as of the start of the 2009 season he had 214 wins against 99 losses. That means he had more than two wins for every loss, a .684 percentage. With that record he is in sixth place in the history of baseball in winning percentage for hurlers with at least 1,000 innings. (The five above him are Spud Chandler, Dave Foutz, Whitey Ford, Bob Caruthers, and Don Gullett. Pedro sits above the greats of today and yesterday, including Lefty Grove, Babe Ruth, and Smoky Joe Wood. Further down the list are Roger Clemens at .658; Sandy Koufax at .655, and Randy Johnson at .648.

And he is also among the all-time leaders in strikeouts. As 2009 began, he was in 13th place with 3,117 Ks, tied with the great Bob Gibson and just one whiff ahead of Curt Schilling.

All of that production out of a man with merely ordinary stature: 5 feet, 11 inches and about 170 pounds; nearly all of the other dominating pitchers of the modern era are six feet or taller and heavier.

Martinez began his career at age 20 as a relief pitcher for the Los Angeles Dodgers in 1992. The Dodgers brass (including manager Tommy Lasorda) had doubts about whether Pedro had the right stuff for a successful career. Near the end of his rookie year, he injured his left shoulder swinging a bat and had surgery; he came back the next year to post a decent record of 10–5 from the bullpen, but after the season the Dodgers traded him to the Montreal Expos for second baseman Delino DeShields, a deal that has to rank up there among baseball's worst decisions. DeShields brought little to the Dodgers, while Martinez won the first of his three Cy Young Awards in 1997 as an Expo with a 17–8 record and a 1.90 ERA. In the off-season that followed, as he was ready to cash in on his success, the Expos traded him to Boston for Tony Armas and then–minor leaguer Carl Pavano.

He never had a bad year with Boston, but if you wanted to look at one very good season, consider 1999. He posted a record of 23 wins and 4 losses, with an ERA of 2.07 and 313 strikeouts and just 37 walks in 213 innings. He won the Cy Young Award again, picked up the pitching Triple Crown (most wins, most strikeouts, and lowest ERA), and came in second in the voting for Most Valuable Player. (He would win a third Cy Young in 2000.)

Depending on which statistic you want to look at his 2000 season was almost as good or better than 1999. He went 18–6 with an ERA of 1.74. Even his losses were impressive, among them a 1–0 complete game with 17 strikeouts and one walk.

Over that two-year, two Cy Young Award seasons, Martinez had a combined record of 41–10 with 597 strikeouts and a 1.90 ERA. And about half his games were at Fenway Park, a place not usually considered friendly to pitchers.

He had so many remarkable games. In the 1999 postseason, Martinez was hurt and did not start the fifth and final game. But neither the Red Sox nor the Indians starters were effective, and Pedro was brought in as an emergency long reliever in the fourth inning with the game tied 3–3. Unable to throw his fastball or changeup well, he relied almost exclusively on curveballs and he shut down the Indians with six innings of no-hit pitching to get the win and advance the Red Sox to the League Championship. There he threw seven shutout innings to beat Roger Clemens and the Yankees for Boston's only win against the eventual World Series champions that year.

And though across his remarkable career he never pitched a no-hitter, he does have one game in the books that is as close to perfect as possible. Pitching for the Expos on June 3, 1995, he retired the first 27 San Diego Padres he faced; that would ordinarily qualify as a perfect game, but unfortunately for Pedro the score was 0–0 after nine innings. The Expos scored a run in the top of the 10th and Martinez came out to try to close out the game and go into the record books. He gave up a double to the first batter however, and was removed for a reliever. Though the Expos won the game 1–0, baseball rules don't allow for a perfect game or a no-hitter that is less than a complete game.

He spent most of the 2001 season on the disabled list with a rotator cuff injury, returning to form in 2002 and 2003 and making an important contribution to the Red Sox 2004 World Championship season. And then in the afterglow of the Series, Pedro was gone to the New York Mets, who offered a four-year $53 million contract. His Red Sox totals were an astounding 117–37, a winning percentage unmatched by any pitcher in baseball history.

Of course there was also the infamous Game 7 of the 2003 American League Championship against the Yankees. Pedro had pitched well and Boston was ahead 5–2, but he was obviously tiring. Then-manager Grady Little came out to check on the pitcher in the eighth inning and Martinez told him he wanted to stay in the game; there are not too many pitchers who get to have a vote in that kind of decision. As it turned out, Pedro was cooked and so were the Red Sox as the Yankees tied the game. In extra innings Boston lost the game and the championship . . . and manager Little.

But the next year the Red Sox got to the World Series and Martinez had another beauty. In Game 3 against St. Louis he shut out the Cardinals through seven innings; he recorded the last 14 outs consecutively.

One more footnote: On June 28, 2006, Martinez pitched for the Mets against the Red Sox in his first appearance at Fenway since leaving. Boston saluted him and the fans cheered him in recognition, but the Red Sox knocked him out of the game with 7 hits and 8 runs in three innings and he was put on the disabled list.

That leaves the Red Sox as the only major league team that Pedro Martinez has not beaten in his career.

Pedro Martinez

Year	Team	Age	W	L	G	GS	CG	SHO	GF	SV	WHIP	ERA	
1992	LAD (NL)	20	0	1	2	1	0	0	1	0	.875	2.25	
1993	LAD (NL)	21	10	5	65	2	0	0	20	2	1.243	2.61	
1994	MON (NL)	22	11	5	24	23	1	1	1	1	1.106	3.42	
1995	MON (NL)	23	14	10	30	30	2	2	0	0	1.151	3.51	
1996	MON (NL)	24	13	10	33	33	4	1	0	0	1.195	3.70	AS
1997	MON (NL)	25	17	8	31	31	13	4	0	0	.932	1.90	CY, AS
1998	BOS (AL)	26	19	7	33	33	3	2	0	0	1.091	2.89	AS
1999	BOS (AL)	27	23	4	31	29	5	1	1	0	.923	2.07	CY, AS
2000	BOS (AL)	28	18	6	29	29	7	4	0	0	.737	1.74	CY, AS
2001	BOS (AL)	29	7	3	18	18	1	0	0	0	.934	2.39	
2002	BOS (AL)	30	20	4	30	30	2	0	0	0	.923	2.26	AS
2003	BOS (AL)	31	14	4	29	29	3	0	0	0	1.039	2.22	
2004	BOS (AL)	32	16	9	33	33	1	1	0	0	1.171	3.90	
2005	NYM (NL)	33	15	8	31	31	4	1	0	0	.949	2.82	AS
2006	NYM (NL)	34	9	8	23	23	0	0	0	0	1.108	4.48	AS

Year	Team	Age	W	L	G	GS	CG	SHO	GF	SV	WHIP	ERA
2007	NYM (NL)	35	3	1	5	5	0	0	0	0	1.429	2.57
2008	NYM (NL)	36	5	6	20	20	0	0	0	0	1.569	5.61
Total			**214**	**99**	**467**	**400**	**46**	**17**	**23**	**3**	**1.051**	**2.91**
Boston			**117**	**37**	**203**	**201**	**22**	**8**	**24**	**3**	**.978**	**3.11**

Year	Team	IP	H	R	ER	HR	BB	K	HBP	WP	IBB	BK
1992	LAD (NL)	8	6	2	2	0	1	8	0	0	0	0
1993	LAD (NL)	107	76	34	31	5	57	119	4	3	4	1
1994	MON (NL)	144.7	115	58	55	11	45	142	11	6	3	0
1995	MON (NL)	194.7	158	79	76	21	66	174	11	5	1	2
1996	MON (NL)	216.7	189	100	89	19	70	222	3	6	3	0
1997	MON (NL)	241.3	158	65	51	16	67	305	9	3	5	1
1998	BOS (AL)	233.7	188	82	75	26	67	251	8	9	3	0
1999	BOS (AL)	213.3	160	56	49	9	37	313	9	6	1	0
2000	BOS (AL)	217	128	44	42	17	32	284	14	1	0	0
2001	BOS (AL)	116.7	84	33	31	5	25	163	6	4	0	0
2002	BOS (AL)	199.3	144	62	50	13	40	239	15	3	1	0
2003	BOS (AL)	186.7	147	52	46	7	47	206	9	5	0	0
2004	BOS (AL)	217	193	99	94	26	61	227	16	2	0	0
2005	NYM (NL)	217	159	69	68	19	47	208	4	4	3	0
2006	NYM (NL)	132.7	108	72	66	19	39	137	10	2	2	1
2007	NYM (NL)	28	33	11	8	0	7	32	2	1	1	0
2008	NYM (NL)	109	127	70	68	19	44	87	6	2	3	1
Total		**2782.7**	**2173**	**988**	**901**	**232**	**752**	**3117**	**137**	**62**	**30**	**6**
Boston		**1383.7**	**1044**	**428**	**387**	**103**	**309**	**1683**	**77**	**30**	**5**	**0**

MANNY RAMIREZ
Manuel Aristides (Onelcida) Ramirez ("Man-Ram")
(Boston 2001–2008; career 1993–2008, active through 2008)

Primary position: LF	
Bats: R	
Throws: R	
Height: 6'2"	
Weight: 190 pounds	
First major league game: September 2, 1993	
Final major league game: Active player	
Born: May 30, 1972 in Santo Domingo, Dominican Republic	

Manny could amaze you. Manny could drive you mad. But Manny being Manny was one of the best shows in baseball.

Although his time in Boston ended on a sour note, he is one of my all time favorites. He was one of the best hitters I have ever seen in my life.

Above all else, Manny is a winner. He played his first eight seasons in Cleveland, and in those years the Indians finished in first place five times and made it to the World Series twice. Through the end of July in 2008, he had played seven-and-a-half seasons in Boston, in the much more competitive American League East division, and the Red Sox finished in first place twice and won the World Series twice. With the exception of his first year in Cleveland, he has never played for a major league team that finished with a losing record.

Through the start of 2009, Manny has played in 21 postseason series (ten division series, seven league championships, and four World Series). Playing for Cleveland, his side came up short twice; in 2004 and 2007 he was essential in bringing home the trophy for Boston.

In 2008, he engineered a way out of Boston and landed on the Los Angeles Dodgers. On August 1, 2008, the first day he was on the roster, the Dodgers were three games behind Arizona in second place in the NL West, with a 54–55 record. By the end of the regular season, the Dodgers had climbed to first place with a record of 84–78.

Photo by Brita Meng Outzen

Manny hit his first home run for the Dodgers on August 2, and for the month he was *en fuego* . . . on fire. He was 44-for-106 with seven doubles, nine home runs, and 25 RBIs for a batting average of .415 and was named National League Player of the Month. For the season in Los Angeles, he posted a .396 batting average with 17 home runs and 53 RBI. We always knew Manny was a great hitter, but numbers like these surpassed most of his hot streaks in Boston. He was even running out ground balls.

And then he advanced, along with the Dodgers, to the postseason, where Manny being Manny is usually the hottest ticket in town. Including his 2008 appearances in the NLDS and NLCS, he currently holds the number-one spot for home runs in the postseason with 28 in 378 plate appearances across 103 games. He passed former Yankee Bernie Williams, who had 22, in 2007; Williams still leads in postseason RBIs with 80, to Manny's 74. (For the record, the all-time leader in World Series home runs is Mickey Mantle; he hit 18 in 273 plate appearances in 65 games in the era before the division and league championships became part of the postseason. Mantle also leads in World Series RBIs, with 40.)

With the Red Sox from 1998 to 2006 Manny put up a remarkable record of production and consistency, with nine straight seasons with at least 30 home runs and 100 RBIs. He occupies second place on the all-time list of career grand slams with 20; at the start of the 2009 season he is just three behind Lou Gehrig in that category.

One of the classic Manny moments as a member of the Red Sox came July 21, 2004, when he made a dive from his leftfield position to cut off a throw by centerfielder Johnny Damon, turning a triple by David Newhan of the Orioles into an inside the park home run. I could watch that over and over again. It was one of the funniest things I have ever seen.

In second place among Manny moments: May 14, 2008 at Baltimore. There were two runners on and one out, and former Red Sox Kevin Millar hit a ball to deep left-center that looked like it would be over Manny's head; the runners were flying around the bases. But Manny ran at full speed toward the wall and grabbed the ball with his glove arm fully extended.

Nice catch, but it didn't stop there. He was still heading toward the cushioned seven-foot wall, and he used his cleats to climb it to stop his momentum. In the split second when he was at the top, Manny had the time to high-five a Boston fan sitting in the stands. Then he pushed off the wall and threw a strike to second baseman Dustin Pedroia, who had come out into short leftfield; Pedroia relayed the throw to Kevin Youkilis to complete a double play before baserunner Aubrey Huff could get back to first base. I know I've never seen that play before, and I'm pretty sure no one else has.

He works at his craft very hard. Some people think he is out to lunch, but that's not true. He is not dumb. He is very aware of his place in the game, not only with the Red Sox but in baseball history. I'll never forget the day of the victory parade in Boston after the 2004 World Series; we were at Fenway and Don Orsillo and I were doing interviews with some of the players at a rally. Ramirez came up to me and whispered in my ear that no Red Sox player had ever been the MVP of the World Series. He knew he was the first.

As a leftfielder, he was very good at Fenway Park and a bit of an adventure on the road. As any Red Sox fan knows, we've got a small left field in Boston and he handled the wall very well. Manny played shallow, which is the right thing to do at Fenway, and he got rid of the ball very quickly on balls that came off the wall or landed in front of him.

Born in the Dominican Republic, Manny grew up in the Washington Heights section of Manhattan, a long fly ball away from Yankee Stadium. He was a star at George Washington High School from 1989 to 1991; he was drafted by Cleveland in the first round of the 1991 amateur draft as the 13th overall pick. (Players drafted ahead of Ramirez included the Yankees' number one pick pitcher Brien Taylor, who never made it above Double-A ball because of an injury suffered off the field. The third pick was David McCarty, who bounced around as a bench player for six major league teams before finishing his career with Boston in 2004 and 2005. None of the other players selected before him had a career even approaching the numbers put up by Manny.)

He played just two seasons in the minors, hitting 44 home runs as he advanced quickly to Triple-A; he was a late-season callup to the Indians in 1993, going hitless as a DH in his first game against Minnesota. His second game, again as the DH, was at Yankee Stadium, and he got his first major league hit (a double) in the second inning and then banged home runs in the sixth and eighth inning. He had an uneven start in the majors in his first month, but he was the opening day rightfielder for the Indians as the 1994 season began and came in second in the Rookie of the Year voting that year. By 1995 Manny was being Manny, superstar.

Manny hit 236 home runs and drove in 804 RBI in 967 games for the Cleveland Indians; he hit a career-high 45 home runs in 1998. The next season was one of his best, with 44 homers plus a career-high 165 RBI, a batting average of .333 and 131 runs scored.

With Boston, Manny helped lead the Red Sox to the postseason in 2004 with 43 home runs, 130 RBIs, a .308 batting average and a slugging percentage of .613. And that year the duo of Ramirez and David Ortiz became the first American League teammates to each hit 40 home runs, have 100 RBI, and bat .300 since Babe Ruth and Lou Gehrig accomplished this for the New York Yankees in 1931. Also in 2004, Ortiz and Ramirez hit back-to-back home runs six times, tying the major league single-season record.

In 2007, Ramirez had a below-average year, finishing with a .296 batting average, 20 home runs, and 88 RBIs; he was injured in late August and missed most of the remainder of the regular season. But the rest must have done him some good when he returned for the postseason. In Game 2 of the American League Division Series against the Los Angeles Angels of Anaheim, Ramirez hit a walk-off three-run home run in the bottom of the ninth inning. And then in the fourth inning of the third and final game of that series, Ramirez followed Ortiz with back-to-back home runs off pitcher Jered Weaver. Overall, Ramirez batted .348 with 4 home runs and 16 RBIs for the 2007 post-season as the Red Sox won the World Series again.

Manny is Manny and would drive you nuts if you were his manager, but I'm also sure you would be thrilled to see him come to the plate. That was the case most of the time he was in Boston.

On May 31, 2008, before Ramirez turned sour on the Red Sox, he hit his 500th home run. It came off Baltimore Orioles pitcher Chad Bradford at Camden Yards. That makes three former Red Sox players in that exclusive club: Ramirez, Jimmie Foxx, and Ted Williams.

Just over a week later, Ramirez got into a public pushing match with teammate Kevin Youkilis that may have had something to do with Youk's intensity. In some ways, the two players are polar opposites. If Youkilis makes an out in a critical situation he's upset and angry; Ramirez would shrug and head for the bench, or the clubhouse, or a few times into the scoreboard room beneath the Green Monster. Manny also had a problem with the team's traveling secretary a bit later in the season.

He went public with complaints about the organization and about the intense fans in Boston; he also complained of a sore knee when medical exams showed no problems. And then on July 25, just a few minutes before a game against the Yankees, Ramirez pulled himself from the lineup. The Red Sox lost the game 1–0.

And so, very quickly, it went from "Manny being Manny" to an intolerable situation. He ticked off management, his teammates, and the fans. He forced the issue. The Red Sox didn't know if he would play the second half; they couldn't trust him.

Over the years, his lack of hustle at times was enough to drive me over the edge; you've got to run out ground balls or take the extra base when you can. On the other hand, when he was happy he had such a likeable personality, and most importantly he had so much talent as a hitter.

And then just before the July 31 trading deadline, he was gone. In a three-way deal, Ramirez went to the Dodgers and the Red Sox obtained Jason Bay from the Pirates. (Boston also sent outfielder Brandon Moss and pitcher Craig Hansen to Pittsburgh.)

Terry Francona held a closed-door team meeting before the next game, something he doesn't do often. The Red Sox went on to win the Wild Card and advance through the playoffs without Manny, but with significant contributions by Bay.

It was a sad ending for a guy who was very popular here in Boston. He ruined his reputation here in a matter of about two weeks. I'm sure he will be booed anytime he comes near Fenway Park or the Red Sox, but on the other hand you can't ignore what he did in Boston; he was a key reason for two World Championships all by himself and his presence in the lineup helped players like David Ortiz and Mike Lowell and others get good pitches to hit.

He's still a Red Sox hero, one of the best right-handed hitters the team ever had. But the ending was not pretty. One thing players, managers, and fans never like is when you quit on them.

Manny Ramirez

Year	Team	Age	G	AB	R	H	2B	3B	HR	RBI	BA	
1993	CLE (AL)	21	22	53	5	9	1	0	2	5	.170	
1994	CLE (AL)	22	91	290	51	78	22	0	17	60	.269	
1995	CLE (AL)	23	137	484	85	149	26	1	31	107	.308	SS, AS
1996	CLE (AL)	24	152	550	94	170	45	3	33	112	.309	
1997	CLE (AL)	25	150	561	99	184	40	0	26	88	.328	
1998	CLE (AL)	26	150	571	108	168	35	2	45	145	.294	AS
1999	CLE (AL)	27	147	522	131	174	34	3	44	165	.333	SS, AS
2000	CLE (AL)	28	118	439	92	154	34	2	38	122	.351	SS, AS
2001	BOS (AL)	29	142	529	93	162	33	2	41	125	.306	SS, AS
2002	BOS (AL)	30	120	436	84	152	31	0	33	107	.349	SS, AS
2003	BOS (AL)	31	154	569	117	185	36	1	37	104	.325	SS, AS
2004	BOS (AL)	32	152	568	108	175	44	0	43	130	.308	SS, AS
2005	BOS (AL)	33	152	554	112	162	30	1	45	144	.292	SS, AS
2006	BOS (AL)	34	130	449	79	144	27	1	35	102	.321	SS, AS
2007	BOS (AL)	35	133	483	84	143	33	1	20	88	.296	AS
2008	*Season*	36	*153*	*552*	*102*	*183*	*36*	*1*	*37*	*121*	*.332*	
	BOS (AL)		100	365	66	109	22	1	20	68	.299	
	LAD (NL)		53	187	36	74	14	0	17	53	.396	
Total			**2103**	**7610**	**1444**	**2392**	**507**	**18**	**527**	**1725**	**.314**	
Boston			**1083**	**3953**	**743**	**1232**	**256**	**7**	**274**	**868**	**.312**	

Year	Team	OBP	SLG	OPS	BB	SO	TB	SB	CS	SH	SF	IBB	HBP	GDP
1993	CLE (AL)	.200	.302	.502	2	8	16	0	0	0	0	0	0	3
1994	CLE (AL)	.357	.521	.878	42	72	151	4	2	0	4	4	0	6
1995	CLE (AL)	.402	.558	.960	75	112	270	6	6	2	5	6	5	13
1996	CLE (AL)	.399	.582	.981	85	104	320	8	5	0	9	8	3	18
1997	CLE (AL)	.415	.538	.953	79	115	302	2	3	0	4	5	7	19
1998	CLE (AL)	.377	.599	.976	76	121	342	5	3	0	10	6	6	18
1999	CLE (AL)	.442	.663	1.105	96	131	346	2	4	0	9	9	13	12
2000	CLE (AL)	.457	.697	1.154	86	117	306	1	1	0	4	9	3	9
2001	BOS (AL)	.405	.609	1.014	81	147	322	0	1	0	2	25	8	9
2002	BOS (AL)	.450	.647	1.097	73	85	282	0	0	0	1	14	8	13
2003	BOS (AL)	.427	.587	1.014	97	94	334	3	1	0	5	28	8	22
2004	BOS (AL)	.397	.613	1.010	82	124	348	2	4	0	7	15	6	17
2005	BOS (AL)	.388	.594	.982	80	119	329	1	0	0	6	9	10	20
2006	BOS (AL)	.439	.619	1.058	100	102	278	0	1	0	8	16	1	13
2007	BOS (AL)	.388	.493	.881	71	92	238	0	0	0	8	13	7	21
2008	*Season*	*.430*	*.601*	*1.031*	*87*	*124*	*332*	*3*	*0*	*0*	*4*	*24*	*11*	*17*
	BOS (AL)	.398	.529	.926	52	86	193	1	0	0	0	8	8	12
	LAD (NL)	.489	.743	1.232	35	38	139	2	0	0	4	16	3	5
Total		**.411**	**.593**	**1.004**	**1212**	**1667**	**4516**	**37**	**31**	**2**	**86**	**191**	**96**	**230**
Boston		**.423**	**.588**	**1.011**	**723**	**973**	**2656**	**10**	**7**	**0**	**41**	**152**	**67**	**144**

JOHNNY DAMON
Johnny David Damon
(Boston 2002–2005; career 1995–2008, active through 2008)

Primary position: OF	
Bats: L	
Throws: L	
Height: 6′2″	
Weight: 175 pounds	
First major league game: August 12, 1995	
Final major league game: Active player	
Born: November 5, 1973 in Fort Riley, Kansas	

Johnny Damon was one of my all time favorites. He came in with his long hair, looking like Jesus, and I said, "How long is this going to last?" Well, it lasted all through the 2003 "Cowboy Up" year and it turned out to be a statement about the "Idiots" who won the World Series in 2004.

That is pretty much the way they were, free spirits. They didn't let anything bother them. They called themselves the idiots. Some looked like they were, some acted like they were.

But Johnny Damon was a very good leadoff hitter. He could hit, he could draw walks, and he could steal and run the bases.

Another of the roles of a leadoff hitter—at least at the beginning of a game—is to see a lot of pitches so that the rest of the lineup can get some idea of the pitcher's stuff that day. In 2004 Damon saw an average of 4.67 pitches per at-bat. His on-base percentage that year was .380, a pretty good number, and he led the team in hits, stolen bases, and runs scored. He also had the third highest number of RBIs on the team, with 94—quite a high number for a leadoff batter. And he was also third in walks, behind Mark Bellhorn and Manny Ramirez. So he could get on base, drive in runs, and score runs.

His biggest weakness was his throwing arm. He couldn't throw a lick, but he sure could track down balls in the outfield. The fact is that you don't have to have a great arm to play centerfield. You can't hide a weak arm in rightfield but in centerfield if you have

speed, you've just got to get to the ball and get it to the cutoff man quickly.

He took offense when he was criticized about his arm, but let's be honest: It wasn't good. But overall he was an exciting and very important member of the team.

Damon had already proved himself as a fine major leaguer in six seasons with Kansas City and one in Oakland. He came to Boston as a free agent, one of former general manager Dan Duquette's final deals.

The four years he spent with the Boston Red Sox, from 2002 through 2005, were exciting to see, and he was a key member of the team that almost won it all in 2003 and then finally did in 2004. In those four years, batting almost exclusively in the leadoff position, he amassed 730 hits (including 136 doubles, 29 triples, and 56 home runs), produced 299 RBIs, and hit for a .295 batting average. He also stole 98 bases.

In one memorable game, against the Florida Marlins on June 27, 2003, he joined the small group of major leaguers who ever managed to pick up three hits in a single inning; in fact he recorded a single, double, and triple in the first inning of what turned out to be a 25–8 blowout.

Damon was the sort of guy who would lay it all on the line. A great example of this came in the 2003 postseason, in the Division Series against Oakland. It was Game 5 and the Red Sox had gone ahead with four runs in the sixth inning on home runs by Jason Varitek and Manny Ramirez.

In the bottom of the seventh, Jermaine Dye of the A's hit a popup to short centerfield. Damon came charging in hard, while Damian Jackson—installed the inning before at second base as a defensive replacement for Todd Walker—ran hard toward the outfield. The two fielders collided hard, and Damon was knocked unconscious. He was taken off the field in an ambulance, but not before giving a thumbs-up to the fans and the players. Damon was unable to return until the third game of the ALCS against the Yankees, and he was clearly not at full strength as the Red Sox fell to New York in seven games.

In the off-season, Damon let his hair grow and stopped shaving; he said it had something to do with migraine headaches he suffered as a result of the collision. In any case, long-haired bearded Damon set the tone for the 2004 season, when he helped lead the "Idiots" to the Promised Land. For the season he batted .304 with 20 home runs and 94 RBIs from the leadoff slot in the lineup.

The Red Sox had a hot-and-cold season in 2004 including a period of nearly three months in which they were a .500 team. But they got hot just when they needed to, in mid-August, and secured a Wild Card ticket to the playoffs. Damon was in fine form against Anaheim, going 7-for-15 with four runs scored as Boston swept the division series in three games.

The ALCS started out very bad for Boston as they lost the first three games to the Yankees. But then the Red Sox got hot again and clawed their way back to force a seventh and deciding game.

Across the first six games, Damon was in a bad slump, going 3-for-29, including eight strikeouts. But in the crucial back-against-the-wall seventh game of the ALCS against New York, Damon hit two home runs, including a grand slam in the second inning that took most of the air out of Yankee Stadium. It was that one shot, just a few rows far enough into the short porch in right field, that sealed the deal to complete Boston's amazing comeback from being down 0–3 in the ALCS and opened the door to the World Series. In the seventh game, Damon went 3-for-6 with six RBIs, two home runs, and a single.

Damon came through one more time in the fourth and deciding game of Boston's sweep of the St. Louis Cardinals in the 2004 World Series. With Red Sox fans all across the Nation cheering, he led off the game with a home run that ended up being the only run the Red Sox needed in a 3–0 shutout thrown by Derek Lowe and the bullpen.

After he left the Red Sox for the, ahem, Yankees, he had to cut his hair and shave regularly. He has also continued to put up some remarkable numbers for a leadoff man even as age has begun to catch up with him.

On June 7, 2008, Damon went 6-for-6 in a New York win against Kansas City, winning the game with a walk-off ground-rule double; with all of the great players who have been in Yankee pinstripes, that was the first time it had been done since 1934 when Myril Hoag knocked six. (Hoag was a reserve outfielder, on the team in Babe Ruth's last season in New York.)

The other thing that happened to Damon in 2008 was also remarkable. On July 6 he was placed on the 15-day disabled list with shoulder problems; it was the first time in his major league career he was shelved. The injury came on the Fourth of July when he collided with Yankee Stadium's leftfield wall trying to catch a long ball by Boston's Kevin Youkilis. The ball landed on top of the wall and then fell back onto the field for a triple; Boston won 6–4 and the Yankees were on their way to finishing out of the playoffs for the first time since 1994.

But we really can't hold a grudge against someone who was so critical to the 2004 Red Sox World Series season.

Johnny Damon

Year	Team	Age	G	AB	R	H	2B	3B	HR	RBI	BA
1995	KC (AL)	21	47	188	32	53	11	5	3	23	.282
1996	KC (AL)	22	145	517	61	140	22	5	6	50	.271
1997	KC (AL)	23	146	472	70	130	12	8	8	48	.275

JOHNNY DAMON

Year	Team	Age	G	AB	R	H	2B	3B	HR	RBI	BA	
1998	KC (AL)	24	161	642	104	178	30	10	18	66	.277	
1999	KC (AL)	25	145	583	101	179	39	9	14	77	.307	
2000	KC (AL)	26	159	655	136	214	42	10	16	88	.327	
2001	OAK(AL)	27	155	644	108	165	34	4	9	49	.256	
2002	BOS (AL)	28	154	623	118	178	34	11	14	63	.286	AS
2003	BOS (AL)	29	145	608	103	166	32	6	12	67	.273	
2004	BOS (AL)	30	150	621	123	189	35	6	20	94	.304	
2005	BOS (AL)	31	148	624	117	197	35	6	10	75	.316	AS
2006	NYY (AL)	32	149	593	115	169	35	5	24	80	.285	
2007	NYY (AL)	33	141	533	93	144	27	2	12	63	.270	
2008	NYY (AL)	34	143	555	95	168	27	5	17	71	.303	
Total			1988	7858	1376	2270	415	92	183	914	.289	
Boston			597	2476	461	730	136	29	56	299	.295	

Year	Team	OBP	SLG	OPS	BB	SO	TB	SB	CS	SH	SF	IBB	HBP	GDP
1995	KC (AL)	.324	.441	.765	12	22	83	7	0	2	3	0	1	2
1996	KC (AL)	.313	.368	.681	31	64	190	25	5	10	5	3	3	4
1997	KC (AL)	.338	.386	.724	42	70	182	16	10	6	1	2	3	3
1998	KC (AL)	.339	.439	.778	58	84	282	26	12	3	3	4	4	4
1999	KC (AL)	.379	.477	.856	67	50	278	36	6	3	4	5	3	13
2000	KC (AL)	.382	.495	.877	65	60	324	46	9	8	12	4	1	7
2001	OAK(AL)	.324	.363	.687	61	70	234	27	12	5	4	1	5	7
2002	BOS (AL)	.356	.443	.799	65	70	276	31	6	3	5	5	6	4
2003	BOS (AL)	.345	.405	.750	68	74	246	30	6	6	6	4	2	5
2004	BOS (AL)	.380	.477	.857	76	71	296	19	8	0	3	1	2	8
2005	BOS (AL)	.366	.439	.805	53	69	274	18	1	0	9	3	2	5
2006	NYY (AL)	.359	.482	.841	67	85	286	25	10	2	5	1	4	4
2007	NYY (AL)	.351	.396	.747	66	79	211	27	3	1	3	1	2	4
2008	NYY (AL)	.375	.461	.836	64	82	256	29	8	2	1	0	1	5
Total		.354	.435	.789	795	950	3418	362	96	51	64	34	39	75
Boston		.362	.441	.803	262	284	1092	98	21	9	23	13	12	22

DAVID ORTIZ

David Americo (Arias) Ortiz ("Big Papi")
(Boston 2003–2008; career 1997–2008, active through 2008)

Primary position: DH, 1B	
Bats: L	
Throws: L	
Height: 6'4"	
Weight: 230	
First major league game: September 2, 1997	
Final major league game: Active player	
Born: November 18, 1975 in Santo Domingo, Dominican Republic	

David Ortiz was just an average player for Minnesota. When you looked at him he was big and strong, but he was not feared; he was a relatively easy out.

The Minnesota Twins released him after the 2002 season; Boston pounced almost immediately, signing him as a free agent. But it didn't look as obvious then as it does now.

The Red Sox were taking a chance on him when they signed him. And he wasn't immediately a starting player in the lineup. On Opening Day for the 2003 season, Kevin Millar was at first base and Jeremy Giambi was the DH. Ortiz got the start at first base the next day and went 0-for-6 in a grinding 16-inning win over Tampa Bay.

When he arrived in Boston he still had a lot of holes in his swing; if a pitcher got a ball up and in on him he'd get an out. That's what Minnesota thought they had; they never would have let him walk if they knew how he would develop. When I saw him playing for Minnesota, I never imagined what he would become.

But the Red Sox worked with him and made him into a totally different hitter than he was with the Twins. And Ortiz also greatly benefitted from sliding into a lineup with Manny Ramirez and other strong hitters around him.

By the end of 2003, Ortiz had 448 at-bats, the most of his career to that point, and 31 home runs with a .288 batting average. And he

Photo by the National Baseball Hall of Fame Library, Cooperstown, N.Y.

went from relative obscurity to becoming a cult hero in Boston. He became Big Papi, Mr. Clutch.

If he had been in the lineup on a weak-hitting team, with nobody behind him, he wouldn't have been pitched to at all. That's what the Angels ran into in the 2007 American League Division Series; manager Mike Scioscia said when it came to the three-four positions in the Red Sox lineup, it was a matter of picking your poison: Do you pitch to Ortiz or to Ramirez?

Once he was on track here in Boston, Ortiz's accomplishments became the stuff of legend; he went through a period when he seemed to be getting the clutch or game-winning hit in almost every game. Nobody would leave the ballpark before the ninth inning if he was due to come up to bat, because they knew the Red Sox had a chance to win.

Ortiz was signed out of high school by the Seattle Mariners in 1992. He put in three years for Seattle's rookie and Single-A minor league teams. In 1996 he was traded to the Minnesota Twins for Dave Hollins (a journeyman infielder who made a brief stop in Boston in 1995, playing in five games before being given free agency and signing with the Twins).

Meanwhile, Ortiz continued to play in the minors, spending another four years advancing from Single-A to the Triple-A affiliate of the Twins and making occasional trips up to the big team. He finally became a regular on the major league team in 2000, hitting a respectable .282 with 10 home runs in 130 games. His average fell off to .234 the next year.

And then in 2002, after a year in which he batted .272 and clubbed 20 home runs and batted in 75 runs, the Twins released David Ortiz. Looking back, the move by the Twins to release Ortiz has to be one of the least successful management decisions in recent history. (The fact that Seattle traded him away earlier in his career doesn't look too great, either.)

We turned on the "way-back" machine to read the news reports in 2003 when the Twins let him go. According to the team, one of the reasons Ortiz was released was to make room for Jose Morban, a shortstop Minnesota selected from the Texas Rangers in the Rule 5 draft of minor leaguers.

Twins general manager Terry Ryan told reporters that they were unable to make a trade of Ortiz and had to release him. "I really would have liked to deal David, but I couldn't find a taker."

Morban, by the way, did not make the Twins team the next spring and ended up playing just one season in the major leagues: In 2003 he got into 61 games for the Baltimore Orioles, batting .141 in 71 at-bats. Morban hit a total of two home runs in his career.

When Ortiz arrived in Boston, the Red Sox had too many infielders. Shea Hillenbrand was splitting time between first and third base. Jeremy Giambi, younger brother of Jason Giambi of the Yankees, was supposed to play first and DH. That left Bill Mueller as an extra third baseman.

Giambi did not perform as expected, and Hillenbrand was traded to the Arizona Diamondbacks in May for pitcher Byung-Hyun Kim. That allowed Mueller to take over at third and opened up first base/ DH for Ortiz. And the rest, as they say, is history.

Ortiz batted fifth in one of the most potent lineups in recent years. Johnny Damon batted leadoff, followed by Bill Mueller for much of the season, and then Nomar Garciaparra. Manny Ramirez had cleanup. Mueller ended up as the American League batting champion, finishing with a .326 average.

Ortiz completed his first season in Boston batting .288 with 31 home runs and 101 RBIs in 128 games. In the magical World Series season of 2004, Ortiz had the DH role for the year, and improved to a .301 average, 41 home runs, and 139 RBIs.

His legend began to grow as he won several postseason games including a walk-off homer to win the Division Series against the Angels. Then in the AL Championship Series, as the Red Sox pulled off the greatest comeback in postseason history, he hit a walk-off home run against the Yankees in Game 4 and then a walk-off single in Game 5.

Since becoming a member of the Red Sox, he has been in the top five in the voting for MVP every year except for his injury-shortened 2008. In 2005 he finished in second place for the honor, barely edged out by A-Rod of the Yankees. The next year he was in third place, as Justin Morneau won the title. And he was fourth in the voting in 2007, as A-Rod won again.

In 2006 he had a monster year with 54 homers. He set a Red Sox record with 54 home runs for the season, passing Jimmie Foxx's mark of 50. (He tied Babe Ruth for the AL season record for homers on the road; 32 of his long balls came away from Fenway Park.) He led the league in both homers and RBIs, and batted .287 with a monster OPS of 1.049. And he continued to prove that he was a clutch hitter of amazing ability. He had five walk-off base hits (three of them homers) that year; that was more than most teams had for their entire roster.

In 2007, he hit "only" 35 big flies but raised his batting average to a career high of .332 despite battling torn cartilage in his right knee as well as injuries to his shoulder and other muscles. He also had 117 RBIs, and he helped lead the Red Sox back to the World Series.

After the end of the 2007 season, Ortiz had arthroscopic surgery on his knee. He came back at the start of 2008 and played well, but some of the pop seemed to be missing from Big Papi. (His protection in the batting order by Manny Ramirez was not as strong as in previous years; Manny was being Manny.) In any case, he started off slow but had a strong May.

But in a game on May 31, 2008 against the Baltimore Orioles, Ortiz suffered an injury to his left wrist—a partial tear of the sheath on the tendon. We could see it happen as he took a swing and fouled off a pitch. At one point it looked like he might have to have surgery, which could have ended his season, but he and the Red Sox chose to treat the injury with rest and rehab.

That was the bad news. The good news was that J. D. Drew stood up and stood in for Ortiz, posting some amazing numbers in June. In 26 games that month, he batted .337 with 12 home runs, 7 doubles, and 2 triples. June included an 11-game hitting streak that began on the day Ortiz was taken out of the lineup, and for the month he delivered 29 RBIs. Drew won his first-ever AL Player of the Month award. It was the perfect time for Drew to come through, and it probably saved the Red Sox season.

Bottom line for Ortiz: He played in about two-thirds of Boston's games in the 2008 regular season and he put up numbers that were about two-thirds of his recent "normal." But he was still a presence in the lineup, and the players around him in the batting order—Kevin Youkilis, Drew, and Jason Bay—benefitted from the caution with which he was approached by pitchers.

In the 2008 postseason, Ortiz was cold, sometimes looking like he was lost at the plate, although near the end of the ALCS he was making some hard-hit outs. Overall, he hit just .186 for the post-season with just a single home run; that long ball, though, was the bomb that put the Red Sox on track for their amazing recovery in the fifth game against Tampa Bay as Boston came back from a 7–0 deficit to win 8–7. Alas, though the Red Sox made it to the seventh game, neither Ortiz nor the other players on the team were able to get them their fourth win and a ticket to the World Series.

We can hope Big Papi will return with strong knees and wrists. His place in Red Sox history is already as solid as the championship hardware that has been hung on the walls since he arrived, and the World Series rings on his fingers.

David Ortiz

Year	Team	Age	G	AB	R	H	2B	3B	HR	RBI	BA	
1997	MIN (AL)	21	15	49	10	16	3	0	1	6	.327	
1998	MIN (AL)	22	86	278	47	77	20	0	9	46	.277	
1999	MIN (AL)	23	10	20	1	0	0	0	0	0	.000	
2000	MIN (AL)	24	130	415	59	117	36	1	10	63	.282	
2001	MIN (AL)	25	89	303	46	71	17	1	18	48	.234	
2002	MIN (AL)	26	125	412	52	112	32	1	20	75	.272	
2003	BOS (AL)	27	128	448	79	129	39	2	31	101	.288	
2004	BOS (AL)	28	150	582	94	175	47	3	41	139	.301	SS, AS
2005	BOS (AL)	29	159	601	119	180	40	1	47	148	.300	SS, AS
2006	BOS (AL)	30	151	558	115	160	29	2	54	137	.287	SS, AS
2007	BOS (AL)	31	149	549	116	182	52	1	35	117	.332	SS, AS
2008	BOS (AL)	32	109	416	74	110	30	1	23	89	.264	AS
Total			1301	4631	812	1329	345	13	289	969	.287	
Boston			846	3154	597	936	237	10	231	731	.297	

Year	Team	OBP	SLG	OPS	BB	SO	TB	SB	CS	SH	SF	IBB	HBP	GDP
1997	MIN (AL)	.353	.449	.802	2	19	22	0	0	0	0	0	0	1
1998	MIN (AL)	.371	.446	.817	39	72	124	1	0	0	4	3	5	8
1999	MIN (AL)	.200	.000	.200	5	12	0	0	0	0	0	0	0	2
2000	MIN (AL)	.364	.446	.810	57	81	185	1	0	0	6	2	0	13
2001	MIN (AL)	.324	.475	.799	40	68	144	1	0	1	2	8	1	6
2002	MIN (AL)	.339	.500	.839	43	87	206	1	2	0	8	0	3	5
2003	BOS (AL)	.369	.592	.961	58	83	265	0	0	0	2	8	1	9
2004	BOS (AL)	.380	.603	.983	75	133	351	0	0	0	8	8	4	12
2005	BOS (AL)	.397	.604	1.001	102	124	363	1	0	0	9	9	1	13
2006	BOS (AL)	.413	.636	1.049	119	117	355	1	0	0	5	23	4	12
2007	BOS (AL)	.445	.621	1.066	111	103	341	3	1	0	3	12	4	16
2008	BOS (AL)	.369	.507	.877	70	74	211	1	0	1	3	12	1	11
Total		.382	.554	.937	721	973	2567	10	3	2	50	85	24	108
Boston		.398	.598	.996	535	634	1886	6	1	1	30	72	15	73

KEITH FOULKE
Keith Charles Foulke
(Boston 2004–2006; career 1997–2008,
active through 2008)

Primary position: P	
Bats: R	
Throws: R	
Height: 6'0"	
Weight: 195 pounds	
First major league game: May 21, 1997	
Final major league game: Active player	
Born: October 19, 1972 at Ellsworth Air Force Base, South Dakota	

The 2003 season had been an uncomfortable and ultimately unsuccessful experiment; it was the year of the infamous bullpen by committee. And so, the Red Sox went out and hired Keith Foulke for the 2004 season. His assignment was clear: Take charge of the last out of the game.

He was a man with a mission, and for that critical 2004 season he was a hero in Red Sox Nation. Foulke appeared in 72 games during the regular season. He finished 61 of those games and earned 32 saves in 39 opportunities, with an ERA of 2.17 and a WHIP of 0.94.

And then there was the postseason, where Foulke pitched in 11 of the 14 games including five of the seven against the Yankees in Boston's amazing comeback in the 2004 American League Championship. He struck out 19 batters in 14 innings. And he yielded a grand total of one run in the postseason, a harmless point in the third game of the Red Sox sweep of the St. Louis Cardinals.

Foulke was not the prototypical fireballing closer, but he threw well enough to get the job done most of the time. He had a little hitch in his delivery, enough to throw off some batters, and his best pitch was his changeup. Most of all, he was a fierce competitor.

If he had retired or gone on to another team after the World Series victory, his place in the pantheon of Red Sox fans would be secure and unblemished—like Derek Lowe and Dave Roberts.

But in 2005, the year I called the "hangover" season, Foulke was less effective and battled injuries and personal problems off the field.

Photo by Brita Meng Outzen

When some fans began booing his lack of success he popped off about "Johnny Burger King."

And by 2006 he was only a bit player in an off year. He filed as a free agent after the season and signed a contract with Cleveland, but to the surprise of the Indians he retired before the 2007 season began; he unretired for 2008, signing a contract with Oakland.

Foulke was never very good at dealing with the media and after his remarks about fans his star was dimmed in Boston. But when he left town, he was saluted by manager Terry Francona. "I don't want to forget, or have anybody else forget, what he accomplished here," he said. "It was phenomenal what he did here in 2004. We don't win anything without him."

Keith Foulke

Year	Team	Age	W	L	G	GS	CG	SHO	GF	SV	WHIP	ERA
1997	*Season*	*24*	*4*	*5*	*27*	*8*	*0*	*0*	*5*	*3*	*1.514*	*6.38*
	SFG (NL)		1	5	11	8	0	0	0	0	1.746	8.26
	CHW (AL)		3	0	16	0	0	0	5	3	1.151	3.45
1998	CHW (AL)	25	3	2	54	0	0	0	18	1	1.087	4.13
1999	CHW (AL)	26	3	3	67	0	0	0	31	9	0.883	2.22
2000	CHW (AL)	27	3	1	72	0	0	0	58	34	1.000	2.97
2001	CHW (AL)	28	4	9	72	0	0	0	69	42	0.975	2.33
2002	CHW (AL)	29	2	4	65	0	0	0	35	11	1.004	2.90
2003	OAK (AL)	30	9	1	72	0	0	0	67	43	0.888	2.08
2004	BOS (AL)	31	5	3	72	0	0	0	61	32	0.940	2.17
2005	BOS (AL)	32	5	5	43	0	0	0	37	15	1.555	5.91
2006	BOS (AL)	33	3	1	44	0	0	0	16	0	1.188	4.35
2008	OAK (AL)	35	0	3	31	0	0	0	9	1	1.323	4.06
Total			**41**	**37**	**619**	**8**	**0**	**0**	**406**	**191**	**1.075**	**3.33**
Boston			**13**	**9**	**159**	**0**	**0**	**0**	**114**	**47**	**1.166**	**3.73**

Year	Team	IP	H	R	ER	HR	BB	SO	HBP	WP	IBB	BK	
1997	*Season*	*73.3*	*88*	*52*	*52*	*13*	*23*	*54*	*4*	*1*	*2*	*0*	
	SFG (NL)	44.7	60	41	41	9	18	33	4	1	1	0	
	CHW (AL)	28.7	28	11	11	4	5	21	0	0	1	0	
1998	CHW (AL)	65.3	51	31	30	9	20	57	4	3	3	1	
1999	CHW (AL)	105.3	72	28	26	11	21	123	3	1	4	0	
2000	CHW (AL)	88	66	31	29	9	22	91	2	1	2	0	
2001	CHW (AL)	81	57	21	21	3	22	75	8	1	1	0	
2002	CHW (AL)	77.7	65	26	25	7	13	58	2	1	2	0	
2003	OAK (AL)	86.7	57	21	20	10	20	88	7	0	2	1	AS
2004	BOS (AL)	83	63	22	20	8	15	79	6	3	5	0	
2005	BOS (AL)	45.7	53	30	30	8	18	34	5	0	1	0	
2006	BOS (AL)	49.7	52	24	24	9	7	36	2	2	0	0	
2008	OAK (AL)	31	28	14	14	7	13	23	1	1	2	0	
Total		**786.7**	**652**	**300**	**291**	**94**	**194**	**718**	**44**	**14**	**24**	**2**	
Boston		**178.4**	**168**	**76**	**74**	**25**	**40**	**149**	**13**	**5**	**6**	**0**	

CURT SCHILLING
Curtis Montague Schilling
(Boston 2004–2008; career 1988–2008, active through 2008)

Primary position: P	
Bats: R	
Throws: R	
Height: 6'4"	
Weight: 215 pounds	
First major league game: September 7, 1988	
Final major league game: Active player	
Born: November 14, 1966 in Anchorage, Alaska	

It's been a long time since anyone in Boston could shake the hand of a pitcher who has pitched on two Red Sox World Championship teams. Curt Schilling came to the Red Sox in 2004 and delivered that year, and again in 2007.

His stay in Boston wasn't long, but it was a very productive one. He was a major contributor to two Red Sox championships and he is one of the greatest postseason pitchers of all time.

Schilling never made it out of the starting gate in 2008 and underwent surgery in June; we don't know if he will pitch again, and if he does, as I write these words we don't know whose uniform he will wear.

But in any case, Curt Schilling was probably the most prepared pitcher I have ever seen. During the game you can see him sitting in the dugout with his notes on the hitters. One of my favorite pieces of video came during the 2007 season: Schilling was hard at work on updating his notebook while Manny Ramirez, sitting next to him, mugged for the camera. One thought about the game all the time; the other just showed up and played. Both have a pair of World Series rings earned in Boston.

Schilling was so intensely focused on days he was pitching; I remember when he first got to Boston he didn't want you to even look at him when he was getting ready to pitch.

Photo by Brita Meng Outzen

Even on days when he was not pitching you would find him in the dugout, watching and talking. That's not the case with all starting pitchers; some of them sit in the clubhouse watching the game on TV.

If I was a pitcher, he is the kind of the guy I would want talking to me on the bench. Any pitcher could benefit from the knowledge he has gained throughout the years and the preparation that he brings to a game. Someone ought to publish his notes when he is done playing; I think they would be very interesting.

In his prime, Schilling could throw a four-seam fastball at speeds as high as 98 miles per hour. His out pitch was a split-finger fastball that usually dropped below the strike zone.

He was clearly a big game pitcher. His record in the postseason was incredible. Including the 2004 and 2007 Red Sox games as well as appearances for Philadelphia in 1993 and Arizona in 2001 and 2002, he won 10 games and lost 2 with a total ERA of 2.23. I think when voters consider his postseason record he should end up in the Hall of Fame.

His performance in 2004, when his ankle was injured—the famous or infamous "bloody sock" game—will always be part of the story of the modern-day Red Sox. Whatever the facts of the injury and the sock, this much is certain: The great pitchers find a way to win even when they are not 100 percent.

Guys like Schilling know how to pitch. They know how to set up hitters. They know how to find something in the course of a game that is going to work for them.

In his time in Boston, he is tied with Pedro Martinez for the most postseason wins, with six. Martinez won his games in 1998, 1999, 2003, and 2004; Schilling's half-dozen came in 2004, 2005, and 2007.

Schilling grew up in Phoenix and attended a community college in state, leading his team to a berth in the Junior College World Series. In 1986, he was selected by the Boston Red Sox in the second round of the amateur draft, the 39th overall pick. But in 1988, as a minor leaguer, he was traded by Boston to the Baltimore Orioles (along with rookie outfielder Brady Anderson) for pitcher Mike Boddicker.

While Boddicker helped the Red Sox win the AL East that season, Boston was swept by the Oakland Athletics in the playoffs; Boddicker performed well for the Red Sox again in 1989 and 1990 before leaving as a free agent for Kansas City.

Meanwhile, Schilling began his major league career with three unspectacular seasons in Baltimore. In 1988 he was 0–3 as a starter, pitching just under 15 innings as a late season callup. The next season was similar, adding only another loss and less than nine innings to his experience. In 1990, working entirely out of the bullpen, he got into 35 games for the Orioles and posted a 1–2 record.

In January of 1991, he was traded with outfielder Steve Finley and another unproven pitcher, Pete Harnisch, to the Houston Astros for first baseman and DH Glenn Davis. In his one year with Houston, he again worked out of the bullpen posting a 3–5 record; he was far from a star but his strikeout numbers began to rise although he gave up 79 hits and 39 walks in just under 76 innings pitched.

Just before the 1992 season he was traded once again, this time from the Astros to the Philadelphia Phillies for Jason Grimsley. (The Astros sent Grimsley to the minors, and he was released after the season; he went on to be a journeyman middle reliever for half a dozen other teams.)

All this adds up to a not very auspicious start to Schilling's career. But it was in his first year with the Phillies that Schilling emerged as a successful starting pitcher. He started 26 times and posted a 14–11 record with a 2.35 ERA; he also dropped his hits and walks per inning to an impressive WHIP of 0.990, meaning an average of less than one per inning pitched.

In 1993, Schilling helped lead the Phillies to the National League pennant, upsetting the Atlanta Braves in the league championship and earning the MVP award for the playoffs. He lost the first game of the World Series to the Toronto Blue Jays, coming back to pitch a five-hit shutout in the fifth game; Toronto won the series 4–2.

In the years that followed, Schilling suffered from arm problems but by 1997 he was a dominant pitcher, striking out more than 300 batters in 1997 and 1998. But the Phillies were not a very good team overall, and Schilling asked to be traded. After the All-Star break in 2000, Philadelphia obliged him in a four-for-one swap: Schilling to the Arizona Diamondbacks for Omar Daal, Nelson Figueroa, Travis Lee, and Vicente Padilla.

It was the 2001 season for Arizona when the legend of Curt Schilling began to be written in large type. He went 22–6 with a 2.98 ERA, and then 4–0 with a 1.12 ERA in the playoffs against St. Louis for the division series and Atlanta for the league championship. And then in a seven-game World Series against the New York Yankees he beat Mike Mussina in Game 1, had a no-decision in Game 4 when Byung-Hyun Kim blew a save and then lost the game, and also had a no-decision in Game 7 as he gave up just two runs in 7.1 innings.

In that seventh and deciding game of the 2001 World Series, Randy Johnson came back from pitching seven innings the day before to win the game as the Diamondbacks beat Mariano Rivera with a walk-off bloop single over a drawn-in infield. Johnson and Schilling were selected as co-MVPs of the series.

After a 23–7 season in 2002 in which the Diamondbacks failed to make it out of the division series, and losing part of the 2003 season to injuries, Schilling was traded to the Boston Red Sox in the off-season. Boston sent three pitchers from their roster to Arizona: Casey Fossum, Brandon Lyon, and Jorge de la Rosa. In return, they got a player who would be key to their return to the Promised Land after 86 years, and again three years later.

Curt Schilling

Year	Team	Age	W	L	G	GS	CG	SHO	GF	SV	WHIP	ERA
1988	BAL (AL)	21	0	3	4	4	0	0	0	0	2.182	9.82
1989	BAL (AL)	22	0	1	5	1	0	0	0	0	1.5	6.23
1990	BAL (AL)	23	1	2	35	0	0	0	16	3	1.239	2.54
1991	HOU (NL)	24	3	5	56	0	0	0	34	8	1.559	3.81
1992	PHI (NL)	25	14	11	42	26	10	4	10	2	0.99	2.35
1993	PHI (NL)	26	16	7	34	34	7	2	0	0	1.237	4.02
1994	PHI (NL)	27	2	8	13	13	1	0	0	0	1.397	4.48
1995	PHI (NL)	28	7	5	17	17	1	0	0	0	1.052	3.57
1996	PHI (NL)	29	9	10	26	26	8	2	0	0	1.085	3.19
1997	PHI (NL)	30	17	11	35	35	7	2	0	0	1.046	2.97
1998	PHI (NL)	31	15	14	35	35	15	2	0	0	1.105	3.25
1999	PHI (NL)	32	15	6	24	24	8	1	0	0	1.126	3.54
2000	*Season*	*33*	*11*	*12*	*29*	*29*	*8*	*2*	*0*	*0*	*1.184*	*3.81*
	PHI (NL)		6	6	16	16	4	1	0	0	1.26	3.91
	ARI (NL)		5	6	13	13	4	1	0	0	1.096	3.69
2001	ARI (NL)	34	22	6	35	35	6	1	0	0	1.075	2.98
2002	ARI (NL)	35	23	7	36	35	5	1	0	0	0.968	3.23
2003	ARI (NL)	36	8	9	24	24	3	2	0	0	1.048	2.95
2004	BOS (AL)	37	21	6	32	32	3	0	0	0	1.063	3.26
2005	BOS (AL)	38	8	8	32	11	0	0	21	9	1.532	5.69
2006	BOS (AL)	39	15	7	31	31	0	0	0	0	1.216	3.97
2007	BOS (AL)	40	9	8	24	24	1	1	0	0	1.245	3.87
2008	BOS (AL)	41	Injured									
Total			**216**	**146**	**569**	**436**	**83**	**20**	**81**	**22**	**1.1374**	**3.4581**
Boston			**53**	**29**	**119**	**98**	**4**	**1**	**21**	**9**	**1.2148**	**3.9467**

Year	Team	IP	H	R	ER	HR	BB	K	HBP	WP	BFP	IBB	BK
1988	BAL (AL)	14.7	22	19	16	3	10	4	1	2	76	1	0
1989	BAL (AL)	8.7	10	6	6	2	3	6	0	1	38	0	0
1990	BAL (AL)	46.0	38	13	13	1	19	32	0	0	191	0	0
1991	HOU (NL)	75.7	79	35	32	2	39	71	0	4	336	7	1
1992	PHI (NL)	226.3	165	67	59	11	59	147	1	4	895	4	0
1993	PHI (NL)	235.3	234	114	105	23	57	186	4	9	982	6	3
1994	PHI (NL)	82.3	87	42	41	10	28	58	3	3	360	3	1
1995	PHI (NL)	116.0	96	52	46	12	26	114	3	0	473	2	1
1996	PHI (NL)	183.3	149	69	65	16	50	182	3	5	732	5	0
1997	PHI (NL)	254.3	208	96	84	25	58	319	5	5	1009	3	1
1998	PHI (NL)	268.7	236	101	97	23	61	300	6	12	1089	3	0
1999	PHI (NL)	180.3	159	74	71	25	44	152	5	4	735	0	0
2000	*Season*	*210.3*	*204*	*90*	*89*	*27*	*45*	*168*	*1*	*4*	*862*	*4*	*0*
	PHI (NL)	112.7	110	49	49	17	32	96	1	4	474	4	0
	ARI (NL)	97.7	94	41	40	10	13	72	0	0	388	0	0
2001	ARI (NL)	256.7	237	86	85	37	39	293	1	4	1021	0	0
2002	ARI (NL)	259.3	218	95	93	29	33	316	3	6	1017	1	0
2003	ARI (NL)	168.0	144	58	55	17	32	194	3	4	673	2	0
2004	BOS (AL)	226.7	206	84	82	23	35	203	5	3	910	0	0
2005	BOS (AL)	93.3	121	59	59	12	22	87	3	1	418	0	1
2006	BOS (AL)	204.0	220	90	90	28	28	183	3	1	834	1	0
2007	BOS (AL)	151.0	165	68	65	21	23	101	2	0	633	1	0
2008	BOS (AL)	Injured											
Total		**3261.0**	**2998**	**1318**	**1253**	**347**	**711**	**3116**	**52**	**72**	**13284**	**43**	**8**
Boston		**675**	**712**	**301**	**296**	**84**	**108**	**574**	**13**	**5**	**2795**	**2**	**1**

GREAT MOMENTS AND
GREAT TEAMS

1967, THE IMPOSSIBLE DREAM

Before there was Red Sox Nation and before the shoulda-coulda-woulda seasons of 1978, 1986, and 2003, there was the Impossible Dream of 1967. This was the team that brought baseball back to Boston.

Now someone out there just read the paragraph above and said: "What do you mean, brought baseball back to Boston?"

Of course I know that the Red Sox have been around since 1908 (and the predecessor Boston Americans since 1901), and that Fenway Park has been in operation since 1912. But let's look at a statistic that is in the box score every day but not usually in the headlines: attendance. The number of fannies in the seats is one of the most direct ways of gauging the level of devotion of the fans, especially in the days before every game was on television.

In 2008, as the Red Sox completed another successful season, moving on to the postseason for the fifth time in the past six seasons, they broke the major league record with their 456th consecutive complete sellout at home.

The total regular season attendance at Fenway in 2008 was also a record: For the first time ever, the Red Sox drew more than three million: 3,048,250 to be precise. That is officially 104 percent of capacity. Fans were shoehorned into the great cathedral of baseball; under the team's new management they have done some very creative things to squeeze more seats onto the Green Monster, on the roof, and in corners we didn't even realize were there. The overcapacity comes from people willing to pay for the privilege of standing for four hours.

Now, turn on the way-back machine. In 1965 the average home game attendance was 8,052 fans, a total of 652,201 for the year. In that season and all the way back to World War II, you could have walked up to the park five minutes before the first pitch of almost any game and bought a ticket.

When the great Ted Williams ended his fabulous career (with a home run) on September 28, 1960, total attendance was 10,454. On Sept. 16, 1965, with Boston limping toward a 62–100 record and

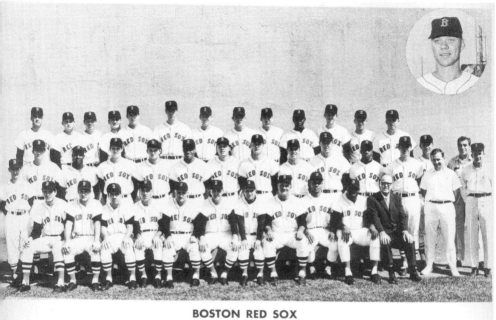

BOSTON RED SOX
1967 AMERICAN LEAGUE CHAMPIONS

BACK ROW: Gary Waslewski, Jose Santiago, Gary Bell, Dave Morehead, Jerry Stephenson, Jim Lonborg, Darrell Brandon, Russ Gibson, Sparky Lyle, John Wyatt, Bill Landis, Lee Stange, Hank Fischer

MIDDLE ROW: Billy Rohr, Joe Foy, Mike Andrews, Ken Harrelson, Elston Howard, Mike Ryan, George Thomas, Dalton Jones, Norm Siebern, Jose Tartabull, Batboy Jimmy Jackson, Dan Osinski, Equipment Manager Vince Orlando

FRONT ROW: Batboy Keith Rosenfield, Tony Conigliaro, Carl Yastrzemski, Rico Petrocelli, Coach Sal Maglie, Coach Bobby Doerr, Manager Dick Williams, Coach Eddie Popowski, Coach Al Lakeman, Reggie Smith, George Scott, Traveling Secretary Tom Dowd, Trainer Buddy LeRoux, Equipment Manager Don Fitzpatrick

INSERT: Jerry Adair

Photo by the National Baseball Hall of Fame Library, Cooperstown, N.Y.

a forgettable ninth-place finish, Dave Morehead pitched a no-hitter against the Cleveland Indians; it's in the record books, so we know it happened. But if you meet someone who tells you he or she was there, be skeptical: The published official attendance was only 1,247.

The teams of the early 1960s were pretty bad; the good news was that not many people seemed to care. From 1960 through 1966, the hometown team finished as follows: seventh, sixth, eighth, seventh, eighth, ninth, and ninth. There wasn't a winning season in any of those seasons; in fact, the previous Red Sox team to finish over .500 was all the way back in 1958 when they battled to a 79–75 record . . . and third place behind those Yankees.

The summer of 1967 was the Summer of Love in San Francisco and the moment when Americans began to hear about "hippies." That year the Beatles released *Sergeant Pepper's Lonely Hearts Club Band* and the Rolling Stones put out "Ruby Tuesday." The Vietnam War was going badly. The first successful heart transplant was accomplished.

And 1967 was the year of one of the most inspiring and heartbreaking teams ever to take the field in Boston. The nickname came from a well-known song—actually called "The Quest"—from the 1965 Broadway hit musical, *Man of La Mancha*.

So what did the Red Sox of 1967 do? They went from almost-worst ninth place the season before (26 games behind the AL champion Baltimore Orioles, just half a game ahead of the cellar-dwelling New York Yankees) to first place. And in the process, they would nearly triple their attendance for the season from a few years before, reaching 1,727,832 in 1967.

It was a white-knuckle ride. In those days, all ten teams in each league competed for just one ticket to the World Series. The Chicago White Sox, who had been in the mix for most of the season, were swept in a three-game series by the lowly Washington Senators. The pennant race came down to the very last game of the season, Boston against Minnesota.

When the last weekend of the regular season began, the Minnesota Twins were in first place, ahead by one game. To win the pennant, the Red Sox had to win on Saturday to move into a tie, and again on Sunday to go ahead. And one more thing: The Detroit Tigers had to lose one of their remaining games to get out of the way.

On Sunday, October 1 at Fenway Park, Jim Lonborg—who already had 21 wins against just 9 losses that season—was up against 20-game winner Dean Chance. Boston fell behind 2–0 in the early innings.

The Red Sox scored all their runs in the sixth inning. It began when Lonborg got a bunt single. Jerry Adair followed with a single to center, and then Dalton Jones had a shallow single to left. The bases were loaded with no outs for Boston's big man, Carl Yastrzemski, who came into the game with a league-leading 44 homers. Yaz didn't reach the fences, but he did stroke a single to center to score both Lonborg and Adair and move Jones to third.

Ken Harrelson reached on a fielder's choice, scoring Jones and moving Yaz to second. Sensing the chance for a big inning, manager Dick Williams sent in Jose Tartabull to run for Harrelson; there were still no outs. On the other side, Chance was replaced by Al Worthington on the mound.

In one of those situations that makes managers old before their time, Worthington proceeded to uncork a wild pitch, allowing Yastrzemski to move to third and Tartabull to second. And then he did it again; Yaz scored and Tartabull moved to third. Four runs were in.

Finally, Worthington got an out, striking out George Scott. But the inning continued. Rico Petrocelli drew a walk, putting runners on the corners. And then Reggie Smith reached on an error by Harmon Killebrew at first base; Tartabull scored. After a ground out by pinch-hitter Norm Siebern, the inning ended with Lonborg up to bat for the second time; he made an out to second. But five runs were in.

In the eighth, the Twins scratched out a run; they had four singles in the inning, but a double play erased the first runner. To show you how differently managers treated ace pitchers in those days, Lonborg was left in to get out of the mess. And Lonborg came out to finish the game: nine innings with seven scattered hits. Final score: 5–3 Boston.

And then Boston fans and Boston players had to sit around and wait for the results of the second game of the second consecutive doubleheader between the Detroit Tigers and the California Angels. Detroit had won the first game in a 6–4 nailbiter, and if they had beaten the Angels for a sweep, they would have ended in a tie with Boston and there would have been a one-game playoff between the teams to decide the pennant. But the Red Sox were on the side of the Angels, who won the second game 8–5 and delivered the AL Championship to Boston.

The Red Sox ended the season just one game ahead of both the Detroit Tigers and the Minnesota Twins. And the Chicago White Sox were just three back. It was the first time they would return to the Promised Land since 1946.

Before we look at the World Series, let's consider the 1967 team on that last day of the year.

Carl Yastrzemski was having his career year, one for the ages. He won the Triple Crown with a batting average of .326, slugging 44 home runs, and driving in 121 runs. He also led the league in on-base percentage, slugging, OPS, runs, hits, and total bases. Oh, and he was selected as Most Valuable Player.

Jim Lonborg, deservedly known as "Gentleman Jim" but also as a fierce competitor who had no fear of pounding the inside of the plate, led the league with 22 wins, in games started with 39, and strikeouts with 246. After the season, he was given the Cy Young Award.

Five of the players on that 1967 team—Yaz, Lonborg, Scott, Petrocelli, and Tony Conigliaro—are on my list as Red Sox Heroes; you can read more about them in this book. Conigliaro did not make it to the postseason; he had been seriously injured late in the season, on August 18.

And there were some other notable players on that team as well: Ken Harrelson, Mike Andrews, and Sparky Lyle among them.

In addition to the great talent on the bench, there had been one other important change in Boston that year. Dick Williams had been hired as manager; it was his first job at the helm of a major league team. He had played in the majors for thirteen seasons as a utility outfielder and infielder, beginning with the Brooklyn Dodgers, then moving to Baltimore, Cleveland, and Kansas City, before finishing his career coming off the bench for the Red Sox in 1963 and 1964. After two years coaching for Boston minor league teams, he was at Fenway and in charge.

Williams was a tough and demanding manager. He stressed the fundamentals and he got the most out of his players, at least from those players who could deal with his style; I know, because he was my first manager when I came up to the California Angels in 1975. I owe him a lot.

The 1967 World Series

The big show that year was a rematch; Boston had lost to the St. Louis Cardinals in 1946, their only other World Series appearance since 1918.

It was in the seventh game of that 1946 series that Johnny Pesky was the relay man on the throw from Leon Culberson; with two outs in the eighth inning, the Cardinals' Enos Slaughter dashed all the way from first on a hit to left-center to score the go-ahead run. Sadly, it was also Ted Williams' only appearance in the World Series and the great hitter played injured and ineffectively, batting only .200 with five singles and one RBI across the seven games. (For the 1946 regular season, he had batted .342 with 38 home runs and 123 RBIs.)

But in 1967, the Red Sox opened the World Series at home riding the wave of emotion that came out of their Impossible Dream season.

Pitching dominated, just as you might expect with Bob Gibson of the Cardinals on one side and Lonborg throwing for the Red Sox. But because Lonborg had started—and finished—the final game of the regular season, it would not be until the seventh game before the two aces faced each other.

That's not to say there weren't some great exhibitions of hitting; Yastrzemski batted .400 for the series with a .500 OBP and .840 slugging. He had 10 hits, including a pair of doubles and 3 homers. Those are incredible numbers, almost enough to carry his team. Almost.

And the Cardinals were no slouches, either. They had won 101 games in the season, and their lineup included Lou Brock, Orlando Cepeda, and Tim McCarver. They also had Roger Maris, a few years past his single-season home run record prime but still a potent hitter.

The first game drew 34,796 fans to Fenway Park on October 4. Bob Gibson, ace of the Cardinals staff, had missed most of July and August with a broken leg. He was matched against Jose Santiago, a right-hander who had a career year for Boston with a 12–4 record with a 3.59 ERA; Santiago put up his best stuff against Gibson—from the mound and at the plate.

The Cardinals drew first blood, scoring a single run in the third inning with a single by Lou Brock, double by Curt Flood, and a runscoring groundout by Roger Maris. In the bottom of the third inning, Santiago settled the score all by himself with a solo homer to left-center.

The score stayed knotted at 1–1 until the seventh inning when the speedy Lou Brock again led off with a single. He stole second base, and then scored on back-to-back groundouts by Flood and Maris. Gibson would end up with ten strikeouts and a complete game; Santiago would give the Red Sox seven fine innings and reliever John Wyatt contributed two more. Final score: 2–1 St. Louis.

A capacity crowd of 35,188 came to Fenway the next day to see Jim Lonborg start against Dick Hughes of the Cardinals for the second game. Hughes, a 29-year-old who was playing in his one and only full season in the major leagues, put up a 16–6 record with a 2.67 ERA during the regular season; he would be named NL Rookie of the Year by the *Sporting News*. He would retire because of injuries after an abbreviated 1968 season.

Lonborg, pitching on short rest after pitching a complete game to win the pennant for Boston, was nearly perfect. He did not allow a single baserunner for seven and one-third innings; Curt Flood worked a walk but no runs scored. With two outs in the eighth inning, he finally gave up a hit, a double by Julian Javier.

The Red Sox got the only run they needed when Carl Yastrzemski hit a solo homer in the fourth; he added a three-run blast in the seventh for good measure. The other Boston run came on a sacrifice fly by Rico Petrocelli in the sixth. Lonborg's line was one hit, one walk, no runs for a complete-game shutout. Final score: 5–0 Boston.

The series moved to St. Louis and resumed on October 7 for the third game. Playing before their home crowd, the Cardinals pulled out in front early and held on to win. They pounded Boston's starter, Gary Bell, for three runs in the first two innings. That was all they needed, as their starter Nelson Briles gave up just two runs and threw a complete game.

The Cardinals used their speed and punch to open the scoring in the first. Lou Brock led off the game with a triple and then came home on a Curt Flood single. The next inning, Mike Shannon hit a two-run homer to leftfield.

Boston scored a single run in the sixth inning when Mike Andrews scored on a hit by Dalton Jones. But in the bottom of that inning Lou Brock shook things up with a bunt hit and then took third on a wild pickoff attempt; he scored on a single by Maris. The Red Sox would score their second run on a solo homer by Reggie Smith in the seventh, but that was matched by a Cardinals run in the eighth. Final score: 5–2 St. Louis.

The fourth game of the Series rematched Bob Gibson against Jose Santiago, with the same results as the first game: a gem by Gibson, who allowed only five hits in a complete game shutout.

The Cardinals brought home four runs in the first inning, with scoring again begun by Lou Brock, who led off the game with an infield single to third base. Curt Flood singled, and then lefty Roger Maris went the other way for a double to left field to score both runs. The other two runs in the first came on singles by Tim McCarver and the light-hitting Dal Maxvill. The Cardinals got two more runs in the third. Final score: 6–0 St. Louis.

Coming into the fifth game, the Red Sox were down 3–1 in the Series, their backs against the wall. That was the bad news; the good news was that Jim Lonborg was ready to pitch again. The not-so-good news was that he was matched up against young Steve Carlton. At age 22, Carlton had just completed his first full year in the majors, posting a 14–9 record and 2.98 ERA; in 1994 he took his career record of 329–244 into the Baseball Hall of Fame.

Boston pushed across a single unearned run in the third inning after Joey Foy (who had singled and advanced to second on an error on a bunt by Andrews) scored on a single by Harrelson. The score stayed at 1–0 until the ninth. Carlton sat down after six innings, replaced by Ray Washburn, who held the Cardinals scoreless for two more frames.

In the top of the ninth, the Red Sox loaded the bases on a George Scott walk, a double by Reggie Smith, and an intentional walk to Rico Petrocelli. Elston Howard, a late-season pickup by the Red Sox in an August trade with the Yankees after thirteen seasons in New York, was in the game as the catcher. The veteran popped a single to right to score Scott, and the throw by Roger Maris to the plate was high, allowing Smith to come in behind him.

Maris partly made up for his error in the bottom of the ninth, hitting a solo home run, but that was the end of the scoring. Final score: 3–2 Boston.

The teams traveled back to Boston for the sixth game, held on October 11. The Red Sox were still facing elimination, down 3–2.

Boston sent out Gary Waslewski, a rookie who had only appeared in 12 games in the regular season; he was matched against Dick Hughes. The Red Sox jumped out to a lead with a solo homer over the Green Monster by Rico Petrocelli in the second inning. But the Cardinals doubled down with two runs in the third: a double by Julian Javier, a run-scoring single by Brock (followed by a steal of second) and an RBI single by Flood. In the bottom of the fourth, Boston showed its power with a set of solo homers by Yastrzemski, Smith, and Petrocelli to go up 4–2.

The Cardinals would tie the score in the seventh inning, when Lou Brock showed the power that went with his speed, hitting a two-run homer into the rightfield bleachers to tie the score.

But once again the Red Sox bounced back, scoring four runs in the bottom of the eighth; ten batters came to the plate against four Cardinal pitchers. The Red Sox scored their runs on base hits, a double, and a sacrifice fly and ended the inning with the bases loaded. Gary Bell pitched the final two innings for Boston without allowing a run. Final score: 8–4 Boston.

And then there was the seventh and final game, one of the most exciting setups in all of sport: two teams prepare for a game, knowing that one of them will go home with the highest trophy and the other will just go home.

The game brought back the two best pitchers on each team: Gibson against Lonborg, each with two wins in the Series. Lonborg was throwing on just two days of rest, while Gibson had been given an extra day off; that may have been the whole story right there. Lonborg struggled, giving up two runs on three hits and a wild pitch in the third inning. In the fifth Gibson hit a home run to help his own cause, and Lou Brock singled and then stole second and third before coming home on a sacrifice fly by Maris.

Boston picked up a run in the bottom of the fifth on a George Scott triple plus an error. But Lonborg could not hold off the Cardinals; in the top of the sixth he gave up a three-run home run to Julian Javier. Boston was able to pick up a second run in the eighth, but it was too little too late. When the game was over, the Impossible Dream had come to an end. Final score: 7–2 St. Louis.

The dream was over, and it would not be until 1986 that the Red Sox would make it back to the World Series and not until 2004 before they would win it all. But the 1967 team captured lightning in a bottle and all of Red Sox Nation owes its thanks to its many heroes.

1967 Boston Red Sox Regular Season

Player	Pos	Age	G	AB	R	H	2B	3B	HR	RBI	BA	
Mike Ryan	C	25	79	226	21	45	4	2	2	27	.199	
George Scott	1B	23	159	565	74	171	21	7	19	82	.303	
Mike Andrews	2B	23	142	494	79	130	20	0	8	40	.263	
Joe Foy	3B	24	130	446	70	112	22	4	16	49	.251	
Rico Petrocelli	SS	24	142	491	53	127	24	2	17	66	.259	
Carl Yastrzemski	LF	27	161	579	112	189	31	4	44	121	.326	MVP
Reggie Smith	CF	22	158	565	78	139	24	6	15	61	.246	
Tony Conigliaro	RF	22	95	349	59	100	11	5	20	67	.287	
Jerry Adair	IF	30	89	316	41	92	13	1	3	26	.291	
Jose Tartabull	OF	28	115	247	36	55	1	2	0	10	.223	
Dalton Jones	3B	23	89	159	18	46	6	2	3	25	.289	
Russ Gibson	C	28	49	138	8	28	7	0	1	15	.203	
Elston Howard	C	38	42	116	9	17	3	0	1	11	.147	
George Thomas	OF	29	65	89	10	19	2	0	1	6	.213	
Ken Harrelson	OF	25	23	80	9	16	4	1	3	14	.200	
Bob Tillman	C	30	30	64	4	12	1	0	1	4	.188	
Norm Siebern	1B	33	33	44	2	9	0	2	0	7	.205	
Don Demeter	OF	32	20	43	7	12	5	0	1	4	.279	
Tony Horton	1B	22	21	39	2	12	3	0	0	9	.308	
Jim Landis	OF	33	5	7	1	1	0	0	1	1	.143	
Ken Poulsen	3B	19	5	5	0	1	1	0	0	0	.200	
Jim Lonborg	P	25	39	99	7	14	1	1	0	8	.141	
Gary Bell	P	30	29	59	7	12	3	0	0	2	.203	
Lee Stange	P	30	35	49	2	3	1	0	0	1	.061	
Bucky Brandon	P	26	39	43	4	8	3	0	0	1	.186	
Jose Santiago	P	26	50	42	5	8	3	0	1	3	.190	
Dennis Bennett	P	27	13	25	1	3	0	0	1	4	.120	
Jerry Stephenson	P	23	8	16	0	4	0	0	0	0	.250	
Dave Morehead	P	24	10	12	1	1	0	0	0	0	.083	
John Wyatt	P	32	60	12	0	1	0	0	0	0	.083	
Gary Waslewski	P	25	12	11	0	1	0	0	0	0	.091	
Billy Rohr	P	21	10	10	0	0	0	0	0	0	.000	
Dan Osinski	P	33	34	9	0	3	1	0	0	1	.333	
Sparky Lyle	P	22	27	8	1	2	1	0	0	0	.250	
Hank Fischer	P	27	9	7	0	1	0	0	0	1	.143	
Galen Cisco	P	31	11	3	0	0	0	0	0	0	.000	
Bill Landis	P	24	21	2	1	0	0	0	0	0	.000	
Don McMahon	P	37	11	2	0	0	0	0	0	0	.000	
Total			162	5471	722	1394	216	39	158	666	.255	

Player	OBP	SLG	OPS	BB	SO	SB	CS	SH	SF	IBB	HBP	GDP
Mike Ryan	.282	.261	.543	26	42	2	0	4	2	5	1	8
George Scott	.373	.465	.838	63	119	10	8	3	6	10	4	13
Mike Andrews	.346	.352	.698	62	72	7	7	18	2	4	2	9
Joe Foy	.325	.426	.751	46	87	8	6	4	0	1	3	14
Rico Petrocelli	.330	.420	.750	49	93	2	4	8	3	9	5	4
Carl Yastrzemski	.418	.622	1.040	91	69	10	8	1	5	11	4	5
Reggie Smith	.315	.389	.704	57	95	16	6	2	3	11	1	7
Tony Conigliaro	.341	.519	.860	27	58	4	6	2	6	2	5	3
Jerry Adair	.321	.367	.688	13	35	1	4	4	2	0	2	10
Jose Tartabull	.287	.243	.530	23	26	6	6	4	2	0	0	4
Dalton Jones	.333	.409	.742	11	23	0	1	1	1	3	0	2
Russ Gibson	.263	.275	.538	12	31	0	0	2	2	3	0	7
Elston Howard	.211	.198	.409	9	24	0	0	1	2	3	1	4
George Thomas	.255	.270	.525	3	23	0	1	1	0	0	2	0
Ken Harrelson	.247	.388	.635	5	12	1	1	0	0	2	0	2
Bob Tillman	.224	.250	.474	3	18	0	0	0	0	0	0	2
Norm Siebern	.300	.295	.595	6	8	0	0	0	0	1	0	1
Don Demeter	.326	.465	.791	3	11	0	0	1	0	0	0	0
Tony Horton	.300	.385	.685	0	5	0	0	0	1	0	0	2
Jim Landis	.250	.571	.821	1	3	0	0	0	0	0	0	0
Ken Poulsen	.200	.400	.600	0	2	0	0	0	0	0	0	0
Jim Lonborg	.175	.172	.347	4	52	1	1	6	0	0	0	0
Gary Bell	.203	.254	.457	0	12	0	0	2	0	0	0	1
Lee Stange	.096	.082	.178	2	14	0	0	6	1	0	0	0
Bucky Brandon	.205	.256	.461	1	16	0	0	5	0	0	0	0
Jose Santiago	.222	.333	.555	2	15	0	0	1	1	0	0	1
Dennis Bennett	.115	.240	.355	0	10	0	0	1	1	0	0	3
Jerry Stephenson	.250	.250	.500	0	7	0	0	0	0	0	0	0
Dave Morehead	.154	.083	.237	1	4	0	0	3	0	0	0	0
John Wyatt	.154	.083	.237	0	6	0	0	0	0	0	1	0
Gary Waslewski	.091	.091	.182	0	7	0	0	1	0	0	0	1
Billy Rohr	.167	.000	.167	2	4	0	0	3	0	0	0	0
Dan Osinski	.333	.444	.777	0	4	0	0	0	0	0	0	0
Sparky Lyle	.250	.375	.625	0	4	0	0	0	0	0	0	0
Hank Fischer	.143	.143	.286	0	4	0	0	1	0	0	0	0
Galen Cisco	.000	.000	.000	0	1	0	0	0	0	0	0	0
Bill Landis	.000	.000	.000	0	2	0	0	0	0	0	0	0
Don McMahon	.000	.000	.000	0	2	0	0	0	0	0	0	0
Total	**.321**	**.395**	**.716**	**522**	**1020**	**68**	**59**	**85**	**40**	**65**	**31**	**103**

Player	Age	W	L	G	GS	CG	SHO	GF	SV	WHIP	ERA
Jim Lonborg	25	22	9	39	39	15	2	0	0	1.14	3.16
Gary Bell	30	12	8	29	24	8	0	3	3	1.15	3.16
Lee Stange	30	8	10	35	24	6	2	2	1	1.12	2.77
Dennis Bennett	27	4	3	13	11	4	1	1	0	1.35	3.88
Dave Morehead	24	5	4	10	9	1	1	0	0	1.47	4.34
Billy Rohr	21	2	3	10	8	2	1	0	0	1.54	5.10
Gary Waslewski	25	2	2	12	8	0	0	1	0	1.29	3.21
Jerry Stephenson	23	3	1	8	6	0	0	1	1	1.21	3.86
John Wyatt	32	10	7	60	0	0	0	43	20	1.18	2.60
Jose Santiago	26	12	4	50	11	2	0	16	5	1.27	3.59
Dan Osinski	33	3	1	34	0	0	0	12	2	1.18	2.54
Sparky Lyle	22	1	2	27	0	0	0	11	5	1.09	2.28
Bucky Brandon	26	5	11	39	19	2	0	11	3	1.31	4.17
Hank Fischer	27	1	2	9	2	1	0	2	1	1.20	2.36
Bill Landis	24	1	0	18	1	0	0	5	0	1.36	5.26
Galen Cisco	31	0	1	11	0	0	0	6	1	1.30	3.63
Don McMahon	37	1	2	11	0	0	0	6	2	1.53	3.57
Ken Brett	18	0	0	1	0	0	0	1	0	1.50	4.50
Total		92	70	162	162	41	7	121	44	1.22	3.36

Player	IP	H	R	ER	HR	BB	SO	WP	HBP	BK	IBB
Jim Lonborg	273.3	228	102	96	23	83	246	12	19	1	5
Gary Bell	165.3	143	70	58	16	47	115	4	4	0	3
Lee Stange	181.7	171	64	56	14	32	101	3	2	0	7
Dennis Bennett	69.7	72	32	30	12	22	34	3	2	0	2
Dave Morehead	47.7	48	24	23	0	22	40	3	2	0	0
Billy Rohr	42.3	43	27	24	4	22	16	3	2	0	2
Gary Waslewski	42	34	18	15	3	20	20	2	1	1	2
Jerry Stephenson	39.7	32	18	17	4	16	24	1	1	0	2
John Wyatt	93.3	71	30	27	6	39	68	6	2	0	5
Jose Santiago	145.3	138	61	58	14	47	109	3	2	0	3
Dan Osinski	63.7	61	19	18	5	14	38	0	0	0	2
Sparky Lyle	43.3	33	13	11	3	14	42	5	2	2	1
Bucky Brandon	157.7	147	86	73	21	59	96	9	7	0	7
Hank Fischer	26.7	24	15	7	3	8	18	1	1	0	0
Bill Landis	25.7	24	16	15	6	11	23	0	0	0	3
Galen Cisco	22.3	21	10	9	4	8	8	0	0	0	0
Don McMahon	17.7	14	8	7	4	13	10	1	0	0	0
Ken Brett	2	3	1	1	0	0	2	0	0	0	0
Total	1459	1307	614	545	142	477	1010	56	47	4	44

1967 Boston Red Sox World Series Statistics

Hitting

Player	POS	G	AB	R	H	2B	3B	HR	RBI	BB	SO	BA	OBP	SLG	OPS	SB
Jerry Adair	2B	5	16	0	2	0	0	0	1	0	3	.125	.118	.125	0.243	1
Mike Andrews	2B	5	13	2	4	0	0	0	1	0	1	.308	.308	.308	0.616	0
Joe Foy	3B	6	15	2	2	1	0	0	1	1	5	.133	.188	.200	0.388	0
Russ Gibson	C	2	2	0	0	0	0	0	0	0	2	.000	.000	.000	0.000	0
Ken Harrelson	OF	4	13	0	1	0	0	0	1	1	3	.077	.143	.077	0.220	0
Elston Howard	C	7	18	0	2	0	0	0	1	1	2	.111	.158	.111	0.269	0
Dalton Jones	3B	6	18	2	7	0	0	0	1	1	3	.389	.421	.389	0.810	0
Rico Petrocelli	SS	7	20	3	4	1	0	2	3	3	8	.200	.292	.550	0.842	0
Mike Ryan	C	1	2	0	0	0	0	0	0	0	1	.000	.000	.000	0.000	0
George Scott	1B	7	26	3	6	1	1	0	0	3	6	.231	.310	.346	0.656	0
Norm Siebern	OF	3	3	0	1	0	0	0	1	0	0	.333	.333	.333	0.666	0
Reggie Smith	OF	7	24	3	6	1	0	2	3	2	2	.250	.308	.542	0.850	0
Jose Tartabull	OF	7	13	1	2	0	0	0	0	1	2	.154	.214	.154	0.368	0
George Thomas	OF	2	2	0	0	0	0	0	0	0	1	.000	.000	.000	0.000	0
Carl Yastrzemski	OF	7	25	4	10	2	0	3	5	4	1	.400	.500	.840	1.340	0
Gary Bell	P	3	0	0	0	0	0	0	0	0	0					0
Ken Brett	P	2	0	0	0	0	0	0	0	0	0					0
Jim Lonborg	P	3	9	0	0	0	0	0	0	0	7	.000	.000	.000	0.000	0
Dave Morehead	P	2	0	0	0	0	0	0	0	0	0					0
Dan Osinski	P	2	0	0	0	0	0	0	0	0	0					0
Jose Santiago	P	3	2	1	1	0	0	1	1	0	1	.500	.500	2.000	2.500	0
Lee Stange	P	1	0	0	0	0	0	0	0	0	0					0
Jerry Stephenson	P	1	0	0	0	0	0	0	0	0	0					0
Gary Waslewski	P	2	1	0	0	0	0	0	0	0	1	.000	.500	.000	0.500	0
John Wyatt	P	2	0	0	0	0	0	0	0	0	0					0
Total		**7**	**222**	**21**	**48**	**6**	**1**	**8**	**19**	**17**	**49**	**.216**	**.276**	**.360**	**0.636**	**1**

Pitching

Player	W	L	G	GS	CG	SV	IP	H	ER	BB	SO	WHIP	ERA
Jim Lonborg	2	1	3	3	2	0	24	14	7	2	11	0.67	2.63
Jose Santiago	0	2	3	2	0	0	9.7	16	6	3	6	1.96	5.57
Gary Waslewski	0	0	2	1	0	0	8.3	4	2	2	7	0.72	2.17
Gary Bell	0	1	3	1	0	1	5.3	8	3	1	1	1.70	5.09
John Wyatt	1	0	2	0	0	0	3.7	1	2	3	1	1.08	4.86
Dave Morehead	0	0	2	0	0	0	3.3	0	0	4	3	1.21	0.00
Lee Stange	0	0	1	0	0	0	2	3	0	0	0	1.50	0.00
Jerry Stephenson	0	0	1	0	0	0	2	3	2	1	0	2.00	9.00
Ken Brett	0	0	2	0	0	0	1.3	0	0	1	1	0.77	0.00
Dan Osinski	0	0	2	0	0	0	1.3	2	1	0	0	1.54	6.92
Total	**3**	**4**	**7**	**7**	**2**	**1**	**61**	**51**	**23**	**17**	**30**	**1.11**	**3.39**

DAVE HENDERSON
David Lee Henderson (Hendu)
(Boston 1986–1987; career 1981–1994)

Primary position: OF	
Bats: R	
Throws: R	
Height: 6'2"	
Weight: 220 pounds	
First major league game: April 9, 1981	
Final major league game: July 29, 1994	
Born: July 21, 1958 in Merced, California	

Eighteen years before The Steal by Dave Roberts, there was The Homer by Hendu. In both great moments in Red Sox history, it was a part-time player who rose to the occasion.

Dave Henderson was acquired by the Red Sox from the Seattle Mariners very late in the season, on August 19, 1986. Boston dealt promising shortstop Rey Quinones—who never lived up to his potential—and some minor league prospects for Henderson and Spike Owen. It was a great short-term trade for the Red Sox.

Hendu filled in from time to time for Tony Armas Sr. in centerfield but didn't bring much of a bat; in 51 regular season appearances he had ten hits and one home run, for a batting average of .196.

But fast-forward to Game 5 of the 1986 American League Championship Series against the California Angels; the Red Sox were one game away from elimination, down 3 games to 1. Henderson had come in to replace an injured Armas in centerfield in the bottom of the fifth inning. The Red Sox were clinging to a 2–1 lead.

In the sixth inning, Henderson went back to the wall to catch a long fly ball by Bobby Grich for what should have been the third out of the inning; instead the ball landed briefly in the palm of his glove and then deflected off and over the wall for a two-run homer that put the Angels up 3–2.

Come the ninth inning, it was the Red Sox who were up against the wall; by this time California was ahead 5–2. Bill Buckner singled to start the inning, and after Jim Rice was called out on strikes,

Photo by the National Baseball Hall of Fame Library, Cooperstown, N.Y.

former Angel Don Baylor hit a two-run homer to bring the Red Sox to within one run, at 5–4.

Dwight Evans popped out to third and the Red Sox were down to their last out. Catcher Rich Gedman kept the game alive when he was hit by a pitch. That brought Henderson to the plate, with the chance to make up for the Grich homer; that is, of course, exactly how the story worked out.

The count went to 2–2; the Red Sox were down to the final strike of the game and the series. Hendu swung and lofted the ball deep to left field to put the Sox ahead 6–5. Henderson was a bit excited, running toward first and even trotting backwards for a few steps, enjoying the arc of the ball over the fence.

Of course, with the Red Sox it was not quite that simple. The Angels managed to tie the score in the bottom of the ninth, and the game extended to the eleventh. Once again the Red Sox received a gift runner, when Don Baylor was hit by a pitch. Evans singled to center, and Gedman reached base on what was ruled a bunt single. The bases were loaded . . . and up came Hendu one more time. He hit a sacrifice fly to centerfield and Baylor scored what turned out to be the winning run.

The shell-shocked Angels returned to Boston for the final two games of the league championship and were blown away 10–4 and 8–1. It would have been an even greater story if the Red Sox had managed to defeat the New York Mets in the World Series that year . . . but that did not happen.

The Red Sox traded Henderson to the San Francisco Giants on September 1, 1987, but Hendu will forever have his moment in Red Sox Nation lore.

Dave Henderson

Year	Team	Age	G	AB	R	H	2B	3B	HR	RBI	BA	
1981	SEA (AL)	22	59	126	17	21	3	0	6	13	.167	
1982	SEA (AL)	23	104	324	47	82	17	1	14	48	.253	
1983	SEA (AL)	24	137	484	50	130	24	5	17	55	.269	
1984	SEA (AL)	25	112	350	42	98	23	0	14	43	.280	
1985	SEA (AL)	26	139	502	70	121	28	2	14	68	.241	
1986	*Season*	*27*	*139*	*388*	*59*	*103*	*22*	*4*	*15*	*47*	*.265*	
	SEA (AL)		103	337	51	93	19	4	14	44	.276	
	BOS (AL)		36	51	8	10	3	0	1	3	.196	
1987	*Season*	*28*	*90*	*205*	*32*	*48*	*12*	*0*	*8*	*26*	*.234*	
	BOS (AL)		75	184	30	43	10	0	8	25	.234	
	SFG (NL)		15	21	2	5	2	0	0	1	.238	
1988	OAK (AL)	29	146	507	100	154	38	1	24	94	.304	
1989	OAK (AL)	30	152	579	77	145	24	3	15	80	.250	
1990	OAK (AL)	31	127	450	65	122	28	0	20	63	.271	
1991	OAK (AL)	32	150	572	86	158	33	0	25	85	.276	AS
1992	OAK (AL)	33	20	63	1	9	1	0	0	2	.143	
1993	OAK (AL)	34	107	382	37	84	19	0	20	53	.220	
1994	KCR (AL)	35	56	198	27	49	14	1	5	31	.247	
Total			1538	5130	710	1324	286	17	197	708	.258	
Boston			111	235	38	53	13	0	9	28	.226	

Year	Team	OBP	SLG	OPS	BB	SO	TB	SB	CS	SH	SF	IBB	HBP	GDP
1981	SEA (AL)	.264	.333	.597	16	24	42	2	1	1	1	1	1	4
1982	SEA (AL)	.327	.441	.768	36	67	143	2	5	1	1	2	0	5
1983	SEA (AL)	.306	.444	.750	28	93	215	9	3	2	6	3	1	5
1984	SEA (AL)	.320	.466	.786	19	56	163	5	5	2	1	0	2	4
1985	SEA (AL)	.310	.388	.698	48	104	195	6	1	1	2	2	3	11
1986	*Season*	*.335*	*.459*	*.794*	*39*	*110*	*178*	*2*	*3*	*2*	*1*	*4*	*2*	*6*
	SEA (AL)	.350	.481	.831	37	95	162	1	3	1	1	4	2	5
	BOS (AL)	.226	.314	.540	2	15	16	1	0	1	0	0	0	1
1987	*Season*	*.329*	*.410*	*.739*	*30*	*53*	*84*	*3*	*1*	*1*	*2*	*0*	*0*	*3*
	BOS (AL)	.313	.418	.731	22	48	77	1	1	1	2	0	0	3
	SFG (NL)	.448	.333	.781	8	5	7	2	0	0	0	0	0	0
1988	OAK (AL)	.363	.525	.888	47	92	266	2	4	5	7	1	4	14
1989	OAK (AL)	.315	.380	.695	54	131	220	8	5	1	6	1	3	13
1990	OAK (AL)	.331	.467	.798	40	105	210	3	1	1	2	1	1	5
1991	OAK (AL)	.346	.465	.811	58	113	266	6	6	1	2	3	4	9
1992	OAK (AL)	.169	.159	.328	2	16	10	0	0	0	0	0	0	0
1993	OAK (AL)	.275	.427	.702	32	113	163	0	3	0	8	0	0	1
1994	KCR (AL)	.304	.404	.708	16	28	80	2	0	1	2	1	1	3
Total		**.320**	**.436**	**.756**	**465**	**1105**	**2235**	**50**	**38**	**19**	**41**	**19**	**22**	**83**
Boston		**.295**	**.396**	**.691**	**24**	**63**	**93**	**2**	**1**	**2**	**2**	**0**	**0**	**4**

DAVE ROBERTS AND "THE STEAL"

David Ray Roberts
(Boston 2004; career 1999–2008,
active through 2008)

Bats: L	
Throws: L	
Height: 5'10"	
Weight: 180 pounds	
First major league game: August 7, 1999	
Final major league game: Active player	
Born: May 31, 1972 in Okinawa, Japan	
Boston Red Sox Hall of Fame: 2006	

The Steal is the most famous act of robbery in Red Sox history, and maybe in all of baseball history.

That stolen base is one of the great moments in Red Sox history. Without Dave Roberts' theft of second base in the bottom of the ninth inning of Game 4 of the 2004 American League Championship, the Red Sox might well have been swept by the Yankees. Instead, the Sox rallied and won the game . . . and the next three . . . and went on to win their first World Series since 1918.

You could not have scripted a more dramatic setting. The Red Sox had lost the first three games of the ALCS, and they were losing 4–3 in what could have been their last game of the season. On the mound for the Yankees was Mariano Rivera, who already has the key to the Hall of Fame as perhaps the greatest closer of all time; he had been brought into the game in the eighth with hopes of a six-out save.

Rivera had not walked a man in the postseason since 2001, and he had mowed down the Minnesota Twins in the division series of 2004, giving up just two hits in 5.2 innings with an ERA of goose eggs: 0.00.

And so, what does Rivera do with Kevin Millar, one of the chief instigators of Boston's band of "Idiots"? He walks him on five pitches.

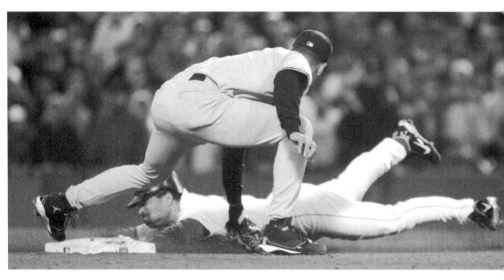

Photo by Brita Meng Outzen

Dave Roberts, age 32 at the time, had been acquired by the Red Sox from the Los Angeles Dodgers just minutes before the July 31 trading deadline; many fans may not have even noticed, since that was also the day that Nomar Garciaparra was traded away to the Chicago Cubs (for Orlando Cabrera and Doug Mientkiewicz).

Roberts was intended as a backup outfielder; Dirt Dog Trot Nixon was injured at the time and Boston needed some help. Roberts, like Nixon, was a left-handed hitter but he did not have much pop at the plate; in parts of five seasons in the majors with Cleveland and then the Dodgers he had hit 13 home runs and had batted about .250. But he had speed, something the Red Sox seriously lacked.

He had made only one appearance in the playoffs, as a pinch runner in the second game of the division series against the Angels, and otherwise had sat on the bench in all three of the league championship games against the Yankees. But when Millar drew the walk, manager Terry Francona sent Roberts to first base as a runner.

"When I was with the Dodgers," Roberts later told *Boston Globe* writer Bob Ryan, "Maury Wills once told me that there will come a point in my career when everyone in the ballpark will know that I have to steal a base. When I got out there, I knew that was what Maury Wills was talking about."

And so came the fourth game of the ALCS on October 17, 2004, at Fenway Park. There was no doubt about why Roberts had been sent in. Rivera threw over to first and Roberts dove back. Rivera threw over a second time and nearly picked him off. And then he threw over a third time.

"I knew that after three throws they weren't going to pitch out," Roberts said. "I took my standard three-and-a-half-step lead, and when he went to the plate, I took off. I got a great jump."

It was actually quite a close play at second base. Jorge Posada made a strong throw and Derek Jeter put down a great swipe tag, but umpire Joe West called Roberts safe.

Of course, The Steal was not enough. The next batter, Bill Mueller, came through with a single to center, and Roberts turned on the jets to score from second to tie the game.

The Red Sox almost ended the game right there. Mientkiewicz batted for Mark Bellhorn and put down a sacrifice bunt that moved Mueller into scoring position at second. Johnny Damon reached base on an error by Yankee first baseman Tony Clark and Mueller moved to third. Orlando Cabrera struck out and Manny Ramirez was walked, which loaded the bases for David Ortiz. All of Fenway waited for Big Papi to give the Red Sox a walk-off win, but instead he popped out to second base.

But in the 12th inning, the Red Sox lineup had gone around once again. Ramirez led off with a single to left, and then Big Papi came through with his second game-winning walk-off home run of the 2004 postseason.

It was a victory for the ages and it set the stage for the end of 86 years of frustration. But it took The Steal to make it possible.

Dave Roberts moved on to the San Diego Padres for the 2005 and 2006 seasons and played for the San Francisco Giants in 2007 and 2008.

On June 15, 2007, he returned to Fenway Park with the Giants for an interleague game, receiving a standing ovation from Red Sox fans every time he came up to bat. Batting leadoff for the Giants, he got a single off a Julian Tavarez fastball. Jason Varitek made a snap throw behind Roberts almost picking him off; Roberts scored on a double.

Dave Roberts

Year	Team	Age	G	AB	R	H	2B	3B	HR	RBI	BA
1999	CLE (AL)	27	41	143	26	34	4	0	2	12	.238
2000	CLE (AL)	28	19	10	1	2	0	0	0	0	.200
2001	CLE (AL)	29	15	12	3	4	1	0	0	2	.333
2002	LAD (NL)	30	127	422	63	117	14	7	3	34	.277
2003	LAD (NL)	31	107	388	56	97	6	5	2	16	.250
2004	*Season*	*32*	*113*	*319*	*64*	*81*	*14*	*7*	*4*	*35*	*.254*
	LAD (NL)		68	233	45	59	4	7	2	21	.253
	BOS (AL)		45	86	19	22	10	0	2	14	.256
2005	SDP (NL)	33	115	411	65	113	19	10	8	38	.275
2006	SDP (NL)	34	129	499	80	146	18	13	2	44	.293
2007	SFG (NL)	35	114	396	61	103	17	9	2	23	.260
2008	SFG (NL)	36	52	107	18	24	2	2	0	9	.224
Total			**832**	**2707**	**437**	**721**	**95**	**53**	**23**	**213**	**.266**
Boston			**45**	**86**	**19**	**22**	**10**	**0**	**2**	**14**	**.256**

Year	Team	OBP	SLG	OPS	BB	SO	TB	SB	CS	SH	SF	IBB	HBP	GDP
1999	CLE (AL)	.281	.308	.589	9	16	44	11	3	3	1	0	0	0
2000	CLE (AL)	.333	.200	.533	2	2	2	1	1	1	0	0	0	0
2001	CLE (AL)	.385	.417	.802	1	2	5	0	1	0	0	0	0	0
2002	LAD (NL)	.353	.365	.718	48	51	154	45	10	6	1	0	2	1
2003	LAD (NL)	.331	.307	.638	43	39	119	40	14	5	0	1	4	0
2004	*Season*	*.337*	*.379*	*.716*	*38*	*48*	*121*	*38*	*3*	*3*	*6*	*0*	*5*	*4*
	LAD (NL)	.340	.356	.696	28	31	83	33	1	2	3	0	4	2
	BOS (AL)	.330	.442	.772	10	17	38	5	2	1	3	0	1	2
2005	SDP (NL)	.356	.428	.784	53	59	176	23	12	11	4	3	1	10
2006	SDP (NL)	.360	.393	.753	51	61	196	49	6	7	5	2	4	5
2007	SFG (NL)	.281	.356	.637	42	66	144	31	5	4	0	1	0	4
2008	SFG (NL)	.341	.270	.621	20	18	30	5	3	1	2	1	0	0
Total		**.342**	**.366**	**.708**	**307**	**362**	**991**	**243**	**58**	**41**	**19**	**8**	**16**	**24**
Boston		**.330**	**.442**	**.772**	**10**	**17**	**38**	**5**	**2**	**1**	**3**	**0**	**1**	**2**

THE 2004 RED SOX: REVERSE THE CURSE

They may not have been the best Red Sox team to play in Boston. They did not have Ted Williams or Carl Yastrzemski or Tris Speaker in the outfield. Their infield lacked Wade Boggs, Bobby Doerr, Rico Petrocelli, and Jimmie Foxx. Babe Ruth and Cy Young and Jim Lonborg were not in the bullpen.

But this band of brothers, these "idiots" did something that no other Red Sox team had accomplished since 1918. Entire generations had come and gone since the last time Boston had won the World Series. There were the tragedies of 1946, 1967, 1975, and 1986; there were the heartbreaks of the one-game playoff in 1978 and the 2003 seventh-game ALCS loss to the Yankees.

All of those tears, as well as the Curse of the Bambino and a thousand other insults were washed away (love that dirty water) at 11:40 p.m. on October 27, 2004. At that moment, Red Sox closer Keith Foulke grabbed a one-bounce comebacker and ran five or six steps to his left before he underhanded the ball to Doug Mientkiewicz at first base.

The 86-year-drought was broken. There were stories about sons visiting the graves of their fathers to bring them the news. Three days later, I was on a Duck Boat as a rolling rally moved through downtown Boston and eventually into that dirty water in the River Charles. I saw old ladies and grown men crying; it was unlike anything I have ever experienced.

The Road to the Promised Land

So, how did all this happen?

The Boston Red Sox had staggered out of Yankee Stadium after the deflating extra-innings loss in the seventh game of the American League Championship Series in 2003. If there is anyone out there who has forgotten the details: Pedro Martinez looked manager Grady Little in the eyes and stayed in the game in the eighth inning.

Photo by the National Baseball Hall of Fame Library, Cooperstown, N.Y.

Unfortunately, that didn't work out; New York scored three runs to tie the game. And then late in the night, Aaron Boone broke the heart of Red Sox Nation with a game-winning home run off Tim Wakefield.

Red Sox management crunched the numbers and made some additions and a subtraction. Goodbye Grady Little, hello Terry Francona. And then they gave Francona some strong arms that ultimately would make the difference. First, the Red Sox signed Curt Schilling, who backed up his bluster with a solid 21–6 season. And they also filled the gaping hole in their bullpen with Keith Foulke, who did not disappoint in this important season.

And the lineup had a bit more punch—and consistency—than the Red Sox had seen in a while. Johnny Damon, Bill Mueller, Mark Bellhorn, and Kevin Millar did a very good job of setting the table.

And then the big boppers came through nicely: Manny Ramirez clobbered 43 long flies and drove in 130 runs and David Ortiz had 41 homers and 139 RBIs.

Overall, the Red Sox ended up as American League leaders in team batting average, on-base percentage, slugging, runs, and doubles.

The Red Sox had pulled out the stops to sign Schilling and Foulke. Schilling probably could have signed with the Yankees or Philadelphia, or a few other teams; Boston management made a pitch that was kind of like this: "You could become a Yankee and be just another cog in their machine, or you could come to the Red Sox and become a hero as we make a run at doing something that hasn't happened to our team in 86 years." Of course, the Red Sox gave him a lot of money, too, but I think Schilling embraced the challenge and I know he enjoyed taking center stage.

Schilling battled his way through injuries, leading by example although he also didn't hesitate to jabber; you can do that when you win. There was a still-effective Pedro Martinez who posted a 16–9 record. Derek Lowe, Tim Wakefield, and fifth starter Bronson Arroyo had good-but-not-great seasons but all of them benefitted from having Foulke ready to come out of the bullpen. Foulke earned 32 saves but also helped put out lots of other fires; he appeared 72 times, nearly half of the games played in the regular season.

And then there was the team chemistry. This had to be one of the loosest clubhouses ever. The ringleaders here were Kevin Millar and Johnny Damon, who between them declared the team a bunch of "idiots." As I understand it, they were not declaring themselves and their teammates to be stupid, but they were announcing to the world that they felt they had more than enough confidence in themselves. As it turned out, they were pretty smart.

Even with all that talent and confidence, there was one more round of subtraction and addition and this one took place at midseason. On July 31, the deadline day for non-waiver trades, the Red Sox parted with one of their franchise players: Nomar Garciaparra. He was a fan favorite and he had put up some great numbers since beginning his career in Boston, but in 2004 he was coming off injuries, and he was unhappy and not all that productive at the plate or effective in the field. Management rolled the dice, and made a trade that would prove to be one of the keys to success. Goodbye Nomar. Hello Doug Mientkiewicz, a steady defensive first baseman.

Hello Orlando Cabrera, a stellar shortstop with some pop in his bat. And, in a separate trade almost unnoticed at the time, hello to outfielder Dave Roberts, who possessed a skill the Red Sox had lacked for a while: speed.

The trades energized the Red Sox and they broke out of a midseason slump to finish strongly. But the Red Sox still had to deal with the New York Yankees. As good as the Red Sox were—they ended up with 98 wins against 64 losses—that was only good enough for second place in the American League East division, three games behind New York, which won 101 games. The good news, though, was that no other team in the AL was close to Boston in the race for the wild card.

The Division Playoffs

The Anaheim Angels (once called the California Angels, now called the Los Angeles Angels of Anaheim) had a good season in 2004, just squeezing past the Oakland A's to win the American League West with a 92–70 record. But the Red Sox had their number: They won the first two games of the best-of-five series pretty handily.

In the first game, Curt Schilling limited them to three runs (two of them earned) over 6.2 innings and then Alan Embree and Mike Timlin shut the Angels down the rest of the way. Manny Ramirez doubled with two outs in the first inning, and the second half of Boston's one–two punch, David Ortiz, singled him home for the lead. In the fourth inning the Sox broke the game open with seven runs; Kevin Millar and Ramirez hit home runs sandwiched around a two-run error on a Johnny Damon grounder that allowed Jason Varitek and Orlando Cabrera to score. Final score: 9–3 Boston.

The only worry: Schilling seemed to aggravate his already-injured ankle in making a fielding play.

In the second game, Pedro Martinez threw seven solid innings. Manager Terry Francona sent in the relief corps—no soulful glances into the pitcher's eyes—and Timlin and Mike Myers set up Keith Foulke for the save. The game was made easier when the Red Sox scored four times in the top of the ninth with big hits by Trot Nixon and Orlando Cabrera. Final score: 8–3 Boston.

Back in Boston for the third game, things were looking dicey as the Angels scored five times in the seventh inning off starter Bronson

Arroyo and relievers Chad Myers and Mike Timlin to tie the game at 6–6. But in the bottom of the tenth, Big Papi blew off the doors with a two-run walk-off homer to promote the Red Sox to the League Championship. Derek Lowe, who had been sent to the bullpen for the playoffs, picked up the win. Final score: 8–6 Boston.

The Championship Series

As dramatic as their win in the ALDS was, Red Sox Nation was deep in the dumps three games into the ALCS against those damned Yankees. Boston lost the first three games of the best-of-seven series. The first two games were close, but the third one was downright ugly.

The first game, at New York, saw Curt Schilling give up six runs in three innings and leave with his ankle worse off. Wakefield, the third reliever, gave up two more. Meanwhile, New York's Mike Mussina carried a perfect game into the seventh inning; Mark Bellhorn broke it up with a double and Boston made it interesting with five runs in the inning and two more in the eighth, but in the end the Yankees' great closer Mariano Rivera shut the door. Final score: 10–7 New York.

In the second game, Pedro Martinez pitched well, but not quite as well as New York's Jon Lieber. Pedro gave up three runs over six innings, while Lieber held the Red Sox to just one in seven frames. Boston tried to mount a rally in the eighth inning with Lieber still on the mound. Trot Nixon singled and the Yankees brought in former Red Sox pitcher Tom Gordon; Jason Varitek greeted him with a double that moved Nixon to third. Orlando Cabrera brought Nixon home on a groundout. Yankee manager Joe Torre went to the well once more, bringing in Mariano Rivera to get the last four outs and his second save in two games. Final score: 3–1 New York.

The third game was water torture. First there was a rainout, delaying the game at Fenway Park. And then the starting pitching— for both teams—was eminently forgettable. New York's Kevin Brown and Boston's Bronson Arroyo each lasted only two innings, and by the third the score was tied 6–6. And then the Yankees pummeled every pitcher Boston sent out there: Ramiro Mendoza, Curtis Leskanic, Tim Wakefield (who volunteered to come in and soak up innings to save the bullpen, giving up his shot at a start in Game 4), Alan Embree, and Chad Myers. There was nothing pretty about this game, and Boston also knew that the blowout had given Mariano Rivera an extra day of rest, and that was not good news. Final score: 19–8 New York.

And the band of idiots woke up the next morning to listen to the sports talk shows going on and on about an unpleasant bit of baseball history: No team had ever come back from an 0–3 deficit in a seven-game playoff or World Series. Not once, not ever.

Derek Lowe, who had been moved to the bullpen for the playoffs because of uneven performance at the end of the regular season, was given an unexpected start for the fourth game. He pitched pretty well, but there was no joy in Beantown in the third inning when Lowe gave up a two-run homer to the Yankees' unloved shortstop Alex Rodriguez.

But the Red Sox took the lead in the fifth on walks by Millar and Bellhorn, an RBI hit by Orlando Cabrera, and a two-run, two-out single by David Ortiz. Lowe pitched into the top of the sixth inning with that 3–2 lead until Hideki Matsui walloped a triple to deep center with one out. Mike Timlin came in to relieve and blew the save and put Boston into a hole: An infield single by Bernie Williams tied the game, and a wild pitch, a walk, a passed ball, and an infield single by Tony Clark put the Yankees ahead 4–3.

That set the stage for the Yankees to bring in Mariano Rivera to shut down the Red Sox; a win would have given the Yankees the league championship. The situation was a little unusual, though; Torre brought in Rivera in the eighth inning and asked him to get six outs.

Rivera set down the Red Sox in his first inning, and when the bottom of the ninth inning began Boston was three outs away from a humiliating sweep by the Yankees. But one of the loosest of the idiots, Kevin Millar, managed to draw a walk to lead off the inning; Boston manager Terry Francona sent in Dave Roberts—the late-season addition who could motor. Everyone in the park and watching on television knew that he was sent in to steal second base; you can read more about The Steal in the chapter about Roberts in this book, but the bottom line is that he got a great break and just barely beat a fine throw by New York catcher Jorge Posada. And then Bill Mueller brought him home with a single to tie the game. The Red Sox almost won the game in the ninth, which ended when Ortiz popped up with bases loaded. The Yankees threatened in the eleventh but did not score. And then in the bottom of the twelfth, Manny Ramirez singled to left, which brought up David Ortiz: a mighty swing and a two-run home run to right field for a walk-off win after five hours and two minutes of baseball. Final score: 6–4 Boston.

Later that same day, Pedro Martínez started against Mike Mussina for the fifth game; Pedro pitched well but Boston was once again facing elimination, down 4–2 after six innings. But in the eighth inning, David Ortiz came through in the clutch again, with a leadoff home run to bring Boston within a run. Millar followed with a walk; Dave Roberts came in as pinch runner. Nixon singled to center and the speedy Roberts moved to third base. The Yankees once again called on Mariano Rivera to save the day, but Varitek lifted a sacrifice fly to centerfield bringing Roberts home with the tying run.

And then back into the mire. The Red Sox bullpen, which had worked into the twelfth inning the night before, shut down the Yankees for the next eight innings: Mike Timlin, Keith Foulke, Bronson Arroyo, Mike Myers, and Alan Embree scattered four hits across five frames, and Tim Wakefield came in for three superb innings, giving up just a single hit and striking out four.

Finally, we reached the bottom of the fourteenth inning; the Yankees had Esteban Loaiza pitching in his fourth inning of relief. Johnny Damon worked a walk with one out. Cabrera struck out. With two outs, Manny Ramirez also drew a walk. And that brought up David Ortiz: He hit a single to center to score Damon and win the game. The five-hour, forty-nine-minute game had begun in the late afternoon and ended before midnight: Ortiz had his second game-winning walk-off hit in one very long day. Final score: 5–4 Boston.

There was no rest for the weary; because a day had been lost to the rainout the teams immediately headed to New York. And the bullpens of both teams were ragged, having thrown 26 innings in 24 hours.

And the Red Sox didn't know if Curt Schilling, their scheduled starter, would be able to answer the bell for the sixth game; doctors said he had a dislocated tendon in his ankle. Although some of the details are a bit murky, the medical report was this: In an unusual procedure, doctors put stitches into the skin around the tendon to relieve discomfort and give him a bit more support. No one knew if it would work, or how long Schilling could pitch.

To the great relief of Red Sox Nation, Schilling gutted it out for seven innings in a cold drizzle with television cameras zooming in on his right ankle and a small red circle on his sock that just might have been blood; he gave up just four hits and one run, a bases-empty home run by Bernie Williams. The Red Sox had accomplished the nearly impossible: They had come back from an 0–3 deficit to tie the playoffs. Final score: 4–2 Boston.

And so it came down to a seventh and deciding game. And even though Boston clearly had the record-setting momentum that comes with rising off the floor from an 0–3 deficit to tie the series, everyone in Red Sox Nation could remember the deflating defeat that had come just a year before. Once again, the Red Sox were in the lion's den, in Yankee Stadium, with the championship on the line.

But this band of idiots was loose and ready; it was the button-down Yankees who were uptight and nervous. In the first inning Johnny Damon singled to left and then stole second. With one out Manny Ramirez singled to left of center and Damon was thrown out at home plate. But Big Papi—David Ortiz—took care of business with a two-run home run to right.

And then in the second inning, after a quick hook took New York starter Kevin Brown out of the game, Johnny Damon got another chance to score a run. This time it was as the back end of a grand slam he hit off reliever Javier Vazquez, bringing home Kevin Millar, Bill Mueller, and Orlando Cabrera. After two complete, it was 6–0 Red Sox and the Yankees were the ones on the floor.

Derek Lowe, who had worked his way back into the starting rotation, was pitching well; he threw six innings of one-hit ball, giving up just one run. Meanwhile, in the fourth inning Damon hit his second home run of the game. In the seventh inning, Pedro Martinez came in as a relief pitcher—partly to get in some work on an off-day, partly to help spell the bullpen, and partly to exorcise past demons; it didn't work out all that well, as Martinez gave up two runs on three hits in one inning, but it didn't matter in the end. The Red Sox scored single runs in the eighth and ninth to pull away; Derek Lowe was the winning pitcher.

The Red Sox had accomplished perhaps the greatest comeback in the history of baseball, maybe in all of sports. After losing the first three games of the ALCS, they won the next four in a row and were now the American League champions. Final score: 10–3 Boston.

The World Series

The Red Sox were in the Promised Land; they were past the New York Yankees and they were back in the World Series. And they came in with the wind at their back, having made their amazing comeback.

Although they tried hard—especially in the first game of the Series—the St. Louis Cardinals never really stood a chance. The Red Sox had broken the Curse of the Bambino in New York, and the rest was mere details.

The World Series opened at Fenway Park on October 23, 2004. The Red Sox were ahead 4–0 before the first inning of the first game was over and 7–2 by the end of the third. But Tim Wakefield had a shaky start and was out of the game after 3.2 innings, and the Cardinals came back to tie the game at 7–7 in the sixth off Bronson Arroyo.

Boston went back into the lead in the seventh with RBI hits by Ramirez and Ortiz to put them up 9–7. In the eighth, Mike Timlin and Alan Embree yielded hits and closer Keith Foulke was brought in with one out; the Cardinals brought home both runners on two consecutive errors by Manny: he bobbled a single to the outfield and then tried to make a diving catch on a fly ball that instead glanced off his glove as he tumbled.

But the seesaw rose again for the Red Sox in the bottom of the eighth against Cardinals setup pitcher Julian Tavarez. Jason Varitek reached on an error and then Mark Bellhorn put the Sox back on top with a home run to right field. The Red Sox tied a World Series record with four errors. It wasn't pretty and it wasn't easy, but it was a win. Final score: 11–9 Boston.

The second game saw the return of the stitched-up ankle of Curt Schilling; actually, one of the sutures was removed before the game because it was causing discomfort. The ones who really felt the pain were the Cardinals, as Schilling pitched six innings, allowing only one unearned run.

Once again, the Red Sox jumped off to a quick start with a triple by Jason Varitek in the first inning to score Manny Ramirez and David Ortiz, who had each reached on walks. After St. Louis picked up a run on an error by Bill Mueller in the top of the fourth, the Red Sox got two more back in the bottom of the inning on Mark Bellhorn's double.

In the top of the sixth, Mueller had the dubious experience of tying an ancient World Series record when he made his third error of the game. And then on the next play, Bellhorn committed a fourth error to put the Red Sox in the record books as the only team ever to make eight errors in the first two games of the World Series. But Schilling pitched his way out of the jam.

In the bottom of the sixth, Trot Nixon singled and Johnny Damon moved him over with another base hit; Orlando Cabrera drove them both home with another single. After Mike Timlin gave up a run in the eighth, Foulke came in to get the last four batters out and secure the second win of the World Series in the last game of the season played in Boston. Final score: 6–2 Boston.

The Series moved to St. Louis for the third game, and it was Pedro Martinez's chance to shine on the big stage. He pitched seven scoreless innings, striking out six and giving up just three hits. Once again, Boston struck first, this time with a huge home run to leftfield by Manny Ramirez.

Mike Timlin pitched a perfect eighth, and Keith Foulke got the save—allowing a bases-empty home run to Todd Walker in the ninth inning. Final score: 4–1 Boston.

And then, on Wednesday, October 27, 2004 the World Series—and an 86-year-long painful drought—came to an end. Once again, Boston set the tone: Johnny Damon homered to right field to lead off the fourth and final game. It would be the only run starter Derek Lowe and the Red Sox would need to win the game, although they also got a pair of RBIs from Trot Nixon in the third inning.

After the third inning, it was a quiet, tense game. Lowe threw seven shutout innings yielding just three hits. Bronson Arroyo and Alan Embree combined for a hitless eighth, setting up the eleventh appearance by closer Keith Foulke in the fourteen postseason games.

Just before the ninth inning, in the skies overhead there was a total lunar eclipse. And then Edgar Renteria grounded back to the mound; Foulke grabbed the ball and ran a few steps toward first before he tossed it carefully to Doug Mientkiewicz at first base. The Boston Red Sox were World Champions. Final score: 3–0 Boston.

The individuals on this team may not have been the best players ever to wear a Boston uniform, but together they accomplished a win for the ages. Heroes all.

2004 Boston Red Sox

Regular Season

Player	Pos	Age	G	AB	R	H	2B	3B	HR	RBI	BA
Jason Varitek	C	32	137	463	67	137	30	1	18	73	.296
Kevin Millar	1B	32	150	508	74	151	36	0	18	74	.297
Mark Bellhorn	2B	29	138	523	93	138	37	3	17	82	.264
Bill Mueller	3B	33	110	399	75	113	27	1	12	57	.283
Pokey Reese	SS	31	96	244	32	54	7	2	3	29	.221
Manny Ramirez	LF	32	152	568	108	175	44	0	43	130	.308
Johnny Damon	CF	30	150	621	123	189	35	6	20	94	.304
Gabe Kapler	RF	28	136	290	51	79	14	1	6	33	.272
David Ortiz	DH	28	150	582	94	175	47	3	41	139	.301
Orlando Cabrera		29	58	228	33	67	19	1	6	31	.294
Kevin Youkilis		25	72	208	38	54	11	0	7	35	.260
Doug Mirabelli		33	59	160	27	45	12	0	9	32	.281
Nomar Garciaparra		30	38	156	24	50	7	3	5	21	.321
David McCarty		34	89	151	24	39	8	1	4	17	.258
Trot Nixon		30	48	149	24	47	9	1	6	23	.315
Doug Mientkiewicz	*Season*	*30*	*127*	*391*	*47*	*93*	*24*	*1*	*6*	*35*	*.238*
	Minn		78	284	34	70	18	0	5	25	.246
	Boston		49	107	13	23	6	1	1	10	.215
Dave Roberts		32	45	86	19	22	10	0	2	14	.256
Cesar Crespo		25	52	79	6	13	2	1	0	2	.165
Brian Daubach		32	30	75	9	17	8	0	2	8	.227
Ricky Gutierrez		34	21	40	6	11	1	0	0	3	.275
Ellis Burks		39	11	33	6	6	0	0	1	1	.182
Andy Dominique		28	7	11	0	2	0	0	0	1	.182
Adam Hyzdu		32	17	10	3	3	2	0	1	2	.300
Sandy Martinez		33	3	4	0	0	0	0	0	0	.000
Earl Snyder		28	1	4	0	1	0	0	0	0	.250
Curt Schilling		37	2	7	0	1	0	0	0	0	.143
Bronson Arroyo		27	3	6	0	0	0	0	0	0	.000
Derek Lowe		31	2	4	0	1	1	0	0	1	.250
Pedro Martinez		32	1	2	0	0	0	0	0	0	.000
Tim Wakefield		37	1	2	0	0	0	0	0	0	.000
Regular season total			162	5720	949	1613	373	25	222	912	.282

Player	OBP	SLG	OPS	BB	SO	TB	SB	CS	SH	SF	IBB	HBP	GDP
Jason Varitek	.390	.482	.872	62	126	223	10	3	0	1	9	10	11
Kevin Millar	.383	.474	.857	57	91	241	1	1	0	6	0	17	16
Mark Bellhorn	.373	.444	.817	88	177	232	6	1	1	3	1	5	8
Bill Mueller	.365	.446	.811	51	56	178	2	2	0	6	1	4	8
Pokey Reese	.271	.303	.574	17	60	74	6	2	6	1	1	0	5
Manny Ramirez	.397	.613	1.009	82	124	348	2	4	0	7	15	6	17
Johnny Damon	.380	.477	.857	76	71	296	19	8	0	3	1	2	8
Gabe Kapler	.311	.390	.700	15	49	113	5	4	1	2	0	2	5
David Ortiz	.380	.603	.983	75	133	351	0	0	0	8	8	4	12
Orlando Cabrera	.320	.465	.785	11	23	106	4	1	1	7	0	1	4
Kevin Youkilis	.367	.413	.780	33	45	86	0	1	0	3	0	4	1
Doug Mirabelli	.368	.525	.893	19	46	84	0	0	0	0	0	3	5
Nomar Garciaparra	.367	.500	.867	8	16	78	2	0	0	1	2	4	4
David McCarty	.327	.404	.731	14	40	61	1	0	0	1	0	2	5
Trot Nixon	.377	.510	.887	15	24	76	0	0	0	2	1	1	3
Doug Mientkiewicz													
Season	_.326_	_.350_	_.676_	_48_	_56_	_137_	_2_	_3_	_2_	_2_	_2_	_4_	_12_
Minn	.340	.363	.703	38	38	103	2	2	2	1	2	3	9
Boston	.286	.318	.603	10	18	34	0	1	0	1	0	1	3
Dave Roberts	.330	.442	.772	10	17	38	5	2	1	3	0	1	2
Cesar Crespo	.165	.215	.380	0	20	17	2	0	0	0	0	0	1
Brian Daubach	.326	.413	.739	10	21	31	0	0	0	0	0	1	1
Ricky Gutierrez	.310	.300	.610	2	6	12	1	0	0	0	0	0	0
Ellis Burks	.270	.273	.543	3	8	9	2	0	0	0	0	1	1
Andy Dominique	.182	.182	.364	0	3	2	0	0	0	0	0	0	0
Adam Hyzdu	.364	.800	1.164	1	2	8	0	0	0	0	0	0	0
Sandy Martinez	.000	.000	.000	0	2	0	0	0	0	0	0	0	0
Earl Snyder	.250	.250	.500	0	1	1	0	0	0	0	0	0	1
Curt Schilling	.143	.143	.286	0	2	1	0	0	0	0	0	0	0
Bronson Arroyo	.000	.000	.000	0	5	0	0	0	1	0	0	0	0
Derek Lowe	.250	.500	.750	0	1	2	0	0	1	0	0	0	0
Pedro Martinez	.000	.000	.000	0	1	0	0	0	0	0	0	0	0
Tim Wakefield	.000	.000	.000	0	1	0	0	0	0	0	0	0	0
Regular													
season total	**.360**	**.472**	**.832**	**659**	**1189**	**2702**	**68**	**30**	**12**	**55**	**39**	**68**	**123**

Team Pitching

Player	POS	Age	W	L	G	GS	CG	SHO	GF	SV	WHIP	ERA
Derek Lowe	SP	31	14	12	33	33	0	0	0	0	1.615	5.42
Pedro Martinez	SP	32	16	9	33	33	1	1	0	0	1.171	3.90
Curt Schilling	SP	37	21	6	32	32	3	0	0	0	1.063	3.26
Tim Wakefield	SP	37	12	10	32	30	0	0	0	0	1.381	4.88
Bronson Arroyo	SP	27	10	9	32	29	0	0	0	0	1.220	4.03
Keith Foulke	Closer	31	5	3	72	0	0	0	61	32	0.940	2.17
Mike Timlin		38	5	4	76	0	0	0	12	1	1.232	4.13
Alan Embree		34	2	2	71	0	0	0	11	0	1.147	4.13
Curtis Leskanic		36	3	2	32	0	0	0	16	2	1.444	3.57
Scott Williamson		28	0	1	28	0	0	0	5	1	1.010	1.25
Ramiro Mendoza		32	2	1	27	0	0	0	12	0	1.042	3.52
Lenny DiNardo		24	0	0	22	0	0	0	6	0	1.661	4.22
Terry Adams		31	2	0	19	0	0	0	1	0	1.519	6.00
Mark Malaska		26	1	1	19	0	0	0	8	0	1.650	4.50
Byung-Hyun Kim		25	2	1	7	3	0	0	2	0	1.387	6.24
Mike Myers		35	1	0	25	0	0	0	5	0	1.467	4.20
Anastacio Martinez		25	2	1	11	0	0	0	7	0	1.776	8.41
Pedro Astacio		34	0	0	5	1	0	0	1	0	2.069	10.34
Jamie Brown		27	0	0	4	0	0	0	3	0	2.468	5.84
Jimmy Anderson		28	0	0	5	1	0	0	2	0	2.167	6.00
Abe Alvarez		21	0	1	1	0	0	0	0	0	2.600	9.00
Phil Seibel		25	0	0	2	0	0	0	0	0	1.351	0.00
David McCarty		34	0	0	3	0	0	0	2	0	0.811	2.43
Bobby Jones		32	0	1	3	0	0	0	1	0	3.333	5.45
Joe Nelson		29	0	0	3	0	0	0	1	0	2.593	16.67
Frank Castillo		35	0	0	2	0	0	0	2	0	2.000	0.00
Regular season total			**98**	**64**	**162**	**162**	**4**	**1**	**158**	**36**	**1.293**	**4.19**

Player	IP	H	R	ER	HR	BB	SO	WP	HBP	BK	IBB
Derek Lowe	182.7	224	138	110	15	71	105	3	8	0	2
Pedro Martinez	217	193	99	94	26	61	227	2	16	0	0
Curt Schilling	226.7	206	84	82	23	35	203	3	5	0	0
Tim Wakefield	188.3	197	121	102	29	63	116	9	16	0	3
Bronson Arroyo	178.7	171	99	80	17	47	142	5	20	0	3
Keith Foulke	83	63	22	20	8	15	79	3	6	0	5
Mike Timlin	76.3	75	35	35	8	19	56	1	5	0	3
Alan Embree	52.3	49	28	24	7	11	37	0	1	0	1
Curtis Leskanic	27.7	24	11	11	3	16	22	0	1	0	3
Scott Williamson	28.7	11	6	4	0	18	28	4	3	0	1
Ramiro Mendoza	30.7	25	12	12	3	7	13	1	1	1	1
Lenny DiNardo	27.7	34	17	13	1	12	21	1	2	0	1
Terry Adams	27	35	19	18	6	6	21	2	1	0	1
Mark Malaska	20	21	11	10	2	12	12	0	1	0	1
Byung-Hyun Kim	17.3	17	15	12	1	7	6	1	2	0	1
Mike Myers	15	16	7	7	2	6	9	1	0	0	1
Anastacio Martinez	10.7	13	10	10	2	6	5	0	1	0	0
Pedro Astacio	8.7	13	10	10	2	5	6	1	0	0	0
Jamie Brown	7.7	15	7	5	1	4	6	0	0	0	0
Jimmy Anderson	6	10	4	4	0	3	3	1	0	0	0
Abe Alvarez	5	8	5	5	2	5	2	0	0	0	0
Phil Seibel	3.7	0	0	0	0	5	1	0	1	0	0
David McCarty	3.7	2	1	1	0	1	4	1	0	0	0
Bobby Jones	3.3	3	2	2	1	8	3	0	0	0	1
Joe Nelson	2.7	4	5	5	0	3	5	0	2	0	0
Frank Castillo	1	1	0	0	0	1	0	0	0	0	0
Regular season total	**1451.3**	**1430**	**768**	**676**	**159**	**447**	**1132**	**39**	**92**	**1**	**28**

THE 2007 RED SOX: CHAMPIONS OF THE WORLD, PART II

Three years after they broke the curse, the Red Sox showed the world two things. First of all, that 2004 was no fluke. And secondly, that for the moment the balance of power in the American League East and indeed, in all of baseball, was tilting toward the hub of the universe: Boston.

The 2007 Red Sox took possession of first place two weeks after the season opened and held on to it for the rest of the season. They finished in first place in the AL East for the first time since 1995; in 2005, Boston and New York had ended the season with identical records but because the Yankees won the majority of the season's games against the Red Sox, they got to claim the division title.

In winning their division, the Red Sox had to hold off a late charge by, yes, New York; the Yankees had to settle for the wild card as their ticket to the postseason. New York was hobbled by injuries, especially to their pitchers; at various points in the season they were starting kids brought up from Double-A and Triple-A.

The Red Sox simply played good, consistent ball all year long. Once the Yankees began to put it together in the final month, there was no panic in Boston, even when New York closed to within one and a half games.

Manny Ramirez suffered an injury late in the season; the team focused on getting him—and the rest of the team—in playing shape for the postseason. Hideki Okajima, who literally came out of nowhere to become a very important member of the team as the bridge to closer Jonathan Papelbon, began to struggle after throwing many more innings than he was used to in Japan; they shut him down for about ten days to give him rest. It was smart thinking by management.

The Red Sox knew there was no need for desperation; they could see a clear path to either the division title or the wild card. Standing above the Yankees on the last day of the season was a bonus, but the real prizes lay ahead in the playoffs.

Photo by Brita Meng Outzen

Jonathan Papelbon

As a result, when the season finally ended Boston's pitching rotation was set up perfectly with 20-game winner Josh Beckett ready to pitch the first game. He would set the tone for the entire postseason.

And one more thing: As it turned out, this time the road to the World Series did not run through New York at all. The Cleveland Indians sent New York home by winning three of the four games; they were aided and abetted by a swarm of midges that flew in from Lake

Erie and disrupted Yankee pitcher Joba Chamberlain in the second game of that series, a contest won by the Indians 2–1.

American League Division Series

The Red Sox, as winners of their division, got to play against the Los Angeles Angels of Anaheim. This rematch from the 2004 post-season ended up with the same results: a three-game clean sweep by Boston.

In the first game, Josh Beckett established his dominance in the postseason by throwing a four-hit complete game shutout. After giving up a single to the first batter of the game, he retired the next 19 hitters in a row, going into the record book tied for the third-longest streak in postseason history. He notched eight strikeouts and issued no walks; he threw 108 pitches, 83 of them for strikes, and it was all over in a neat and tidy two hours and thirty-seven minutes.

The only run the Red Sox needed came when their second batter came to the plate in the first inning; Kevin Youkilis put a John Lackey pitch over the Green Monster. In the third inning, David Ortiz continued his postseason heroics with a two-run shot, and later in the same frame Mike Lowell drove in Manny Ramirez from second. Final score: 4–0 Boston.

The second game, also at Fenway, was by no means as easy a win. Boston went ahead, then fell behind before they tied the game and set the stage for a dramatic bottom-of-the-ninth. In the first inning, J.D. Drew came up to the plate with the bases loaded and two outs; Drew had not reached expectations in his first regular season in Boston, but he was showing signs of getting hot at the right time. On the second pitch he saw, he hit a ground ball up the middle to score Youkilis and Ramirez.

Meanwhile, Daisuke Matsuzaka's first postseason game was not going well. In the second inning, he gave back three runs on a walk, a single, and a pair of doubles; he was back on the bench with two outs in the fifth inning. But the bullpen came through, shutting down the Angels for the remainder of the game while Boston tied the game in the bottom of the fifth.

The bottom of the ninth arrived and Angels manager Mike Scioscia had to pick his poison. Julio Lugo led off the inning with a single, and Dustin Pedroia grounded out to first base to move the potential winning run into scoring position at second. Scioscia brought in his hard-throwing right-handed closer Francisco Rodriguez. K-Rod tried a pickoff move on Lugo but then concentrated on Youkilis at the plate, striking him out on four pitches.

With two outs Scioscia faced this tough choice: should he allow K-Rod to pitch to David Ortiz or Manny Ramirez? He chose to bypass Ortiz with an intentional walk.

Up came Manny. He watched the first pitch come in low and outside. And then he swung at the next pitch, a 96-mile-per-hour fastball on the inside of the plate; he kept his hands inside the ball and launched it onto Lansdowne Street for a three-run walk-off homer. Final score: 6–3 Boston.

The third game took place in Anaheim, and it started out as a pitcher's duel but ended as a laugher. Surgically repaired Curt Schilling tossed seven innings of six-hit shutout baseball; the Boston bullpen would keep the Angels off the scoreboard until Eric Gagne allowed a single, meaningless run in the ninth.

Boston's twin poisons scored one apiece in the fourth inning. Ortiz led off with a bomb to right field; Manny Ramirez took a strike, then fouled off three pitches and took three balls to work the count to full. Then he crushed a 76-mile-per-hour changeup from Jered Weaver, sending it into the artificial mountain and stream over the centerfield wall.

The score remained tight at 2-0 into the top of the eighth inning; the Red Sox put together three doubles, two singles, two walks, and a couple of productive outs to score seven runs and put the game—and the Division Series—out of reach. Final score: 9-1 Boston.

American League Championship Series

Cleveland had dispatched the Yankees, but now they had to come to Fenway to face Josh Beckett and the Red Sox. Although the Indians managed to touch up Beckett for a solo home run in the first inning of the first game, Boston came back immediately to tie the game and then put together a double handful of runs to win.

Josh Beckett had been given more than a week off after disposing of the Angels, and he was well rested and sharp. He limited the

Indians to just four hits and two runs, striking out seven and giving up no walks.

On the other side, C.C. Sabathia was gone after four-and-a-third innings, giving up eight runs and the game. Boston's power punchers Ortiz and Ramirez reached base ten times in ten appearances at the plate. They had two hits apiece, plus five walks, and Ortiz was hit by a pitch. This time they let others drive them in.

In the third inning Julio Lugo led off with a ground-rule double to right field and Dustin Pedroia moved him to third with a sacrifice bunt. Youkilis drew a walk to put runners at the corners, bringing up Big Papi. This time it was Cleveland manager Eric Wedge's chance to decide whether to pitch to Ortiz or wait for Manny. He chose to have Sabathia pitch to Big Papi, but that didn't work out well: On a 1-1 count, he threw one way inside and hit Ortiz in his kitchen. That brought up Manny with the bases loaded; down two strikes, Ramirez showed a great eye as he took the next four pitches for balls and drew an RBI walk. And then Mike Lowell brought home two more runs with another ground-rule double. The fourth run of the inning came on a groundout by Varitek.

Boston picked up three more in the fifth inning when reserve outfielder Bobby Kielty—put in the lineup because he had good numbers against Sabathia—singled to rightfield to drive home two more runs. And Varitek brought in one more with a run-scoring double. And the Red Sox brought in their ninth and tenth runs in the sixth when Ramirez once again drew a bases-loaded walk and Mike Lowell lifted a sacrifice fly.

Eric Gagne, a late-season pickup who never seemed to find his rhythm, was brought in to finish the game and he made things interesting by loading the bases on a single, double, and walk, but he managed to strike out Grady Sizemore to end the game. Final score: 10–3 Boston.

The second game in the ALCS did not work out the way Boston had hoped. Old warhorse Curt Schilling was matched up against young fireballer Fausto Carmona. Neither made it past the fifth inning, and the score was tied 6–6 going into the sixth. Schilling gave up a three-run homer to Jhonny Peralta in the fourth inning, and Carmona a two-run shot by Manny Ramirez and then a solo moon shot by Mike Lowell in the top of the fifth. But young Red Sox reliever Manny Delcarmen gave back the lead.

The score stayed knotted until the eleventh inning and the bullpen had been well used by that time; after Delcarmen came Okajima, Timlin, and Papelbon. Finally, Red Sox manager Terry Francona had to go to the shaky Eric Gagne to start the eleventh. Things unraveled quickly from there: Grady Sizemore singled with one out and Asdrubal Cabrera followed with a walk. The Indians sent up old Red Sox favorite Trot Nixon as a left-handed pinch hitter; Francona pulled Gagne and replaced him with lefty Javier Lopez. Nixon poked at a 79-mile-per-hour breaking ball and blooped it into centerfield to put the Indians ahead.

From there it got truly ugly. A wild pitch by Lopez allowed another run, a couple of hits added to the mess, and when Jon Lester came in as the third reliever of the inning he gave up a three-run homer to Franklin Gutierrez. The Indians scored seven times in the inning. Final score: 13–6 Cleveland.

The third game, at Cleveland, was close but Boston received no cigar. Daisuke Matsuzaka was out-dueled by Jake Westbrook. Matsuzaka threw a lot of pitches early; he was gone after 101 pitches in just 4 2/3 innings, giving up six hits and four runs. Westbrook got the Red Sox to hit into one groundball out after another. Boston's only offense came on a two-run homer by Varitek in the seventh inning. Final score: 4–2 Cleveland.

The fourth game started out promisingly, with Tim Wakefield baffling the Indians with his knuckleball for the first four innings of the game; then the wheels fell off as Cleveland scored seven runs off Wakefield and Delcarmen in a painful 35-minute fifth inning. On their side, the Indians won with soft-tossing Paul Byrd, whose breaking pitches and old-fashioned full windup threw Boston hitters off their timing.

The only Red Sox runs came in a spectacular show in the top of the sixth, with back-to-back-to-back home runs by Youkilis, Ortiz, and Ramirez. The only other team to do that in postseason history was the 1997 Yankees in Game 1 of the ALDS, also against the Indians. After that, nothing. Final score: 7–3 Cleveland.

That left the Red Sox in the precarious position of being down 1–3 after four games in a best-of-seven series; but Boston was hardly the sort of team to panic in that situation. After all, in 2004 the Red Sox pulled off their miracle against the Yankees, coming off the mat down 0–3 to win the championship series.

The wheel had gone around full circle, and it was time for Josh Beckett to come out and pitch the fifth game. And he did not disappoint, although he started off a bit rough. In the first inning, as he worked to find his rhythm, he started off allowing runners at the corners; a run came home on a double play . . . and that was all the Indians would score that night.

Playing at Cleveland, Kevin Youkilis had put the Red Sox ahead for the moment with a homer in the first. Boston took back the lead in the third with three runs including a disputed play on a long drive by Ramirez that landed on the top of the yellow line above the wall in right field before bouncing back into play. Manny only made it to first base, but Ortiz scored the go-ahead run.

And then Boston started hitting in the last third of the game. Pedroia led off the sixth with a double and then Youkilis drove him in with a triple; Ortiz hit a sacrifice fly to left to make it 4–1. The Red Sox went on to score three more runs in the eighth. Final score: 7–1 Boston.

Back home at friendly Fenway, Curt Schilling found his form. Schilling had pitched five times in his career when his team had faced elimination in the postseason. His record coming into the sixth game of the ALCS was 4–0 with a 1.37 ERA; by the end of the day it was 5–0.

Dustin Pedroia led off the first with an infield single to first and Kevin Youkilis followed with another infield hit, this time to short. Fausto Carmona threw hard but ultimately wide to David Ortiz, walking him to load the bases. Things looked very promising with Manny Ramirez up at the plate, but he struck out. Then Mike Lowell could do no better than a shallow fly to right field. That left it to J. D. Drew; he rewarded the team and fans when he turned around Carmona's fifth pitch, a 97-mile-per-hour heater, and sent it over the camera well above the wall in centerfield for a grand slam.

Schilling settled in and held the Indians to just six hits and two runs over seven innings, walking none and striking out five.

Boston put the game out of reach in the bottom of the third inning, scoring six runs. In that inning, Ramirez and Lowell opened the inning with walks and then J. D. Drew stroked an RBI single up the middle. Jacoby Ellsbury, making his first postseason start, blooped an RBI single into center. Julio Lugo slashed a two-run double down the leftfield line. Pedroia drew a walk and then Youkilis hit an RBI single off the wall in left; Youk got caught in a rundown between first and second but second baseman Asdrubal Cabrera's throw hit him on the helmet and Pedroia came home. Two more scored in the bottom of the eighth. Final score: 12–2 Boston.

And thus it came down to a seventh and final game, at Fenway, for the American League Championship. Daisuke Matsuzaka pitched well, holding Cleveland to just two runs and six hits over five innings. Jake Westbrook was almost as good, yielding three runs in six frames.

The difference came when each team's bullpen took over. Boston's Hideki Okajima and Jonathan Papelbon each pitched two scoreless innings. Cleveland's Rafael Betancourt and Jensen Lewis gave up a total of eight runs in the seventh and eighth innings.

Boston's rookie outfielder Ellsbury started a seventh inning rally when he reached on a fielding error by Indians third baseman Casey Blake. Julio Lugo bunted him over to third. And then second baseman Dustin Pedroia—who would be named the American League's Rookie of the Year after the season was over—put one of his big swings on a 95-mile-per-hour fastball and drove the ball into the Monster seats in leftfield to make it 5–2 Red Sox. In the bottom of the eighth, Boston settled the issue of which team would be going to the World Series and which team would be flying home to clean out their lockers. Boston scored six runs on a double by Lowell, single by Drew, double by Varitek, double by Pedroia, and a two-run homer by Youkilis. Final score: 11–2 Boston.

2007 World Series

Just like 2004, the Red Sox came into the World Series with a head of steam. Their opponents, the Colorado Rockies, had won 21 out of their previous 22 games, including sweeps of Philadelphia and Arizona in the playoffs. But then they had to sit around and wait eight days after clinching the National League Championship until Boston had gotten past Cleveland; the Rockies never really got on track.

Once again, the pitching rotation was set up just the way Boston wanted: Josh Beckett was ready for the first game, quite ready, actually. In the first inning, he struck out the side on fifteen pitches, all of them in the range of 95 to 97 miles per hour. For his night, he gave up just 1 run and 6 hits while striking out 9 over 7 innings.

At the plate, this solid Boston team showed up to play and win. Dustin Pedroia, batting leadoff, swung at the second pitch he saw from Rockies pitcher Jeff Francis and parked it in the leftfield seats for a leadoff round-tripper. Pedroia became only the second player in World Series history to lead off the first inning of Game 1 with a homer, joining Don Buford of the 1969 Orioles in the record book. The Red Sox never trailed in the game.

The Sox scored twice more in the first inning on a double by Youkilis, RBI single by Ramirez, single by Varitek, and a run-scoring line drive double by J. D. Drew. The Rockies got one run back—their only run in the game—in the top of the second, on a pair of doubles by Garrett Atkins and Troy Tulowitzki. But Boston took back their three-run lead in the bottom of that inning when David Ortiz hit a two-run double to center field, driving in Youkilis, who had reached base on a walk. Two more Boston runs crossed the plate in the fourth inning when Varitek hit a ground-rule double to left, bringing home David Ortiz and Manny Ramirez.

The following all happened with two outs in the bottom of the fifth inning: double by Youkilis, double by Ortiz, single by Ramirez, double by Lowell, walk by Varitek, single by Drew, and then three consecutive run-scoring walks (Lugo, Ellsbury, and Pedroia). Thirteen batters came to the plate and seven runs scored. The Sox set a World Series record with nine doubles in the game. Final score: 13–1 Boston.

The second game of the World Series was anything but a blowout; it was a tense, well-pitched game. Curt Schilling answered the call once more, pitching five and a third innings and giving up just one run and four hits before turning it over to the spectacular bullpen combination of Hideki Okajima (two and a third innings, no hits and no runs) and Jonathan Papelbon (one and a third innings, one hit, and no runs).

The game began with Colorado going ahead on a questionable call and a shaky play: Colorado's first batter, Willy Taveras, may have been hit on the hand—he certainly convinced home plate umpire Laz Diaz, but not the Red Sox. After an out Matt Holliday singled to deep third and both runners moved up a base on a rare throwing error by Boston third baseman Mike Lowell. And then Taveras came home on a fielder's-choice grounder to first.

The Rockies hung on to a 1–0 lead into the fourth inning on the strong pitching of rookie Ubaldo Jimenez, whose fastball approached

100 miles per hour at times. Boston tied the game in the fourth inning after Lowell walked and showed some smart base running crossing over to third on J. D. Drew's single. He came home on a sacrifice fly by Jason Varitek.

And then in the fifth inning, with two outs David Ortiz drew another walk and then Manny Ramirez moved him to second with a hard groundball single into left. Lowell put the ball down the left field line for an RBI double.

After Schilling gave up a single and a walk in the sixth inning, he was replaced by lefty Hideki Okajima, who gave Boston two and a third perfect innings. And then Terry Francona asked Jonathan Papelbon to give him four outs to close out the game; the score was 2–1 with two outs in the eighth inning.

On his third pitch, Papelbon gave up a groundball single to Matt Holliday, which put the potential tying run on base; Holliday has some speed and was a threat to steal a base. From the Red Sox dugout, bench coach Brad Mills flashed a sign to catcher Jason Varitek, who relayed it to Papelbon on the mound. Mills said later that Boston's advance scouting had determined that when Holliday tries to steal a base he usually runs on the first pitch. Instead of throwing home, Papelbon wheeled and fired a strike to Youkilis at first and Holliday was picked off base easily.

It was Papelbon's first pickoff of a runner in his major league career; it was also one of those little details, well thought out and well executed, that wins games and World Series. The inning, and the last threat of the night by the Rockies, was over. Final score: 2–1 Boston.

The third game of the 2007 World Series came three years to the day after the Red Sox broke their 86-year drought in the 2004 World Series. This game was the closest contest between the Red Sox and the Rockies.

Daisuke Matsuzaka pitched one of his better games in his first season with Boston, but once again he was gone pretty early. He gave up just three hits and two runs in five and a third innings.

The shift from Boston to Colorado also presented manager Terry Francona with a difficult decision: Since the pitcher had to be in the lineup, which one of his three stars did he want to sit down? Francona chose to give Kevin Youkilis the game off, at least for the start, sending David Ortiz to first base with a glove and keeping Mike Lowell in position at third base. The change also resulted in a shuffle of the lineup, putting speedy rookie Jacoby Ellsbury in the leadoff spot, followed by Boston's other rookie star Dustin Pedroia. It was a change that mattered: The pair went seven for ten between them, including three doubles for Ellsbury.

Boston built up a 6–0 lead in the third inning. Ellsbury led off with a line drive double and moved to third when Pedroia laid down a safe bunt hit. And then Rockies manager Clint Hurdle had to face the same tough question opposing managers had been facing for years: Should he pitch to David Ortiz or Manny Ramirez?

He chose to let Ortiz take his cuts; Big Papi swung at reliever Josh Fogg's first pitch, doubling on a line drive to score Ellsbury. With runners now on second and third, Ramirez was intentionally walked; that didn't work out either, as Mike Lowell singled into leftfield to score Pedroia and Ortiz. After a pop-up by J. D. Drew, Jason Varitek singled to leftfielder Matt Holliday; Ramirez rounded the corner at third base (tossing off his helmet and then kicking it as he ran) and was thrown out at the plate on a very close call.

In games played under National League rules (with no DH), managers like to have the number eight batter make the third out of the inning so that a weak-hitting pitcher leads off the next frame. But Fogg was unable to put away Julio Lugo, walking him on four straight pitches.

And so Daisuke Matsuzaka came up to the plate with bases loaded and two outs. He had been up to bat just four times in the regular season during interleague play, and he was hitless in his brief career as a major leaguer. But he swung at the first pitch he saw, a 78-mile-per-hour breaking ball; the result was a grounder through the left side of the infield for a two-run single. Ellsbury, the tenth man up, struck his second double of the inning, bringing home Lugo with the sixth run. In doing so he joined Matt Williams of Arizona (Game 6 of the 2001 World Series against the Yankees) as the only players to hold that particular record.

The Rockies scored two runs off reliever Javier Lopez in the sixth, and then in the seventh Mike Timlin got into trouble: a safe bunt, a stolen base, and a single to put runners at the corners. Francona gave the ball to reliable setup man Hideki Okajima, but his first pitch—a changeup to slugger Matt Holliday—went all the way back, over the centerfield wall. The score had narrowed to Boston 6, Colorado 5.

But in the bottom of the inning, Boston answered. Ellsbury doubled home Julio Lugo and then Pedroia doubled home Crisp and

Ellsbury. In the ninth, a sacrifice fly by Jason Varitek brought home the tenth run, and the Red Sox were up three games to none. Final score: 10–5 Boston.

The fourth and final game of the 2007 World Series was a personal and team triumph and in the end, a nailbiter that hung in the balance until the last out of the ninth inning. Actually, that's the way these sorts of games are supposed to be.

It began with an affirmation of the courage and accomplishment of Boston's talented young pitcher, Jon Lester. Just a year before, Lester was undergoing chemotherapy treatments for anaplastic large cell lymphoma, a rare form of cancer. Here he was, back in the major leagues, pitching in the World Series.

Lester was the real thing, throwing five and two-thirds shutout innings, earning the win. The Sox scored just enough runs—one each in the first, fifth, seventh, and eighth—and then held on for dear life as the Rockies came within a run of tying the game while Rockies pitcher Aaron Cook hung tough. Once again, the Red Sox scored early. Jacoby Ellsbury led off with a double and moved to third on a groundout by Pedroia; he scored on a single to right by Ortiz.

In the fifth, Mike Lowell hit a leadoff double to center and then slid home head first after a single to right by Varitek. And then Lowell hit a solo homer in the top of the seventh to give Boston a 3–0 lead. But in the bottom of that inning, Brad Hawpe answered with a shot of his own off Boston's Manny Delcarmen.

In the top of the eighth inning, Francona sent up Bobby Kielty as a pinch hitter for Mike Timlin. It was Kielty's only appearance at the plate in the World Series—the first of his career—and he made the most of it. He swung at the first pitch he saw from reliever Brian Fuentes and put it over the leftfield wall for a home run.

Although Hideki Okajima and Jonathan Papelbon had both pitched the day before, they were at the ready in the bullpen. When you have the chance to end a Series, you don't hold your horses.

Okajima came in to start the bottom of the eighth inning, and he may have been out of gas. With one out he gave up a single to Todd Helton, and five pitches later he left a fat pitch right over the plate for Garrett Atkins; the result: a two-run homer that cut the score to 4–3. In came Jonathan Papelbon for the final 5 outs of the game: 23 pitches, 18 strikes, 0 hits, 0 runs, and his 3rd save in the World Series. Final score: 4–3 Boston.

Mike Lowell would be selected World Series MVP for his timely hitting and steady play at third base. Manny Ramirez and David Ortiz did their thing. Josh Beckett earned his star as a great postseason pitcher; he was set up to pitch Game 5 if one had been necessary and Jonathan Papelbon would have answered the bell to pitch with any game on the line. Dustin Pedroia didn't know it yet, but he was about to be named Rookie of the Year for his play during the regular season. And Red Sox Nation and the world was introduced to the talent and potential of youngsters Jon Lester, Jacoby Ellsbury, and others.

The year 2007 was a year of affirmation, a team of heroes.

2007 Boston Red Sox

Player	Pos	Age	G	AB	R	H	2B	3B	HR	RBI	BA
Jason Varitek	C	35	131	435	57	111	15	3	17	68	.255
Kevin Youkilis	1B	28	145	528	85	152	35	2	16	83	.288
Dustin Pedroia	2B	23	139	520	86	165	39	1	8	50	.317
Mike Lowell	3B	33	154	589	79	191	37	2	21	120	.324
Julio Lugo	SS	31	147	570	71	135	36	2	8	73	.237
Manny Ramirez	LF	35	133	483	84	143	33	1	20	88	.296
Coco Crisp	CF	27	145	526	85	141	28	7	6	60	.268
J. D. Drew	RF	31	140	466	84	126	30	4	11	64	.270
David Ortiz	DH	31	149	549	116	182	52	1	35	117	.332
Alex Cora	IF	31	83	207	30	51	10	5	3	18	.246
Eric Hinske	IF/OF	29	84	186	25	38	12	3	6	21	.204
Wily Mo Pena	OF	25	73	156	18	34	9	1	5	17	.218
Jacoby Ellsbury	OF	23	33	116	20	41	7	1	3	18	.353
Doug Mirabelli	C	36	48	114	9	23	3	0	5	16	.202
Bobby Kielty	OF	30	20	52	6	12	2	0	1	9	.231
Kevin Cash	C	29	12	27	2	3	1	0	0	4	.111
Brandon Moss	OF	23	15	25	6	7	2	1	0	1	.280
Jeff Bailey	IF	28	3	9	1	1	0	0	1	1	.111
Royce Clayton	IF	37	8	6	1	0	0	0	0	0	.000
David Murphy	OF	25	3	2	1	1	0	1	0	0	.500
Josh Beckett	P	27	3	11	1	2	1	0	0	1	.182
Daisuke Matsuzaka	P	26	2	4	0	0	0	0	0	0	.000
Julian Tavarez	P	34	2	4	0	1	0	0	0	0	.250
Curt Schilling	P	40	1	2	0	1	0	0	0	0	.500
Tim Wakefield	P	40	1	2	0	0	0	0	0	0	.000
Regular season			162	5589	867	1561	352	35	166	829	**.279**

Player	OBP	SLG	OPS	BB	SO	SB	CS	SH	SF	IBB	HBP	GDP
Jason Varitek	.367	.421	.787	71	122	1	2	0	4	9	8	9
Kevin Youkilis	.390	.453	.843	77	105	4	2	0	5	0	15	9
Dustin Pedroia	.380	.442	.823	47	42	7	1	5	2	1	7	8
Mike Lowell	.378	.501	.879	53	71	3	2	0	8	4	3	19
Julio Lugo	.294	.349	.643	48	82	33	6	8	4	0	0	9
Manny Ramirez	.388	.493	.881	71	92	0	0	0	8	13	7	21
Coco Crisp	.330	.382	.712	50	84	28	6	9	5	1	1	12
J. D. Drew	.373	.423	.796	79	100	4	2	0	6	10	1	12
David Ortiz	.445	.621	1.066	111	103	3	1	0	3	12	4	16
Alex Cora	.298	.386	.684	7	23	1	1	7	2	2	9	5
Eric Hinske	.317	.398	.714	28	54	3	0	0	1	2	3	7
Wily Mo Pena	.291	.385	.675	14	58	0	1	0	0	0	2	5
Jacoby Ellsbury	.394	.509	.902	8	15	9	0	0	2	0	1	2
Doug Mirabelli	.278	.360	.637	11	41	0	0	1	0	0	1	4
Bobby Kielty	.295	.327	.622	5	17	0	0	0	3	0	1	3
Kevin Cash	.242	.148	.391	4	13	0	0	0	1	0	1	2
Brandon Moss	.379	.440	.819	4	6	0	0	0	0	0	0	1
Jeff Bailey	.111	.444	.556	0	1	0	0	0	0	0	0	0
Royce Clayton	.000	.000	.000	0	3	0	0	0	0	0	0	2
David Murphy	.500	1.500	2.000	0	1	0	0	0	0	0	0	0
Josh Beckett	.182	.273	.455	0	1	0	0	0	0	0	0	0
Daisuke Matsuzaka	.000	.000	.000	0	2	0	0	0	0	0	0	0
Julian Tavarez	.400	.250	.650	1	3	0	0	0	0	0	0	0
Curt Schilling	.500	.500	1.000	0	1	0	0	0	0	0	0	0
Tim Wakefield	.000	.000	.000	0	2	0	0	0	0	0	0	0
Regular season total	**.362**	**.444**	**.806**	**689**	**1042**	**96**	**24**	**30**	**54**	**54**	**64**	**146**

Team Pitching

Player	POS	Age	W	L	G	GS	CG	SHO	GF	SV	WHIP	ERA
Daisuke Matsuzaka	SP	26	15	12	32	32	1	0	0	0	1.324	4.40
Tim Wakefield	SP	40	17	12	31	31	0	0	0	0	1.349	4.76
Josh Beckett	SP	27	20	7	30	30	1	0	0	0	1.141	3.27
Curt Schilling	SP	40	9	8	24	24	1	1	0	0	1.245	3.87
Julian Tavarez	SP	34	7	11	34	23	0	0	2	0	1.500	5.15
Jon Lester	SP	23	4	0	12	11	0	0	0	0	1.460	4.57
Kason Gabbard	SP	25	4	0	7	7	1	1	0	0	1.122	3.73
Jonathan Papelbon	Closer	26	1	3	59	0	0	0	53	37	0.772	1.85
Hideki Okajima		31	3	2	66	0	0	0	13	5	0.971	2.22
Javier Lopez		29	2	1	61	0	0	0	11	0	1.327	3.10

Player	POS	Age	W	L	G	GS	CG	SHO	GF	SV	WHIP	ERA
Mike Timlin		41	2	1	50	0	0	0	19	1	1.085	3.42
Kyle Snyder		29	2	3	46	0	0	0	17	0	1.418	3.81
Manny Delcarmen		25	0	0	44	0	0	0	5	1	1.023	2.05
Joel Pineiro		28	1	1	31	0	0	0	15	0	1.618	5.03
Clay Buchholz		22	3	1	4	3	1	1	0	0	1.057	1.59
Brendan Donnelly		35	2	1	27	0	0	0	4	0	1.159	3.04
J. C. Romero		31	1	0	23	0	0	0	5	1	1.950	3.15
Eric Gagne		31	2	2	20	0	0	0	11	0	1.872	6.74
Bryan Corey		33	1	0	9	0	0	0	2	0	1.075	1.94
Devern Hansack		29	0	1	3	1	0	0	0	0	1.818	4.68
Regular season total			**96**	**66**	**162**	**162**	**5**	**3**	**157**	**45**	**1.273**	**3.87**

Player	IP	H	R	ER	HR	BB	SO	WP	HBP	BK	IBB
Daisuke Matsuzaka	204.7	191	100	100	25	80	201	5	13	0	1
Tim Wakefield	189	191	104	100	22	64	110	10	4	0	1
Josh Beckett	200.7	189	76	73	17	40	194	3	5	0	0
Curt Schilling	151	165	68	65	21	23	101	0	2	0	1
Julian Tavarez	134.7	151	89	77	14	51	77	4	7	0	4
Jon Lester	63	61	33	32	10	31	50	1	1	0	0
Kason Gabbard	41	28	17	17	3	18	29	0	4	0	0
Jonathan Papelbon	58.3	30	12	12	5	15	84	0	4	0	0
Hideki Okajima	69	50	17	17	6	17	63	0	1	0	2
Javier Lopez	40.7	36	16	14	2	18	26	1	4	0	2
Mike Timlin	55.3	46	23	21	7	14	31	0	3	0	3
Kyle Snyder	54.3	45	29	23	7	32	41	4	6	0	2
Manny Delcarmen	44	28	11	10	4	17	41	0	2	0	1
Joel Pineiro	34	41	20	19	3	14	20	3	1	0	0
Clay Buchholz	22.7	14	6	4	0	10	22	0	1	0	0
Brendan Donnelly	20.7	19	8	7	0	5	15	2	4	0	0
J. C. Romero	20	24	7	7	2	15	11	0	0	0	3
Eric Gagne	18.7	26	14	14	1	9	22	0	0	0	0
Bryan Corey	9.3	6	2	2	0	4	6	0	0	0	0
Devern Hansack	7.7	9	5	4	2	5	5	0	0	0	0
Regular season total	**1438.7**	**1350**	**657**	**618**	**151**	**482**	**1149**	**33**	**62**	**0**	**20**

2008: HEROES IN THE MAKING

One season does not a hero make, but today's Red Sox fans have been so very lucky to see a quartet of homegrown talent come up from the minors and develop into stars before our very eyes.

Only time will tell if these four players will stay healthy, stay strong, and stay with Boston. We do know that each of them played an important role in propelling the Red Sox to the postseason in 2007 and again in 2008. They give us hope.

And there's a fifth hero in the making, the man who has managed the show on one of the most demanding stages in all of baseball.

Dustin Pedroia
Dustin Luis Pedroia ("Pedey")

Primary position: 2B	
Bats: R	
Throws: R	
Height: 5'9"	
Weight: 180 pounds	
First major league game: August 22, 2006	
Final major league game: Active player	
Born: August 17, 1983 in Woodland, California	

Pedroia is off to a spectacular start. He won the Rookie of the Year award in 2007 in his first full year in the major leagues. And then in 2008 he became only the eighth man in American League history to win the Most Valuable Player award as well as Golden Glove and Silver Slugger in one season. And he also became the first-ever Red Sox second baseman to be named MVP, which is pretty remarkable when you think of the greats who have stood at that position, including Bobby Doerr. Pedroia is only the tenth Red Sox MVP winner. He is the first to bring home the award since Mo Vaughn in 1995. The

Photo by Brita Meng Outzen

previous winners from Boston were Jimmie Foxx (1938), Ted Williams (1946 and 1949), Jackie Jensen (1958), Carl Yastrzemski (1967), Fred Lynn (1975), Jim Rice (1978), and Roger Clemens (1986).

He's just a really good player. He brings a level of intensity and energy to the team that is infectious to everybody. He's not intimidated by anything. I honestly believe that every time he walks on the field he wants to have a better game than the other second baseman.

He began his professional career having to shift over from shortstop to second base. A guy of his size has had to battle at every step of his career, and he has certainly proven all the naysayers wrong.

And his defense should not be overlooked. I don't know a second baseman who played better defense than he did in 2008. Depending on how long he stays in Boston, he may end up as the best second baseman in Red Sox history after Bobby Doerr.

Dustin Pedroia

Year	Team	Age	G	AB	R	H	2B	3B	HR	RBI	BA	
2006	BOS (AL)	22	31	89	5	17	4	0	2	7	.191	
2007	BOS (AL)	23	139	520	86	165	39	1	8	50	.317	ROY, AS
2008	BOS (AL)	24	157	653	118	213	54	2	17	83	.326	GG, SS, AS, MVP
Total			327	1262	209	395	97	3	27	140	.313	

Year	Team	OBP	SLG	OPS	BB	SO	TB	SB	CS	SH	SF	IBB	HBP	GDP
2006	BOS (AL)	.258	.303	.561	7	7	27	0	1	1	0	0	1	1
2007	BOS (AL)	.380	.442	.822	47	42	230	7	1	5	2	1	7	8
2008	BOS (AL)	.376	.493	.869	50	52	322	20	1	7	9	1	7	17
Total		.369	.459	.828	104	101	579	27	3	13	11	2	15	26

Kevin Youkilis
Kevin E. Youkilis ("Youk")

Primary position: 1B/3B

Bats: R

Throws: R

Height: 6'1"

Weight: 220 pounds

First major league game: May 15, 2004

Final major league game: Active player

Born: March 15, 1979 in Cincinnati, Ohio

Youkilis is a guy who seems to take every at-bat as if it is going to be the last one of his career. He is a real tough out who grinds it out every single day.

And I'm so impressed with his remarkable versatility in switching back and forth between first base and third whenever it is needed for the team. He earned a Gold Glove playing first base in 2007 and then showed Gold Glove–like skills at both corners in 2008 after he was asked to fill in for the injured Mike Lowell.

Moving back and forth across the infield—sometimes during the course of a single game—didn't affect Youk's time at the plate. He had his best offensive year in 2008, with career highs in hits, home runs, RBIs, and slugging. He moved smoothly into the cleanup spot after Manny Ramirez left.

Youk wears his emotions on his sleeve, but that's okay when you come through every day. Everything Youk does is above and beyond the call of duty, and he does it all with great intensity.

Kevin Youkilis

Year	Team	Age	G	AB	R	H	2B	3B	HR	RBI	BA	
2004	BOS (AL)	25	72	208	38	54	11	0	7	35	.260	
2005	BOS (AL)	26	44	79	11	22	7	0	1	9	.278	
2006	BOS (AL)	27	147	569	100	159	42	2	13	72	.279	
2007	BOS (AL)	28	145	528	85	152	35	2	16	83	.288	GG
2008	BOS (AL)	29	145	538	91	168	43	4	29	115	.312	AS
Total			553	1922	325	555	138	8	66	314	.289	

Year	Team	OBP	SLG	OPS	BB	SO	TB	SB	CS	SH	SF	IBB	HBP	GDP
2004	BOS (AL)	.367	.413	.780	33	45	86	0	1	0	3	0	4	1
2005	BOS (AL)	.400	.405	.805	14	19	32	0	1	0	0	0	2	0
2006	BOS (AL)	.381	.429	.810	91	120	244	5	2	0	11	0	9	12
2007	BOS (AL)	.390	.453	.843	77	105	239	4	2	0	5	0	15	9
2008	BOS (AL)	.390	.569	.959	62	108	306	3	5	0	9	7	12	11
Total		.385	.472	.857	277	397	907	12	11	0	28	7	42	33

Jon Lester
Jonathan Tyler Lester

Primary position: P

Bats: L

Throws: L

Height: 6'2"

Weight: 190 pounds

First major league game: June 10, 2006

Final major league game: Active player

Born: January 7, 1984 in Tacoma, Washington

Jon Lester has the potential to be a number one, top of the rotation guy. That was the Red Sox view from the day they signed him: In his minor league career they had ranked him higher than Jonathan Papelbon, and that's pretty impressive.

He came up in 2006 and pitched well for the equivalent of about half a season until the end of August, when he was scratched from a game because of a sore back. After undergoing tests the diagnosis was scary: anaplastic large cell lymphoma, a rare form of cancer. He spent the rest of the year and the off-season not on the mound but instead in hospital rooms receiving chemotherapy. He came back to the Red Sox on July 23 of 2007, went 4–0 down the stretch, and then he was the starting and winning pitcher in the fourth and deciding game of the World Series against the Colorado Rockies.

In 2008 we saw him begin to blossom, and he did so in style. On May 19, less than two months into the season, Lester threw a no-hitter against the Kansas City Royals at Fenway Park. He had the strength to throw 130 pitches, allowing only two walks and striking out nine batters. It was the first no-no by a Red Sox lefty since Mel Parnell in 1956.

He went on to post a 16–6 record in 2008. It was remarkable to watch him gain strength all through the season. He became an absolute bull, throwing the most innings on the team: 210 innings in the regular season and 26 more in the postseason.

In the 2008 Division Series, Lester was the starter and winning pitcher for the Red Sox in Game 1, allowing Josh Beckett some extra time to rest a strained oblique muscle. His line: seven innings, six hits, seven strikeouts, and one unearned run.

Lester pitched even better in the fourth and final game of the series, giving up no runs and just four hits across seven games. If Boston's bullpen had not coughed up two runs in the top of the eighth to tie the game, Lester would have won his first three postseason starts with the Red Sox. In Red Sox history, only Babe Ruth and Luis Tiant have accomplished that.

He has a picture perfect delivery. Fundamentally, he's got it all: no extra motion, the way a pitching coach would teach it.

He has gotten his velocity back and learned to use the outside part of the plate. He started as a fastball pitcher and later added a cut fastball, slider, changeup, and a good curve.

I didn't know what exactly we're going to get from Lester. But I think we're watching the development of one of the top left-handers in baseball.

Jon Lester

Year	Team	Age	W	L	G	GS	CG	SHO	GF	SV	WHIP	ERA
2006	BOS (AL)	22	7	2	15	15	0	0	0	0	1.65	4.76
2007	BOS (AL)	23	4	0	12	11	0	0	0	0	1.46	4.57
2008	BOS (AL)	24	16	6	33	33	2	2	0	0	1.27	3.21
Total			**27**	**8**	**60**	**59**	**2**	**2**	**0**	**0**	**1.39**	**3.81**

Year	Team	IP	H	R	ER	HR	BB	SO	HBP	WP	IBB	BK
2006	BOS (AL)	81.3	91	43	43	7	43	60	5	5	1	0
2007	BOS (AL)	63.0	61	33	32	10	31	50	1	1	0	0
2008	BOS (AL)	210.3	202	78	75	14	66	152	10	3	1	1
Total		**354.6**	**354**	**154**	**150**	**31**	**140**	**262**	**16**	**9**	**2**	**1**

Jonathan Papelbon
Jonathan Papelbon ("Paps")

Primary position: P	
Bats: R	
Throws: R	
Height: 6'4"	
Weight: 230 pounds	
First major league game: July 31, 2005	
Final major league game: Active player	
Born: November 23, 1980 in Baton Rouge, Louisiana	

Look into those eyes when he's on the mound: He's got the makeup to be a closer and the fastball to prove it.

He has a great fastball and the ability to put it where he wants. In 2008, he went away from throwing his splitter, which is a critical pitch for him; I think the Red Sox were trying to limit his innings. They're very concerned that he not get injured. At the end of the ALCS in 2008, in Papelbon's last outing of the season, he was exhausted, on fumes; he got the outs, though.

There are very few pitchers who can get away with just one pitch; Mariano Rivera is the most obvious exception.

But the bottom line is that as long as Papelbon can stay healthy, there is no reason he cannot be one of the top closers in baseball for a long time to come.

Jonathan Papelbon

Year	Team	Age	W	L	G	GS	CG	SHO	GF	SV	WHIP	ERA
2005	BOS (AL)	24	3	1	17	3	0	0	4	0	1.47	2.65
2006	BOS (AL)	25	4	2	59	0	0	0	49	35	0.78	0.92
2007	BOS (AL)	26	1	3	59	0	0	0	53	37	0.77	1.85
2008	BOS (AL)	27	5	4	67	0	0	0	62	41	0.95	2.34
Total			**13**	**10**	**202**	**3**	**0**	**0**	**168**	**113**	**0.93**	**1.84**

Year	Team	IP	H	R	ER	HR	BB	SO	HBP	WP	IBB	BK
2005	BOS (AL)	34	33	11	10	4	17	34	3	1	2	0
2006	BOS (AL)	68.3	40	8	7	3	13	75	1	2	2	0
2007	BOS (AL)	58.3	30	12	12	5	15	84	4	0	0	0
2008	BOS (AL)	69.3	58	24	18	4	8	77	0	2	0	0
Total		**230.0**	**161**	**55**	**47**	**16**	**53**	**270**	**8**	**5**	**4**	**0**

Terry Francona
Terry Jon Francona ("Tito")

Primary position: Manager, former OF/IF
Bats: L
Throws: L
Height: 6'1"
Weight: 190 pounds
First major league game: August 19, 1981
Final major league game: April 19, 1990
Major league manager: Philadelphia 1997–2000, Boston 2004–present
Born: April 22, 1959 in Aberdeen, South Dakota

There's no arguing with Terry Francona's record of success: In his first five years at the helm of the Boston Red Sox, he brought them to the Promised Land for the first time in 86 years with a World Series Championship in 2004, and then guided them to a second trophy just three years later in 2007. Thus far, the Red Sox have made it to the postseason four out of the five years of the Francona Era.

It's a pressure cooker in Boston, and I think Francona was on edge a bit in his first year. Winning a championship helps you relax, and he has grown a lot in the job.

He is without a doubt a player's manager. He never publicly embarrasses a player; when he's upset with someone, he keeps it quiet and takes care of it in the clubhouse.

That said, I think the happiest day in his life was when Manny Ramirez was sent to Los Angeles. He honestly thought that when Manny was gone he had a team he could win with, and they made it into the second round of the playoffs. The players love playing for him, and we've got the trophies and the rings to prove it.

Francona, the son of former major-leaguer Tito Francona, had a ten-year MLB career of his own. He came up with Montreal in 1981 at the age of 22 and went on to play for the Chicago Cubs, the Cincinnati Reds, and the Cleveland Indians. His last full season was with the Milwaukee Brewers in 1989; his playing days ended four games into the 1990 season.

Working mostly as a utility player, he had 304 games at first base and 203 as an outfielder. His career batting average was a respectable .274 (his father had a lifetime average of .272).

And here's the answer to a trivia question: Terry Francona has a perfect record as a pitcher. On May 15, 1989, as the Milwaukee Brewers were being pounded 12–2 at Oakland, Francona was brought in to pitch the eighth inning. The results: no hits, no walks, no runs, one flyball out, one popup, and one strikeout. The unlucky batter who whiffed was Stan Javier.

Terry Francona

Year	Team	G	W	L	WinPct	Finish	
1997	PHL (NL)	162	68	94	.420	5	
1998	PHL (NL)	162	75	87	.463	3	
1999	PHL (NL)	162	77	85	.475	3	
2000	PHL (NL)	162	65	97	.401	5	
2004	BOS (AL)	162	98	64	.605	2	WS Champ
2005	BOS (AL)	162	95	67	.586	2	
2006	BOS (AL)	162	86	76	.531	3	
2007	BOS (AL)	162	96	66	.593	1	WS Champ
2008	BOS (AL)	162	95	67	.586	2	
Total		**1458**	**755**	**703**	**.518**		
Boston		**810**	**470**	**340**	**.580**		

American League Division Series

Year	Team	G	W	L	WinPct
2004	BOS (AL)	3	3	0	1.000
2005	BOS (AL)	3	0	3	.000
2007	BOS (AL)	3	3	0	1.000
2008	BOS (AL)	4	3	1	.750
Total		**13**	**9**	**4**	**.692**

American League Championship Series

Year	Team	G	W	L	WinPct
2004	BOS (AL)	7	4	3	.571
2007	BOS (AL)	7	4	3	.571
2008	BOS (AL)	7	3	4	.429
Total		**21**	**11**	**10**	**.524**

World Series

Year	Team	G	W	L	WinPct
2004	BOS (AL)	4	4	0	1.000
2007	BOS (AL)	4	4	0	1.000
Total		**8**	**8**	**0**	**1.000**

ABOUT THE AUTHORS

Jerry Remy has been the color analyst for Boston Red Sox television broadcasts since 1988. He played ten years at second base in the major leagues for the California Angels and the Boston Red Sox, compiling a .275 lifetime batting average. He can be reached through his Web site at www.theremyreport.com

Photo by Brita Meng Outzen

Corey Sandler is the author of more than 150 books on sports, business, history, and travel. A former newsman for the Associated Press and Gannett Newspapers, he lives in Nantucket, Massachusetts. He can be reached through his Web site at www.econoguide.com.

Photo by Tessa Sandler